THE DOMINO EFFECT

How to Grow Sales, Profits, and Market Share through Super Vision

THE DOMINO EFFECT

How to Grow Sales, Profits, and Market Share through Super Vision

by Donald J. Vlcek, Jr.
with Jeffrey P. Davidson

BUSINESS ONE IRWIN
Homewood, Illinois 60430

This publication is designed to provide accurate and
authoritative information in regard to the subject matter
covered. It is sold with the understanding that neither the
author nor the publisher is engaged in rendering legal, accounting,
or other professional service. If legal advice or other expert
assistance is required, the services of a competent
professional person should be sought.

*From a Declaration of Principles jointly adopted by a Committee
of the American Bar Association and a Committee of Publishers.*

Sponsoring editor: Jeffrey A. Krames
Project editor: Jean Lou Hess
Production manager: Ann Cassady
Jacket designer: Image House, Inc.
Compositor: Eastern Graphics Typographers
Typeface: 11/13 Electra
Printer: R. R. Donnelley & Sons Company

Library of Congress Cataloging-in-Publication Data

Vlcek, Donald J.
    The domino effect : how to increase sales, profits, and market
share through super vision / by Donald J. Vlcek, Jr., with Jeffrey
P. Davidson.
        p.   cm.
    Includes bibliographical references and index.
    ISBN 1-55623-602-6
    1. Domino's Pizza (Firm)   2. Sales management.   3. Industrial
management.   I. Davidson, Jeffrey P.   II. Title.
HF5438.4.V53   1991
658.8—dc20   91–30687

Printed in the United States of America

1 2 3 4 5 6 7 8 9 0 DOC 8 7 6 5 4 3 2 1

To Vee, Suzie, Jimmie, Torrie, my parents, our family, and friends for their everlasting support and sacrifices.

To the entire Domino's Pizza family—our franchisees, executives, team members, communities, and suppliers—without you there is no story.

And to Tom Monaghan . . . your dedication, foresight, patience, and trust have been the inspiration to grow.

Foreword

By any measure, Domino's Pizza, Inc., is one of America's most successful corporations of the past 10 years. Every major newspaper in the nation including the *New York Times, Washington Post, Wall Street Journal*, and most business magazines, including *Nation's Business, Business Week, Forbes, Fortune, Success, Inc.*, and *Barron's* have chronicled the story of Domino's Pizza, Inc.

Domino's Pizza is a company of superlatives, as reflected by a brief potpourri of its accomplishments and activities:

- It holds the record for most stores opened in one year by a retail chain—over 1,000!
- It ranks seventh of all restaurant chains in total sales.
- It has been honored as "Franchisor of the Year" and acknowledged as one of the best companies in the world with which to franchise.
- It opened its 5,542nd store in October, 1991, representing spectacular growth since its 400th store opened in 1981.
- At the height of the 1988 presidential race, the George Bush campaign headquarters ordered an average of 40 Domino's pizzas daily.

- Across the Potomac in northern Virginia, the average age of Domino's store managers is 23; their average annual income is $90,000.

- Domino's College of Pizzarology has awarded 500 associate degrees, 600 bachelor degrees, 100 masters, and 3 doctorates.

Using time and motion analysis, the company's typical pizza maker can now make and bake a pizza with all the trimmings in 10 minutes or less; with a guaranteed delivery time of 30 minutes, this allows drivers 20 minutes to travel safely an average of one to two miles.

As a company, the accomplishments go on and on.

AN INSIDE LOOK

What you are about to read is the story behind the story. *The Domino Effect* offers a behind-the-scenes look at the company's leadership and distribution system, the heart and driving force behind the parent corporation.

In the 1980s, of U.S. companies or divisions with revenues of $10 million or more and at least 1,000 employees, Domino's Pizza Distribution, a subsidiary of Domino's Pizza, Inc., grew the fastest. During the 12 years that Don Vlcek has been president of Domino's Pizza Distribution, the company has gone from $5 million in annual revenue to over $600 million, growing even faster than the parent company.

In one eight-year stretch, as a measure of its increase in productivity, Distribution raised annual sales per employee from $100,000 to $180,000 and expanded the number of commissaries (supply centers) from 3 to 32.

Since the early 1980s, both Domino's Pizza, Inc., and Domino's Pizza Distribution have received phone calls and letters annually from top executives, managers, and entrepreneurs worldwide. These professionals seek advice on how they can run their organizations more effectively. Many businesspeople even visit Domino's world headquarters to observe the company.

For years, Domino's replied to each of the phone calls and letters individually and served as host to visitors. Soon, however, the numbers became unwieldy and Distribution initiated the Innovation Network to provide one-on-one guidance to client firms. In only two years, the success of firms working with the Innovation Network—ranging from Stew Leonard's world-famous dairy in Norwalk, Connecticut, to Navistar International, a Fortune 500 manufacturer—has made it abundantly clear that what works for Domino's Pizza Distribution works for businesses of all sizes and endeavors.

Don Vlcek is widely known for being committed to running the best company he can and to helping others, both inside and outside his company, do the same. He believes, and rightly so, that there is a larger social good in empowering others. Don's mission in writing *The Domino Effect* is to share the company's innovations and help others. All of his royalties from this book will be donated to wildlife causes.

WORKABLE IN YOUR COMPANY

The success of Domino's Pizza Distribution lies in the constant development of its leadership system and its strong employee communication. The process works because top management challenges people and has installed the Super Vision system to both support and reward individual initiative. As you'll see, every element of Distribution's system, including its open and innovative atmosphere, is transferable to your company. What works for Distribution will work for you.

This book discloses what it takes for any company to efficiently provide its product or service and to virtually guarantee end-user satisfaction. You'll learn how Distribution amasses the innovation and energy of its employees while keeping them focused on the company's corporate mission, assuring rapid delivery with high customer satisfaction. You'll discover firsthand how you can apply Domino's leadership principles and strategies in your own company or department to achieve outstanding, measurable results.

I hope you enjoy reading *The Domino Effect* as much as I did, because it's a treasure trove of innovations for successful business practice.

Steve Fraser
1984 Olympic Gold Medalist,
U.S. Olympic Team

Acknowledgments

Among the many people who contributed to this effort, I would like to especially thank Peter Niedbala for coordinating the project, rounding up tons of data and supporting materials, and assisting with writing and editing. I am also grateful to Steve Fraser for planting the seeds that led to this book, and Yvonne Lorenz for copyediting. Special thanks to Tom Monaghan for his continual inspiration, Dave Black and the Domino's Pizza executive team for their support, my assistant Marilyn Roe for her ongoing great help, and the entire Domino's Pizza Distribution team for accomplishing every goal I've asked them to attain.

I would also like to thank Jeff Davidson for meritorious writing and editing assistance, Ron Wagner for editorial help, Juliet Bruce for expert copyediting, and Judy Dubler for word processing.

Thanks also to the hard-working team at Business One Irwin, including Jeffrey A. Krames for his enthusiasm, guidance, editing, and overall support, and Rick Riddering, Kathryn Wickham, Michael Desposito, Carol Deselm, Sharon Miller, Margie Hoekstra, Barbara Novasol, Ruth Bachtell, Louis Dewinter, Jean Lou Hess, Ralph Rieves, and Jeffrey O. Sund.

Introduction

Humankind has increased its life span, accelerated its speed of travel, and ventured into space. Human beings have a special gift—the drive and the power to continually better themselves. Of all creatures on Earth, only humans consistently control their surroundings. Businesses need to understand and acknowledge each day that people need to have the freedom to put this special power into motion.

In large corporations today, unfortunately, many executives tend to develop restrictive systems that hinder the drives, power, and aspirations of their employees. Employees may then have no choice but to turn to interpersonal or interdepartmental rivalries to maintain some semblance of power. Sensing turmoil, corporations use management specialists to design systems to enable employees to have a greater perception of power. Ironically, these systems often fail because top management is unwilling to grant employees any real power.

At Domino's Pizza Distribution Corporation (Distribution), we take a different approach.

Everyone at our company receives a share of up to 20 percent of profits if we attain the reasonable and realistic performance goals set at the start of the month. Team members receive a bonus check every four weeks—that's immediate reward for accomplishing goals. We make all painstaking effort to thoroughly explain to our people, "Here is the potential, and here is what you have to do to get your share of the rewards," and then we let them be.

We have found that employees usually do what it takes to earn the reward. If they fail to earn the reward, we—the top executives and leaders—see it as our fault for not offering the direction for accomplishment and the rewards that will follow. The top executives in any size company share the same responsibility.

SHARING WHAT WE'VE LEARNED

Our goal in this book is to provide you with some basic answers concerning the dilemmas you face in business. It offers an inside look at what makes Distribution run, and how its approaches to leadership can be used in other businesses. It describes how to use Super Vision to run a streamlined, responsive, self-managing company and how to maintain employee spirit and energy.

Many companies believe they have to spend large sums to solve pressing problems. We believe the solution is to empower trusted employees with freedom and tools. Even in small companies, individuals who have achieved success can be given the freedom to pursue what they think will work for the benefit of the company. That freedom usually leads to rewards.

The freedom to let people try new things often requires only new perspectives and better uses of existing resources. With us, freedom for team members (we don't use the term *employee* because it is not descriptive of the relationship) can show up in many ways. For production personnel, it is giving them a voice on how to prepare a particular product.

Everyone in the company has a particular skill and has to do what they do best. Leaders need to lead, not manage, by clearly presenting the company's mission, offering incentives for other team members to fulfill it, and allowing them to do their job.

People have a powerful, natural ability to elevate themselves continually. That's why humankind can survive in so many varied climates. That's why we've been able to extend our life expectancy and overcome droughts, famines, and most diseases. A leader has to tap this inherent human force and allow people to rise to their highest level. Managers usually get in the way; true leaders never do.

Take truck driving and product delivery, for example. If you ask who knows the most about semi trucks, one of the fundamental components in our distribution system, many people may say it is the national transportation director or head of safety for the organization. Actually, the person who knows the most about semi trucks is the one who drives them each day. If this person has the freedom to interact with the fleet leadership, the result will be a more productive, safe, and efficient approach to driving and delivery.

Similarly, if the head of fleet operations is faced with particular challenges regarding the transportation system, he or she should rely on the experience of and insight from the drivers. The exchange of information between frontline personnel and company leaders needs to be barrier free and actively encouraged.

PROVEN STRATEGIES

While a historical perspective may help explain how aspects of our leadership system developed, the book doesn't dwell on or retell the story of the origins of the corporation. This is a "how-to" book. It focuses on proven strategies that result in more profitable operations and which can be initiated by leaders within organizations of all sizes.

At the same time, *The Domino Effect* reflects the reality of building a business. You may detect some similarities between what we do and the leadership practices of Japanese companies or the work of Tom Peters, Mike Vance, Ichak Adizes, Dale Carnegie, or others. We've learned from all of these sources, but we believe our system is unique and provides key advantages. Like every corporation, Domino's Pizza Distribution has had its share of failures. We'll share those with you as well, because we've learned from our mistakes, too.

Battling our way to what works, we've become more competitive over the years, as have the companies that now employ our strategies. We believe we have a great system and have a responsibility to share this success with the rest of the world. We offer this to you in hopes it results in improved quality, increased efficiencies, higher profits, or just plain increased morale and satisfaction.

Don Vlcek, Jr.
Ann Arbor, Michigan
November 1991

Contents

PART
I

A Question of Balance

Managers of large corporations face an overwhelming task if they attempt to directly handle every aspect of their company. There are so many factors to keep up with that important matters can drop through the cracks. If you believe you cannot manage everything going on around you, trade in your management position for something better.

The best way to oversee the direction of a large group of people is to have a vision for where they should go and convey that vision clearly to every member of the group. Your task then becomes giving them resources and incentives while monitoring their progress toward that vision, making adjustments as conditions change.

I call this Super Vision.

Chapter One
Super Vision

Trying to handle everything in a company or division is a nightmare; one person cannot do it, but it is possible for one person to control the direction of everything in an organization of any size. When you employ Super Vision, you step back from handling everything directly and look at the overall priorities. Your vision for the company has to focus on the few items that most contribute to your success. Once those key factors are identified, you turn them into "battle cries," tie them together, then lead the charge.

Let's establish some working definitions. The term *supervision* means to watch over everything or ensure it is coordinated. It is that daily series of hundreds of small decisions affecting every detail of an operation. A supervisor characteristically makes an admirable quantity of decisions. Those details and decisions may at times be overwhelming or seem to contradict themselves. A supervisor also rarely has time to strategize or inspire.

Super Vision means getting involved only when there is a crisis or cause for celebration—the rest of your time is spent strategizing and inspiring your team toward a well-thought-out vision. It is the "big picture" perspective, looking only for successes or failures and reacting appropriately to each. As a SuperVisor, your job is to actively communicate your vision so everyone knows where you want them to go. You cannot afford to spend time watching over people and saying, "No, that's not what I want." Life for the SuperVisor is a series of weekly, monthly, or even annual direction-setting sessions. Rather than a focus on "quantity" decisions, it is "quality" dreaming.

One of the best examples of a SuperVisor I can think of is in the movie *Patton*. You may recall the scene where Patton's jeep is delayed behind a stalled convoy. Patton, realizing that a stagnant army is an army in crisis, speeds to the front of the column. He discovers two convoys converging at a crossroads, no sense of order, and no individual taking control of the situation. Patton jumps from his jeep and takes control by directing traffic and moving the convoy out of crisis. As soon as order is restored, Patton pulls back and doesn't interfere. In another scene, Patton is found drinking vodka with the Russian soldiers to celebrate a victory. Clearly, he is genuinely happy and taking the time to congratulate and honor the soldiers.

These two incidents, however, seemed to be an exception to Patton's behavior rather than the norm. Throughout the movie, Patton was typically off with his key strategists or alone studying maps and planning foolproof campaigns. One role of a leader is to study the big picture and remove himself or herself from the day-to-day activities of the people. The leader's other role is to leave the strategizing and planning session to celebrate truly exceptional bravery or to roll up his or her sleeves and assist people out of a crisis. A true SuperVisor helps his or her team fight a crisis and celebrate a victory.

A VISION FROM A VISION

My introduction to Domino's Pizza began when I saw Tom Monaghan's dream. In 1978, when he interviewed me for the job of president of Distribution, he had 168 stores, yet he told me his vision was to be the largest pizza company in the world. When I asked him how many stores Pizza Hut had, he told me they had more than 4,500. I thought he was off his rocker. But during the six hours he articulated his vision, including the 30-minute delivery guarantee and his commitment to providing fresh, hot pizzas made from the highest quality ingredients and sold at a fair price, I became so excited about the company that I would have taken a lower position had I not been hired as president.

In the early days, Domino's Pizza Distribution Corporation was small enough that I could keep an eye on everything, and I was good at it. I knew everything that went on in the company. However, when I looked to the future, I got worried.

While we were still small, I had a vision of our becoming a $200 million corporation. I wondered what the executives in established, large food-service companies did. My research into their jobs made me quickly realize I could not run the company I envisioned by managing it. I had to depart from my old ways to keep up with all we would soon face.

THE IDEAL SUPERVISOR

Ideally, a company SuperVisor would come in on Monday, look over a few pages in a short report to determine that everyone is on track, and then play golf or fish the rest of the week while dreaming up new visions for the company. If things are in crisis or people have been performing at exceptional levels, he or she must stay to either lead a task force or throw a party.

The only time the SuperVisor would need to stay beyond lunch Monday would be if the reports were not favorable. If that were the case, he or she would need to find out why others in the company didn't see the vision, then communicate it more clearly. Then, the SuperVisor would have to make sure he or she had provided the resources team members needed and get out of the way to allow them to fulfill the vision on their own.

The purpose of SuperVisory communication is to get all the other team members who work for you to "be of like mind" with your vision. That's all a leader needs to do. There is no need for a leader to "handle" the company's daily affairs.

While it took considerable effort to get it in such shape, today my system for Super Vision is a concise, seven-step process that results in a self-managing system. While it works well for us, I had never considered that others might find it useful.

One day I was invited to speak about my leadership system at a meeting of some Harvard University business school graduates. I couldn't figure out what I could possibly say that they would find interesting. I had only a bachelor's degree from the University of Michigan's business school and most of these people held Harvard MBAs or PhDs. The University of Michigan has an excellent business program and I'm proud of my alma mater, but addressing a roomful of Ivy League executives was an intimidating thought.

As I presented my seven-step process, I quickly gained confidence as I read their body language. I could easily tell they were intrigued by the concept. After my speech, I offered to send more information to all who left their business cards. I received 40 cards from an audience of 80. Their enthusiastic response confirmed for me that I had a winning system that would apply to companies far removed from the pizza distribution business. That experience was the catalyst for my writing this book.

THE SEVEN STEPS OF SUPER VISION

I want to show you how to apply the seven-step process to your company. You don't have to be a large company or have a large staff to try the suggestions in this book. To describe Super Vision, I'll first list and briefly describe each step:

(1) Gather a thorough inventory of your publics and the groups that make up your publics.

(2) Conduct a thorough investigation and inventory of each group's needs.

(3) Sort the identified needs within each group into major patterns.

(4) Write a concise, detailed wording of those need patterns into a mission statement.

(5) Transfer the patterns into key indicators—numbers used to measure performance and to establish accountability.

(6) Compare performance numbers to the desired levels.

(7) Build in an automatic reward and corrective action system based on the performance as measured by the key indicators.

The process is a repeating cycle. The first two steps where you identify your public and their specific needs drive the Super Vision system. What you learn there enables you to sort the identified needs, Step 3, and create a vision of how you'll serve your public. In Steps 4 and 5, you communicate how to fulfill that vision to others in your company and show them how you'll hold them accountable for the performance you expect. The sixth step is your major leadership task where you verify the system is working. The final step ensures that others have incentive to keep the company functioning productively, without you "handling" everything.

Step 1: Gather a Thorough Inventory of Your Publics and the Groups that Make up Your Publics

Your "publics" are those people or groups of people who are affected by your actions and whose needs, understood and met by you, are the cornerstone of your own success. At Distribution, our publics include our Distribution customers (Domino's pizza stores and franchisees), Distribution team members, the communities in which we operate, Distribution suppliers, and our parent company (Domino's Pizza, Inc.). In Chapters 2 through 6, we will discuss the groups that Distribution affects and how we strive to serve them the best we can.

Because all other steps are built on the work you do identifying your publics, it's essential that you identify them accurately and thoroughly. While this may seem simple, it's not easy to be thorough. For example, all businesses will list customers as part of their public; that's an obvious component. Yet, many people miss some subtleties.

A great place to start is to audit your phone calls over a month or so. Many phone messages are logged in booklets that keep a record automatically; it's simply a matter of reviewing this log. Who is calling you? What group does each call represent? You'll start noticing recurring patterns or groups. These groups need to be considered as your publics.

Next, don't overlook other simple records such as your own calendar. With whom have you been meeting? What group or groups of people come to mind when you need to address vital areas of your operation? Look at an accounts payable log. What firms or individuals does your company depend on to accomplish goals? Examine your own business. Are you a public company with shareholders? Is your firm privately held? Directed by a board? Is your organization funded by tax money? As with the phone calls, organize your findings into groups and determine which publics are represented.

As you discover all the people and groups who have a stake in your success, you may find the list is large and perhaps overwhelming. (If you have found the opposite to be true, you are either very lucky or not thorough!) Examine the groups you've listed and see if two or three actually represent one larger group. At Distribution, we consider con-

Sample Organizations and Groups They May Consider as "Publics"

Grocery Stores	Law Firms	Universities
Customers	Clients	Faculty
Vendors	Bar association	Students
Neighborhood groups	Court officers	Alumni
Health departments		Financial contributors
Grocer associations		Regents
		General public

sultants in the same light as our cheese vendors as a "supplier." Similarly, we group federal regulatory agencies, local municipalities, and the public at large in our "community" group. You may find similar opportunities to pare your list.

Once you've compiled your list of publics, it's time to examine their needs.

Step 2: Conduct a Thorough Investigation and Inventory of Each Group's Needs.

When this step is complete, you will have identified both the groups and what they need. But how do you discover what people truly need? To begin with, recognize that not every member of each public has the same needs or the same way of expressing needs. Yet every member of your public is vital to your success. Understanding their needs and keeping them happy is no easy task. To make this a more efficient process, here are some common subsets to publics that I have discovered:

Largest. Among customers, for example, who are your largest customers? Obviously, these people are essential to your business so you'll want to thoroughly understand their buying habits to learn what they demand in quantity and quality. Who are your largest suppliers? What is the job classification in your company with the largest number of people? You'll need to know what it is like to be in their shoes.

Most Vocal and Most Critical. These people, if not satisfied, will air their complaints to others, thereby "poisoning" other people who were viewing your operation positively or at least neutrally. Which members of your public (customer base, employee group, etc.) are always complaining? It is natural to want to avoid them, but what if their input is a true representation of a needed change in your organization? You must face the fire—it isn't as hot as you think it is, especially if your goal is to please all your publics.

Most Influential.   Within every group of people there will be a few who carry much influence over others. Those people are not always the largest customer or supplier or do not always represent the largest job classification. Sometimes the person may have "connections" in the form of friends and relatives in organizations that can affect your operations. The person may simply have the respect of the entire group for any number of reasons. His or her posture magnifies and should not be ignored.

Most Supportive.   Carefully watch for those members of your public who support you and who can spread the word to other members. There's no way to predict who these will be. Sometimes it's based on personalities in your company that "click" with someone in the supportive group. Often, only your intuition is your guide. Look for the source of positive letters and comments about your organization. You can tap the value of their positive comments by using testimonial letters, interviewing them for your company newsletter or newspaper, or asking them to provide input at your meetings. You'll know you've discovered members of this subset when the thought of disappointing one of them makes you feel sick! And it's a sure sign something may be wrong when you see an abrupt end to support from someone with a long history of supporting you.

Most Visionary.   When contacting members of your public, take mental note of the ones that seem to be tuned into the future and who offer useful predictions or suggestions. I've been lucky: many of our franchisees, most notably Ted Arnovitz from Dayton, Ohio, understand our company and consistently offer invaluable advice from an "outside" perspective. Find a person or persons from your publics who can offer such valuable insight.

Most Nit-picking.   Many businesses avoid the nitpickers and penny-pinchers. It's a natural human reaction. You can run from them and protect your sanity if you choose. However, we've found it valuable to relish the penny-pinchers and nitpickers, looking carefully at every detail of their business and yours. Once you discover what makes these people happy, you'll know how to satisfy everyone down to their most finite needs. You'll be surprised to see the depths of understanding these people have about your business—they dig deeper than most paid consultants would! Your ability to serve everyone else by listening to this group will be greatly enhanced.

Most Active in Associations. While catering to professional, trade, or labor organizations is an obvious path to understanding your publics, look into the backgrounds of the people within those organizations. Often, such leaders also are on other boards. They can serve as valuable allies whose influence extends beyond their formal role with you. Caution: If you disappoint these people, they can share their disappointment with a wide group. If your staff are not members of some type of employee group, encourage them to join one because ideas and fresh approaches come from sources such as these.

Smallest. Many companies ignore their small customers, preferring to coddle the executives of one or two large customers. That tactic misses the point that all your small customers added together often will collectively be your largest customer. All the time spent focusing on one large customer can be wasted if that customer takes its business elsewhere. However, your small customers probably won't all disappear instantly, thereby serving as a steady and reliable base of business. Similarly, which job classification has the smallest number of people? Often these people are ignored, yet, if you don't direct your company to satisfy them, you'll never please everyone in your organization.

Most Vital. When evaluating who the most important members of your supplier public are, don't review them solely on the basis of size. Our flour suppliers are a good example of some misleading numbers. As a line expense item, flour is only 8 percent of our cost of goods budget, yet it represents the major ingredient in our manufacturing process. Without a high quality level and steady supply of flour, we would be out of business. Similarly, our doughmakers do not represent the largest or smallest group, but if they perform poorly, the resulting loss in business would be devastating.

Now that you have some idea how to approach the members of each group, it's time to start the process.

There's no substitute for personal meetings. While you can't handle everything, there are some things you can't afford not to handle—first person-contact with people who can supply you with valuable insights is one of them. In my earlier days with Distribution, I was on the road more than 15 days a month for more than three years. I became so familiar with my customers and team members that I knew their dogs' names and their dogs knew me. I developed relationships with suppliers so deep that I've retained friendships with vendors who no longer supply us. I practically lived with these people so I would know their deepest needs.

No executive can claim to be in touch with the needs of his or her organization's publics unless he or she has logged many hours carefully listening to them in person. You can hand off almost everything else, but you've got to have face-to-face contact on the front lines. Without it, you'll miss some of the most important needs you could serve. Tom Peters, among others, has lauded this as "MBWA"—manage by walking around.

Here's a story that taught me the value of being there. At one point, I began hearing complaints that our sliced pepperoni was sticking together, wasting time in store kitchens. I believed it was not resolvable, thinking, "I've been in the meat business for many years. I'm an experienced pepperoni maker and was manager of a plant that manufactured thousands of pounds of pepperoni. Pepperoni slices naturally stick together; those people don't know they are asking for the impossible."

As part of my job, I traveled extensively, often meeting people on their turf. One day, while making pizzas in the Trowbridge store in East Lansing, Michigan, I was slowed considerably by pepperoni that stuck together. It was so frustrating that I slammed a fistful onto the meat tray and yelled, "This damn stuff keeps sticking!"

Joyce White, a corporate area supervisor, was standing next to me and laughed like crazy. She had been one of several who had forwarded the complaints about the pepperoni to me. That incident confirmed for me the importance of getting information directly from the field. I called John Ezzo, the pepperoni supplier, immediately.

I found out exactly how frustrated I was making my customers: John didn't believe me. I wanted to scream. I realized that's precisely how my customers had felt for months as I didn't respond to their valid complaints.

There was only one thing to do: I put John in a store and made him make pepperoni pizzas.

He changed his formula for pepperoni. It stopped sticking, and two experienced meat people learned a lesson by putting themselves in the shoes of the customer.

But I have two warnings. I have just described the success I had while practicing MBWA. In a new leadership role, it is vital to get face-to-face readings of your publics' needs. As you become familiar with these needs and resolve long-standing issues, you'll discover fewer and fewer surprises and learn less with each trip. At some point, you may spend much time practicing MBWA and learn very little. There comes a time to stop gathering information and start leading people toward success. If I still maintained the travel schedule I started with, I'd never get anything done. In other words, how many people need to tell me that the pepperoni is sticking—all 5,000 store managers and 1,000 franchisees? No, probably three to five similar comments from sources proven to be insightful are enough. Often, a single comment from one seldom-incorrect, respected source is enough to know it's time to sit down at the drawing board or spend a day in the think tank. Super Vision dictates striking a balance between listening and resolving.

Second, listen at every opportunity as if you were trying for a PhD in listening—regardless of how tough the message may be. Especially in our early days, we would hold meetings with our customers where we asked them how we could improve as a company. I recall a particular meeting where Eric Marcus, one of our largest franchisees, went on for what seemed like days listing areas where we could improve our operations and service to his stores. While many executives cringe at hearing so much "dirty laundry" aired, we benefited from Eric's honesty and candid comments. Moreover, Eric is also the first in line to roll up his sleeves and help when it comes to turn potential improvement points into reality.

Another key to listening is building relationships. When taking customers out for events don't rattle on in their ear about your latest development or newest product. How can you learn what your customer needs when you are doing all the talking? When you take customers out to the ball game, simply enjoy them as human beings and say nothing about your company. There are only two valid business-related topics in these social situations: their biggest needs and how they feel about your business and how you're treating them.

If you're happy running in the middle of the pack, then you can continue to ram sales talk down their throats. If you choose to be the best in the world at what you do, then diligently listen to and learn customers' deepest needs. Once you have, you will have done the homework for the next step: identifying patterns that emerge from the blend of those needs.

Step 3: Sort the Identified Needs within Each Group into Major Patterns

Sorting needs into permanent patterns can be tricky. You may hear complaints that you regard as temporary and fail to recognize an underlying pattern or the larger issue behind them. For example, if I've already made changes that will alleviate a problem with fringe benefits, and I hear a team member continue to complain about fringe benefits, it is tempting to glide past that guidepost and not read what the sign truly says.

The true message may not be a pervasive problem with a particular aspect of our fringe benefit package. The message is those fringe benefits, in general, represent a continuing area of need for team members. I can count on the issue of fringe benefits resurfacing in future discussions I have with team members. Even if I was to go a year without hearing a complaint about fringe benefits, I can never take them off the list of most important needs/patterns that apply to team members.

The pepperoni incident discussed above was short-lived. The supplier changed the formula, and those complaints have not resurfaced in any magnitude. That incident was a lesson in patterns—the complaint was not about pepperoni, it was about speed in assembling pies in the stores. Store managers must deliver the Domino's Pizza guarantee to their customers: deliver a hot, tasty pizza in 30 minutes or less while driving safely at legal speeds. Speed, in the Domino's Pizza system, comes from efficient "making and baking" of the fresh pizza itself, not on the road. Store managers don't care what the source of the problem is they'll complain about anything we do wrong that cuts production speed. Again, think of their needs as a public: they are producing a fresh, made-to-order product. Their work is an art, and they need to make pizzas at high speed without high-speed equipment or mass manufacturing processes. As a result of my pepperoni education, I am much more sensitive to any complaint that seems to fit into the pattern of speed reduction in the stores.

At the least, complaints reflect a temporary problem with your public. A lack of complaints does not invalidate the pattern but indicates your performance is at the level your public expects. At Distribution, we've turned this into terms called the *expected zone* or *sleep zone*, which will be discussed later.

Step 4: Write a Concise, Detailed Wording of Those Need Patterns into a Mission Statement

A mission statement is a simple set of guidelines for decision making at all levels. It makes the company's mission public, allowing every member of the team to know the leader's vision and to assist in making it a reality.

The wording of the mission is critical and must be easily understood by every education level of your organization because it must touch everyone in your organization, not only the highly educated MBAs or executives. The wording must enable someone who is uninformed about your company to fully understand your commitments. Remember, people in your organization may have very low reading and comprehension skills, and if you don't speak in a language meaningful to these people, you've lost them from your team. It must address the major needs of your publics and be applied daily to accomplish your corporate objectives. Our mission statement (the focus of Chapter 7) is provided below:

Domino's Pizza Distribution Corporation Mission Statement

Through continuous innovation and living the Golden Rule, we will attain:

- Customers' belief that we're the best place to shop for their needs.

- Team members who can't think of a better company to work for.

- Community (government) that considers us a fine example of what business should be.

- Parent company proud to have us as part of their team.

- Suppliers excited enough to call us their favorite account,

resulting in constant improvement in those key operational areas so vital for our success.

As you can see, we have a component within the statement that addresses each of our publics. Recently, we introduced a new sentence. It includes having every member of our public group look forward to a brighter tomorrow for themselves (mentally, socially, spiritually, physically, and financially) and believe,

> *"Because I am a part of Domino's I know that my life will get better."*

Since part of our mission statement is for our customers to regard us as "the best place to shop," I could easily imagine customers seeking a supplier that provided pepperoni slices that did not stick together.

An effective mission statement must address your public's feelings. When you learn the deepest needs of your public, you will also learn their feelings. Tapping feelings is more powerful than all the intellectual statements you could ever write.

A good example of tapping into feelings resulted in a program we call Touchdown Dough. Carl Vaughan, one of our franchise customers in Virginia, told us we needed to improve our dough quality. Carl said, "Pizza Hut came up with a big improvement in dough and scored three points against us. Don't give us a field goal. Give us a touchdown and the extra point." We adopted Carl's analogy and called our new, improved product *Touchdown Dough*.

The Touchdown Dough battle cry worked so well it also tapped into the feelings of our team members. Soon after we adopted the name, John Vallero and the team members from our Hawaii commissary, acting on their own, painted football scenes on the walls of their facility, and the team members proudly called themselves the "makers of touchdown dough." No one would have painted a mural if we had asked them to produce "new and improved dough."

Similarly, in crafting your mission statement, you want to use unique words that generate feelings in your customers and other publics. You want to use words that convey to others, words that evoke feelings, not trite words that people will automatically pass over.

Step 5: Transfer the Patterns into Key Indicators— Numbers Used to Measure Performance and to Establish Accountability

Step 5 is crucial because once completed, you will be ready to begin implementation. You will know who your public is, what it needs, how to fulfill those needs in concert with your mission statement, and how to measure your performance toward meeting your goals. An example is provided on page 172.

For a long time, we tracked customer satisfaction on our products by simply asking our customers when we talked to them. They seemed satisfied, yet we started to receive random complaints about dough quality. I realized our team members received bonuses that were not affected by any measure of the quality of our dough. We developed a monthly survey we called the "ideal service survey" to get specific, measured information on customer satisfaction in the areas of product, price, service, and relations. Now we had a way to tie performance in these areas to bonuses (as a side note, tying bonus dollars to dough quality scores has led to a continuous seven-year upward trend in dough quality—more on the significance of rewards later).

Through this specific survey and a simple and objective scoring system, we quickly discovered critical points to improve in our dough quality. It wasn't enough to ask, "Are you satisfied with the dough, yes or no?" We found that many customers scored us low because of problems they encountered months earlier. Don't forget: Customers have long memories and do not easily forget disappointments. The better question was, "Were you satisfied with the last shipment of dough you received from us?" Now you have data you can use. You track how each customer responds each time, compute the average score of all customers, and establish a target score you want to achieve with the next shipment, and so forth. Without knowing if their dissatisfaction was current or not, we didn't know if we should adjust our formulas based on survey results. In short, take the most pressing needs you've uncovered from contacts with your publics, pose specific questions, and you'll be able to set the goals to meet these needs.

Target the scores you'd like to achieve to the level that indicates you are serving your customers (or other publics) the best they have ever been served. It is human nature to fall short of goals. If you target performance that satisfies minimum requirements, falling short will place you below average, or in a crisis zone. Set levels of performance that require your company to be *mejor del mundo*. Tom Monaghan took a Spanish class and liked that phrase because it means "best in the world." Tom doesn't do anything unless it's the best in the world. That's why we adopted it.

People will respond to inspiring goals and tough expectations. But if you do fall short of lofty goals, you'll still remain in the comfort zone of average, or what we call sleep zone, performance (the sleep zone is that level of performance that may not require celebration, but it doesn't keep you up at night worrying about the health of your business). To set your *mejor del mundo* goal or expectation, plan on going one step beyond what any other business that serves your public has ever done. The following experience I had dramatically affected the way I think, communicate, analyze, and reward. I think it will illustrate my point:

Dave Board, vice president of our international division, asked me to hold a group meeting for some international franchisees. Dave reported that some of our Canadian store owners were having difficulty getting along with some of the people from corporate headquarters. Dave suggested I call an international peace summit to get to the core of the troubles.

When we got the meeting assembled, it went routinely; no major points of complaint were brought up by any of the Canadian people. In fact, they seemed laid back and aloof, participating but saying nothing was wrong. I didn't buy it for a minute. There was no way they wanted a powwow on this level without having some major complaint. I was determined to get to the bottom of whatever annoyances had prompted this meeting. After a second day of getting nowhere, I took one of the franchisees, Mike Schlaiter, to a hockey game. We didn't talk business; instead we relaxed and enjoyed the game with a few beers. But I did sneak in the one crucial question.

"Mike," I asked, "now what is really going on here? It seems like everything is fine, but it can't be. You wouldn't have called a meeting for the little stuff we've been discussing."

He would only say, "You're going to have to talk to David Gausden because it has to do with something your regional director, Doug Anderson, said to him." It was commendable that he wouldn't discuss it any further, but I was glad to have a compass to steer the next meeting by.

The next day, as we were wrapping up the final session, I decided to use part of the methodology developed by Ichak Adizes to draw out what was bothering people. I said, "OK, we're about through here. If you've put everything you've got out on the table, that's fine. But if you haven't, then after you leave here you can't talk about it anymore. This is your time to clear the air."

Nobody budged, so I continued, "If there's anything bothering you that you don't bring up now, then if you do later, we're going to say,

'Hey, you had your chance.' This is your chance." Still, no one even flinched. So that I wouldn't single out the franchisee I knew had the complaint with Doug, I followed the Adizes method and went around the room one by one.

It worked. When I got to David Gausden, he finally opened up by saying, "Well, I did have something happen. I've never been so humiliated in my life. Because of something really insulting that Doug Anderson said to me, I've been thinking of getting out of this company."

When I asked him what Doug had said, he continued.

"Well, my store had been doing about $6,000 a week in sales and Doug came in and read me the riot act. He said the store should be doing $10,000 a week. He called me on having a new company car and on some vacations I had recently taken and on the fact that I had not been in my store much lately.

"He said I'd better work on it and get my sales up to $10,000. So I told my family, canceled other vacation plans, and began working long hours throughout the weekends. Before Doug's next visit, I had gotten my sales up to $10,000.

"When he came the next time, I picked him up at the airport and he asked me what my sales were. When I told him I'd reached $10,000, his response was that every store in my city should be doing $20,000 a week! That was all he had to say to me."

I turned to Doug Anderson and asked if he agreed that that was what had happened. He said, "Yes, he's exactly right."

"Doug, can you tell me why you said that to him?"

"Sure. Our competition is doing $20,000 per store in similar situations. Our stores should do $20,000."

I pressed Doug further, "Well, what about the $10,000 goal he reached that you set for him?"

"Hey, I know he must have worked his butt off. He made a lot of sacrifices, and he did a great job. He got his advertising act together, and he was on top of what was going on in his store. I was impressed he'd gotten up to $10,000, but let's not kid ourselves. His store should be doing $20,000."

I turned back to David and asked, "Do you think your store was doing poorly at $6,000?"

"Yep."

"Do you think it should do $20,000?"

"Yep."

"So you both agree that $6,000 was a terrible crisis. You agree that he was fair in asking you to get up to $10,000. And you agree that you should be doing $20,000. What's the disagreement about then?"

AGREEMENT WITHOUT UNITY

It seemed a dilemma. We had a set of three levels of performance on which everybody agreed. But no one had been happy, even though they agreed.

That's when it hit me. For the first time, I saw the need for a system of multiple goals. We couldn't depend on a single set of numbers to gauge our progress.

In this case, everyone agreed the lower number indicated a crisis was at hand and it was serious enough to justify canceling vacations and working overtime and weekends.

The next higher number was something everybody was content with as being "OK." David was making a comfortable living, seemed fairly happy with it, and was ready to renew his vacation plans to celebrate climbing out of the cellar. Further, Doug no longer worried about the stability of the store.

Yet, there was another number everyone believed could be reached. Doug knew better than anyone that $20,000 was possible for that store, but David didn't seem to want to make the extra push to attain it.

Here was a situation in which we had a big blowup and nearly lost a franchisee, although he agreed with Doug's assessment of his performance. He simply wanted some recognition for pulling out of the slump.

That was the first time we all worked with a set of three numbers for our business goals. The international crisis passed and the summit ended peacefully. From that meeting evolved the Distribution concepts of exceptional, expected, and crisis performance ratings, which is now the basis of every rating system we employ (more on this later).

LAYING A FOUNDATION

In construction, you need to properly lay the foundation for a new building. With a solid and properly oriented foundation, you can modify the original plans and change the building's function. However, if you didn't set the foundation in the right place, it's difficult to relocate the entire building later without great expense. Steps 1 through 5 are laying the foundation. Steps 6 and 7 enable you to monitor and evaluate the work you've done in the first five steps.

Step 6: Compare Performance Numbers to Your Desired Levels

At an International Franchise Association seminar I attended, a speaker provided some valuable insight on the topic of human nature and how it relates to customers. The point he made applies to all publics, not merely customers.

The speaker updated Abraham Lincoln's famous quotation: "You can't please all the people all the time." The speaker said, "Between 5 and 7 percent of the people you serve are totally critical. Their natural state is to be unhappy. They will respond negatively to almost all questions. If your goal were to satisfy 100 percent of your customers, to be realistic you would have to scale that back to between 93 and 95 percent."

Conversely, 10 to 12 percent of the people you serve are relatively happy no matter what. With them, you can expect approval of nearly anything you do.

At Distribution, we respond to the feelings of our publics as measures of our success. Therefore, overall statements of happiness from our customers, team members, suppliers, community officials, and parent company leaders are important to us. As I mentioned, we evaluate our performance as being either exceptional, expected, or crisis. Since 5 to 7 percent of any particular public is not going to be happy no matter what you do, as a rule of thumb, measure your performance on an adjusted scale where 93 to 95 percent is perfect. We still insist on 100 percent compliance with product standards and other areas not dependent on measuring feelings.

It would be a crisis if, say, one third of your customers were dissatisfied; that would be a clear message that many people are thinking of finding another supplier. You might regard everything that falls between those two extremes as expected performance. The chart on page 26, corresponding to the example provided just before it, reveals how numbers are applied to the three levels of performance to serve as key indicators.

We apply the exceptional, expected, or crisis concept to virtually every aspect of our operations. Even individual team members rate their own performance according to those criteria. We'll explore in depth in Chapter 8 how we analyze our performance data and turn them into useful information that can be used to refine day-to-day business strategies.

Step 7: Build in an Automatic Reward and Corrective Action System Based on the Performance as Measured by the Key Indicators

While compensation is essential, few people take jobs simply for the money. Many studies show that many people will gladly switch to a lower paying but more satisfying job. At Distribution, we offer and our team members seek three forms of reward: normal pay for normal performance, bonuses or compliments for better than average performance, and the opportunity for high praise and special recognition for truly exceptional performance.

Described at length in Chapters 10 and 11, our normal compensation and benefits packages provide the essentials, individual performance objectives reward team members for better than average performance, our internal olympics program offers corporatewide praise and large bonuses for the top performers, and our national performance objectives filter out rewards that might otherwise go to individuals who do not carry a fair share of the workload. In other words, our system is designed both to reward hard work and to prevent laggards from being rewarded when the overall group excels despite carrying dead weight.

A REPEATING CYCLE

The seven-step system is not static. You will continually return to Steps 1 and 2 to update the information on your publics and their needs. When significant changes are noted, you will alter the patterns previously identified in Step 3, which will lead to changes in how to apply your mission statement. By constantly balancing and fine-tuning your understanding of your publics, their needs/patterns, your mission statement, and your key indicators of performance through continual surveys, your company can become and remain a leader in your industry.

After repeating the seven steps, you'll often find you missed some of your publics or overlooked some of the needs of those you did identify. Naturally, you'll update your mission statement if necessary to incorporate the improved picture of your mission.

Further, not all changes in your publics or their needs will result in changes in the mission statement. You may only have to alter the key indicators you use to measure company performance better to support an existing component of your mission.

A SMALL-SCALE APPLICATION

The seven-step Super Vision process applies to even a single project. As a small-scale example of how we apply it in our company, the subject of the rest of the book, I'll explain here how I employed it in writing this book. I had never written a book but had success employing this system in other aspects of my life, so why not with the book!

Step 1: Identifying Publics

The first step is to identify the publics that will be affected. For this book, the most obvious publics are buyers and readers. Book "owners" are a second public. They include the publisher, distributors, retailers, and authors—those who have a vested interest in seeing that it sells. The third public consists of the Domino's Pizza family, whose accomplishments are chronicled in this book.

Step 2: Understanding Needs

Once these publics are recognized, the next step is to identify their needs from this book. What would each want to get out of it? It is not uncommon that these needs and wants will overlap (as is the case in many applications of the seven-step method). Each group, however, will have one or two unique needs. Without an opportunity to MBWA thousands of members of these publics, I went to the most critical as a sounding board. These included business writers such as Jeff Davidson, editors like Jeff Krames, the Domino's Pizza executive team, and franchisee president's council members, and my own executive staff. After this input, I thought I had a clear view of all my publics needs (I did, however, miss a critical one—see Epilogue, page 261).

Step 3: Organize into Patterns

Group One: Buyers and Readers. They want the book to:

- Elevate their knowledge of business management.
- Be easy to understand and reader friendly.
- Give some solid how-to concepts backed by examples.
- Give complete information on a documented success story without holding anything back.

Group Two: Book Owners (Distributers, Retailers, Publishers, Authors). They want the book to:

- Sell successfully.
- Develop repeat customers.

Group Three: Domino's Pizza Family. They want the book to:

- Train new team members on how Distribution works.
- Attract more top-quality team members from the book's readership.
- Give recognition and credit to those contributing to our success.
- Increase pride for being part of Domino's Pizza.
- Share success within the Domino's Pizza family so the franchisees and related companies can use and refine the system.
- Generate contacts for the Domino's Pizza Innovation Network.
- Be positively regarded by readers (maybe even sell some pizzas!).
- Not be a distraction that takes my time away from the company.

Needs of Publics for This Book

Publics	Groups	Major Needs/Patterns
Book buyers and readers	Learners (those seeking to improve) Teachers (professors and consultants) Community at large	Elevate their knowledge of business management Easy to understand Reader friendly Good "how-to" concepts backed by examples Contain complete information, holding nothing back Donations to charity
Book owners	Publisher Distributor Retailer Authors	Sell books Attract repeat business Donations to charity
Domino's Pizza family	Franchisees Team members Suppliers	Recognize and credit them for their achievements Gain a sense of pride for being part of Domino's Enhance their knowledge of Distribution's methods Attract new, top-quality team members from the book's readership Don't be a distraction from company goals Contacts for the Innovation Network Positive regard for company by pizza-buying public

Step 4: The Mission Statement

From the patterns I identified among the public's needs for the book, I then created these three statements that sum up my overall mission, which is to publish a book that:

- Readers find enjoyable and stimulating, and that contains concepts that are easy to understand and apply.

- Shares the positive attributes and methods of the Domino's Pizza family in a "how-to" style.

- Sells enough copies for the authors, publisher, and distributors of the book to consider it having been worth the time and effort.

How do you take a long and varied list of needs from many members of your publics and boil it down to a few short statements. The key is to focus only on the few statements that seem to say it all and serve to set attitude, climate, and cultural behavior when used as a guideline.

If I were an author by trade, these three statements would be on a plaque on the wall, and everyone involved with my writing would know these statements. People would be able to recite them, and I would have tests to ensure they could. Once those were known by everyone, I would trust and let people attend to completing the other steps in the process that fulfill the components of the three sentences.

Steps 5 and 6: Establishing Key Indicators, Comparing Performance Numbers

A mission statement must be turned into something tangible that can be used to gauge your progress toward achieving all the goals it identifies. In this step, actual performance targets are set so that every member of your corporate or project team will always know how you are doing.

Step 5 and Step 6 are closely linked. While Step 5 must be completed first, it's quickly followed by developing a method to determine the target numbers you seek. Remember, each key indicator will use three numbers, representing exceptional, expected, and crisis performance. The chart illustrates the mechanics of Steps 5 and 6. It lists both the key indicators adopted for the book project in Step 5 along with the methods in Step 6 that we chose to measure those indicators.

Keep in mind that the first time you choose key indicators for a single project or your organization's entire performance, you are choosing numbers based on your best understanding and your feelings about the situation. For example, I'm calling 15,000 books sold in the first year expected performance. I don't have hard data to predict sales of a book written by me, but based on my understanding of business book sales, I believe the book can hit that performance level. After the first year's results are complete, for the second year or next book, armed with hard data from the first year, I might revise the expected level of sales to 5,000 or 20,000, depending on my increased understanding of the situation. Every level set to evaluate the performance of this first effort has been set based on understanding and feeling.

You'll notice a pattern to some of the response percentage targets I've established, (i.e., the basic 40, 60, 80 percent ranges). Often the numbers will be fairly uniform across many indicators, and you'll find many of your own will fit these ranges. (However, some areas of your operation will be so critical to your success that you may set 98 percent as exceptional, 95 percent as expected, and 92 percent as a crisis. With Distribution, for example, we would soon be out of business if we considered it expected performance for 80 percent of our deliveries to stores to arrive on time. Our current on-time delivery performance is 99.9983 percent.)

Key Indicators for this Book

Identified Need	Crisis	Expected	Exceptional	Measurement Method
Positively regarded by all readers	50%	65%	85%	Reader survey
Readers understand "how-to" system	40%	65%	85%	Reader survey
Increased reader knowledge	60%	80%	90%	Reader survey
Readers will use some part of what they learned	60%	80%	95%	Reader survey
Enjoyable to read	60%	70%	85%	Reader survey
Increase sense of pride in being part of Domino's Pizza	40%	60%	80%	Corporate survey
Inquiries for Innovation Network	10	20	30	Count
Recognizes and mentions:				
Franchisees	10	15	20	Count
Corporate executives	10	15	20	
Team members	10	15	20	
Suppliers	2	5	10	
Number of books sold in first year	10,000	15,000	25,000	Publisher's audit
Dollars donated to charity from profits	$0	$5,000	$10,000	Our checkbook
Résumés received	50	75	100	Count

Again, you'll often tackle a new project and you won't have a scientific basis for establishing key indicator numbers, such as my estimate for book sales. Another example is when I thought about the percentages for "Positively regarded by all readers." I had no scientific basis for a number to assign to that key indicator.

When you invade new territory, you have to set numbers by gut feelings. When I need to use my intuition to set a new standard, I approach it with these three thoughts: (1) Crisis is the level that would make me feel I couldn't go home at night until it was fixed; (2) exceptional is the level that will make me want to throw a party and pop some champagne corks; and, (3) expected is the level that feels like performance is supporting our goals and is according to plan.

Apply extra vigilance to your indicators when you set them by intuition because they will likely need refining. Feedback from the ongoing surveys will help you adjust the figures for the three zones if the need becomes apparent.

The quickest way to recognize you've erred on the low side is if you find you easily achieve exceptional scores. Exceptional will never be easy. Similarly, if you are easily meeting the expected scores, yet receiving a lot of negative feedback, you'll know your key indicators do not reflect the perceptions of the only people who count: your public! You'll have to increase the score needed to reach the expected level.

Whenever you set key indicator numbers without historical data, eliminate your intuitive guesses as soon as possible, replacing them with figures based on scientific analysis of surveys of your publics.

The methods to count all but four of the key indicators for this book already existed within our system. However, existing channels provided no way to obtain answers to the four questions regarding the value readers got from the book. To that end, the last page of the book is a reader survey card for you to complete and mail. How could I judge my success in these areas if I didn't ask the reader? After finishing this book, please remove or duplicate the survey at the end of the book, complete and mail to my attention at the address on the survey. If you include your name and address, we'll send you a copy of the results and we'll respond to the most frequently aired concerns or questions that come out of the survey.

In the survey, I ask what you believed to be the three best ideas or chapters, as well as three missing points. There also are direct "yes" and "no" questions that will be used to generate the percentage scores to measure the key indicators.

I will get a clear picture of whether the book met the goals established in its mission statement by reading the responses from your survey cards, the surveys of our internal public, and by counting the résumés received and the contacts we make with business leaders.

Step 7: Reward System

Any good seven-step process has an integral reward system. Reward systems have to give people something they truly want to receive, not what you would like to give them. This book is no exception.

I remember a conversation I had with one of my college roommates, Andy Koploy. He and I both agreed that our chief goal in life was to own a company in which every employee would share up to 50 percent of the profits. We believed that sharing the ownership with the entire team—i.e., giving everyone a stake in the success or failure of the organization—would lead to success for everyone concerned. Ten years later, I listened to Tom Monaghan whose philosophy echoes the goal Andy and I set for ourselves. Tom has let me build a company where the team members own up to 20 percent of the profits and where we can innovatively reward and recognize top performers. Rewards, especially for me and the team helping write this book, are not always financial.

One of the rewards will be self-generating. As we wade through history and relearn lessons from our successes and failures, we will gain the satisfaction of better understanding the Domino's Pizza Distribution system of Super Vision, which will provide many benefits. For instance, I'll be able to more clearly and simply explain the concepts found in this book to all members of the Domino's Pizza family and, hence, be a better leader. The team members helping assemble this book will be much better suited for leadership roles through the ongoing dissection of and exposure to these principles.

Another reward will be the charitable contributions the community (the national community, in this case) will receive from the profits of the book. Too many people have been involved in making the Distribution management system what it is today for me to take full credit and retain the profits personally. As with any reward system, I hope my incentive programs for this book will increase readership. The profits will be distributed among these charities:

- The Domino's Pizza Partners—this is a special nonprofit charity set up to disburse funds to Domino's Pizza team members who have suffered a tragedy.

- Environmental agencies, such as Ducks Unlimited, the most cost-efficient wildlife charity in North America with 82 cents from every dollar going directly to the cause, not administration (*Money*, December 1990).

- Vlcek Family Wildlife Foundation—established to protect and enhance wildlife habitats.

Let's turn now to Part II to discuss the groups we affect, our publics, and how we aspire to meet their needs, thereby giving you ideas so you can impact your publics effectively.

PART

II

Know Thy Publics

I don't see how you can be successful, let alone survive, if you don't understand the needs of the groups you impact. At Distribution, we never take the needs of publics lightly. In some cases, we understand their needs better than they do—we have to. Regardless of what business you're in, most people will get along quite well without you because your competitors undoubtedly will gather up whatever market share you had.

In the next five chapters, we'll look at what we do to better know our publics, starting with Distribution customers.

Chapter Two

What Do Our Customers Need?

C learly, Step 1 of Super Vision (identifying publics) is relatively easy when it comes to customers. We can recognize our largest, most influential, most visionary, etc. The trick comes in Step 2—the careful inventory of customer needs. Customers take on many forms and characteristics, and without careful attention to and understanding of their needs any company will fail. Domino's Pizza Distribution is no exception. I could tell hundreds of stories about how we discovered or continue to monitor our customer's needs and the steps we've taken to meet these needs—many of these appear throughout the book—but certain key ones best illustrate what we learned and the patterns that emerged.

THE NEED FOR QUALITY AND CONSISTENCY

Annually, we sponsor a special challenge to our team members to be the best in the company in their particular job. We pose competitions to determine who is the best (we call these our olympics, which will be discussed later). Following the 1986 finals, Ron Conkey, one of our customers who volunteered to judge the dough competition, looked at me and said, "Don, there's a problem you need to know about. I judged both the regional competitions, which involved seven dough-making competitions, and the nationals, where there were five.

"But I have to tell you, Don," he continued, "that of the 12 teams of people I watched, there were a number who weren't following the formula to a tee. In fact, in the national competition, one competitor put yeast into hot water, which we all know kills it."

As I listened, I remembered some recent complaints we were getting about dough quality. It was clear we were letting our customers down.

FAIL-SAFE SERVICE

The need for unmatched, error-free service became clear to me after a conversation with Dick Mueller, our former vice president of operations, when he was leaving the corporation to become a franchisee. Dick's new contract obligated him to build so many stores that he would become our largest customer. Other members of the executive team were troubled about his intentions because Dick had the money, the leverage, and the knowledge to open his own commissary. Dick had told me he wouldn't do that, but I could not allay the fears of the other executive team members without more carefully verifying his intentions.

To ensure I wasn't being shortsighted, I flew to Mississippi and met with Dick. I told him of the lingering concerns over his departure and asked that he level with me. His answer gave me not only his personal guarantee but also a terrific insight into his needs when he said, "Don, we're dealing with food and with items you have to get from other suppliers. I cannot expect you to have perfect quality day in and day out.

"I know you're going to disappoint me sometimes. All I care about is that when you do, you promptly correct it. I also know you won't have the best price on every item every day. All I ask is that you work to correct it when your prices are out of line."

Then he paused before continuing in a more somber tone, "But, Don, if you ever force me to temporarily close one of my stores by failing to deliver on time, then I will consider opening my own commissary."

About the same time as my meeting with Dick, a truck from our Georgia commissary showed up late for deliveries in South Carolina. As a result, all seven stores in that state had to close for an entire night. While it was only seven stores at the time, it was devastating to think that no one could buy a Domino's Pizza in the entire state of South Carolina because of a glitch in our performance. The commissary leader, Ken McPherson, remembers the incident well: "I have never known Don to be so angry. I was thankful that there was a phone line between us because, beyond threatening me with my job, he seemed mad enough to threaten me with my life."

By the next day, news of my tantrum had spread hundreds of miles throughout our commissary system. I received a call from a commissary leader two states away from Ken who told me he and his team have pledged never to close a store and were in the midst of a proactive planning meeting. Two great things have come from this incident: We have not closed stores to this magnitude again in over 10 years since this incident, and Ken McPherson has been promoted several times and is one of our key operations people.

READING OTHER STRONG MESSAGES

In addition to an annual survey (we call it our "summer survey" and it is the focus of Chapter 9), we use our Ideal Satisfaction Survey (ISS) to take a random sample of 10 percent of our customers every month, with the goal of covering each store at least twice a year. Since 1982, we also hold regular meetings with franchisees we call "CommFrans" or "DistFrans" where our customers have come to expect that we'll hold nothing back. At Distribution, that means we've got to be willing to answer any question openly and completely. It also means we can count on some tough questions, including specific questions on our pricing, our efficiencies, and times we've failed. This relationship is valued by both our customers and ourselves.

We prepare for the meetings by imagining we are in the shoes of our customers. We try to anticipate what they'll hit us with and prepare answers before we get the questions. We try to think like our customers and imagine what gripes we would have if we were them. These practice sessions have been great tools for us because many times we see problems and fix them before the meetings.

SORTING IT ALL OUT

Through experiences such as those listed above and hundreds more like them, we've come to understand what our customers need from us and can sort these needs into four basic patterns (Step 3). We've determined that Distribution needs us to be leaders in the areas of quality, service, customer relations, and price. Collectively, we use the battle cry "the Package" to philosophically describe what we can offer our customers:

- *Quality*—We will provide goods that are of unlimited quality, consistent nationwide, and never falling below Domino's Pizza specifications and standards.

- *Service*—We will provide service that is unsurpassed in convenience, to all Domino's Pizza stores, with the correct, undamaged product arriving no later than when the customer needs it.

- *Customer relations*—We will be open and honest with our customers: listening, treating them equally, furnishing them with necessary information and requested training, and inviting their input into our decision-making process.

- *Price*—We will price our foods and services so that our customers cannot find alternatives offering them a better overall financial return. We back up our prices with a rebate guarantee if they are overcharged.

We further communicate these steps to our entire company in a concise, easily understood mission statement (Step 4): "Customers' belief that we're the best place to shop for their needs."

Needs of Distribution Customers

Public	Groups	Major Needs/Patterns
Distribution customers	Franchise stores Corporate stores	"The Package" Highest quality goods Unmatched service Unquestionable relationships Best value pricing
Our mission statement:	Customers' belief that we're the best place to shop for their needs.	

To measure our success at how well we are fulfilling our mission and providing our Package, we have built a system of key indicators (Steps 5 and 6) and use surveys to monitor our progress and success. Like the measures used to determine the success of this book (see Chapter 1), we express three different performance levels to determine our success: crisis, expected, and exceptional. These are measures of results, not efforts. Later in the chapter, I'll discuss efforts in place to achieve our results.

The surveys are scored at corporate headquarters and the results are entered into our computer system, becoming immediately available to every member of the Domino's family. The numbers generated by the results are further used to calculate the monthly bonuses that are an integral part of the total compensation package for every Domino's team member, both at the commissaries and at corporate headquarters.

The pattern of needs and a key indicator for each that we've identified is used as the first column on the chart on page 38 with each level of performance detailed and the current method we use to measure ourselves in subsequent columns:

INSPIRING HEROICS AND SATISFYING NEEDS

Step 7 of the Super Vision process calls for establishing automatic rewards systems for teams. We use a monthly bonus system that rewards fulfilling our customers' needs (as well as the needs of all of our publics) that will be detailed in a later chapter. The lessons for this chapter and its focus on customers are the remarkable efforts, outstanding results, and downright heroics our team members display to ensure that Domino's Pizza Distribution is "the best place customers can shop for their needs."

THE "SECRET WEAPON"

Tom Monaghan has referred to Distribution as the parent company's "secret weapon." If this is so, it's because highly motivated people in our commissary system allow store managers to focus on making, baking, and taking pies to the pizza public by providing value-added service that is both timely and consistent. This support system allows pizza stores to concentrate on what they do best.

Key Indicators for Distribution Customers

Customers' Identified Needs	Crisis	Expected	Exceptional	Measurement Method
Overall satisfaction				
Is Distribution the best place to shop for your needs?	30% no	10–15% no	<10% no	Monthly ideal service survey
Market share calculation	<95.5%	No lower than last year end	.2% better than last year end	Financial records, market share reports
Unmatched service				
No store closings calculation	30 per year	15 per year	<10 per year	Incident reports
Can you get the same or better service from companies other than Distribution?	30% yes	10–15% yes	<10% yes	Monthly ideal service survey
Product quality and value				
Can you find the same or better quality products from companies other than Distribution at the same price?	20% yes	10–15% yes	<8% yes	Monthly ideal service survey
Distribution's dough audit	<90% score	90–94% score	>94% score	Dough process audit
Superior customer relations				
Is it difficult to deal with Distribution?	30% yes	7–11% yes	<7% yes	Monthly ideal service survey
Fair prices				
Do we meet or beat competition?	Competition beats us on any like product	Best in the market on all products	Best in the market for 6 months	Competitive pricing surveys
Can you find better prices than from Distribution?	>10% yes	4–8% yes	<4% yes	Monthly ideal service survey

With 250 state-of-the-art refrigerated trucks and trailers, 1,600 team members (including 50 at the home office) are collectively responsible for ensuring 600,000 timely store deliveries each year. That's 600,000 opportunities to satisfy a customer; that's 600,000 times to meet a crucial need. And we have the best score in the industry with a 99.99983 on-time delivery average.

As of August 1991, 95.5 percent of all Domino's franchisees choose to order from Distribution, even though they don't have to. Why aren't franchisees mandated to order from our commissaries? With a captive market—i.e., all franchisees forced to order exclusively from Distribution—quality and service ultimately would suffer because the commissaries wouldn't be challenged to be the best they can be.

With the franchisees having total freedom in choosing their supplier, Distribution has to strive continually to be the vendor of choice. In this manner, we force ourselves to constantly improve and upgrade products, services, and delivery and offer the type of support the franchisees require and demand. A few of the accomplishments that keep our customers loyal include:

- We're the industry leader in on-time deliveries.

- We're the industry leader in customer pricing and service guarantees.

- We're the industry leader in recognizing our team members as being professionals and giving them the tools and the freedom they need to best serve our customers.

Many other successful fast-food franchises negotiate agreements with their franchisees for the corporate system to supply food, operating supplies, equipment, and related items. With Distribution, that is not the case. Our strength is gained by delivering our "Package"—quality, service, customer relations, and price. That's how we grow and prosper with what seems like a limited market.

We've achieved a 95.5 percent market share using a system that is, according to our franchise attorney, Joe Sheyka, "the purest in the industry," by allowing the franchise customers to choose or not choose to buy from us. And as far as we can tell, this is the highest noncontracted market share in the history of franchising. Because we have to be as competitive as any business, we approach our mission for our customers as if we could make anything happen. Remember, with Super Vision, you set high standards so that even if you miss the mark, you still end up comfortably somewhere between expected and exceptional performance. While we know we're not perfect, our goal is to satisfy everybody 100 percent of the time.

When our customers are in a pizza war with local competition, we have to be a partner in the pizza war with them. If a customer is unhappy for a day because you make a mistake, it need not upset your mission to serve that customer. You can still maintain the integrity of the relationship. You can continue to be the "best place to shop" even if you are not perfect.

If you maintain your vision for them over the long term, in the face of other suppliers who also will make mistakes, despite foul-ups, you'll still have the edge. Too often, business goals and strategies are designed with short-term objectives in mind. It's easy to lose some of your customers if your objectives are short term and you rarely ask them how you're doing.

Consider the difference if you strike the proper balance between short- and long-term objectives. With long-term objectives in mind, ask customers periodically, as we do, how they think you're doing in serving them. With the latter strategy, you can quickly discover the source of any discontent they may have. Then let them know it was an exception to the long-term vision of your relationship with them. You can correct the problem long before they have time to find a new supplier.

IT'S A TWO-WAY STREET

Our challenge is getting the most out of what other corporations would see as a market with limited growth potential. Our opportunity for growth comes from being an outstanding supplier, helping every store achieve higher sales, and incessantly streamlining operations.

It's precisely the same with your business: If your customers grow, you grow. Maybe you've concentrated on adding new customers and have missed the growth opportunities you could enjoy by becoming an integral player with your existing customers.

If your products or services help your customers double in size, you might more than double your own size. Not only is your current customer base buying more, but new customers will want to associate with you based on your own and your customers' successes.

OUR QUALITY PLEDGE

We believe that author and consultant Phil Crosby is exactly right when he says quality is conformance to standards set by your customers. Therefore, we let our customers evaluate our success at providing quality products by their votes on our surveys and, more dramatically, their votes with their checkbooks. Here are a few of our programs to assure we win those votes!

Quality Guarantee

Distribution guarantees all its customers 100 percent satisfaction with our products because that's one of their key areas of need. Any customer can return any unsatisfactory goods for a full refund, at any time. We respect and admire grocer Stew Leonard's customer satisfaction guarantee that he has carved in stone at the entrance to his store: Rule #1—The customer is always right. Rule #2—If the customer is wrong, refer to Rule #1. There's no question that a guarantee is necessary to be considered the best place for your customers to shop. The customer and his or her perception are always right. You'll never achieve long-term success by proving them wrong.

Dough Certification

Dough is an absolutely critical item. If we allow rookies to solo on a batch of dough or don't conform to the highest standards of quality and product formulation, we're headed for trouble. If a store gets a lot of complaints about dough on a busy Saturday night, you can bet that owner will wonder if we're the best place to shop.

Remember franchisee Ron Conkey's observations as he judged our olympic dough event? He helped me see the need for a "doughmaker certification" process and a "master doughmaker" program. Everyone must earn their wings before they can be certified as a Domino's Pizza doughmaker. This includes extensive hands-on training, classroom instruction, and rigorous tests. To drive home the importance of perfect doughmaking, we raised the standards of the olympic judging and doubled the prize money awarded. The master doughmaker program further supports this: to be a master doughmaker in our company requires at least 10,000 hours in the dough room, consistently high scores on their product as rated by customers, and nomination by a regional manager. The payoff to the company to have master doughmakers is clear: we have the best people making the best dough. In fairness, the payoff to the master doughmaker is substantial. Anyone reaching this status gets a retroactive dollar-an-hour raise for their 10,000 hours: a check for $10,000 presented in front of hundreds of people at our annual awards. That is a small price to pay for having the best people making the best products for our customers.

Supplier Planning and Review Sessions

Supplier planning and review sessions are held regularly between members of our executive team at Distribution headquarters and those businesses that supply our commissaries. In these meetings, we review our mission statement for suppliers with those who attend, ensuring that each supplier understands the quality standards Domino's has established for its products. Such sessions help us get a consistent quality product from our suppliers.

"But wait," you say. "We're supposed to be discussing customer relations not supplier relations." That's where the interplay comes in. The products we deliver to our customers certainly can't exceed the quality of the goods we receive from our suppliers.

Because our customers know we hold these regular sessions, they can rest assured the products delivered to their stores are made from the best ingredients we can get. It's a part of being the best place for our customers to shop.

Even if one customer calls me up in a screaming fit over a botched delivery, the overall consistency of our deliveries gives me ammunition to fend off possible threats to take his or her business elsewhere. If a store manager knows we buy the best products available from raw materials suppliers, is he or she going to knowingly downgrade the quality of the product permanently because we slipped up today?

Independent of the size of your business, you can conduct your own supplier planning review sessions. You have only to make your sessions commensurate with the size of your orders. An established and regular telephone contact policy may suffice. The power in the process is that your customers know the materials you use are subject to regular, in-depth reviews with your suppliers.

OUR SERVICE PLEDGE

Following our quality pledge to customers, we also developed a rigorous service pledge, including:

- "Three-point landings."
- Commissary field representatives.
- Keys to the store.

Three-Point Landings

Among the worst things a supplier can do to one of its customers is to cause it to lose business. Most often this happens because of untimely delivery or nondelivery of sufficient quantities of product for the customer to fill orders. To underscore the importance of this service pledge, David Materne, head of our equipment division, described it as "three-point landings." A three-point landing means we promise to deliver: (1) What they want, (2) when they want it, and (3) where they want it.

While it may be unlikely that your business will require a nationally advertised promise like Domino's Pizza's 30-minute delivery guarantee, your customers will admire you for making such a bold delivery pledge. Our pledge to "three-point landings" is backed up with this guarantee: If we're late with a delivery to a store, meaning we deliver outside of the window we commit to, the next delivery is free. Making and keeping a promise like that has meant strong long-term business relationships with our customers.

By Land, Sea, or Air. After Dick Mueller warned me never to close one of his stores and the subsequent disaster in South Carolina, I made a clear statement to my team: We will do anything at any cost to prevent a store from closing. I was determined never to commit the cardinal sin of having a customer (a Domino's Pizza store) lose orders because of any problem due to a misstep by us. Most Domino's Pizza stores are small and have limited physical resources, including small coolers. Lacking the ability to store a large cache of food makes a steady stream of on-time deliveries essential to continuous operation.

The business lost when a caller is turned away multiplies many times over—that caller may not try those unreliable folks at Domino's next time and dial a competitor's number thereafter. The store may never get the customer back.

One of our commissary managers, Kevin Moran, heard my message to pull out the stops to prevent a store closing and once delivered pizza dough by a chartered plane to make up for an equipment failure his commissary experienced. That kind of dedication has become representative of our philosophy, and since Kevin set the standard, others have followed, using helicopters and even snowmobiles to maintain our delivery pledge to our customers.

How did we do financially on a batch of dough delivered by chartered plane? Terrific! We lost a lot of money on that particular order, but what do you think it did for our long-term image in that customer's eyes? We easily could have said, "Look, we're sorry, but the only way to get you any dough is to charter a plane and that wouldn't be cost-effective. How about if I give you a discount on your next order to make up for the business you lose until we can get you supplied again?" Not really meeting their needs, is it?

The real financial return from this episode came from the proactive plans our commissary team members put into place to prevent incurring the costs associated with emergency deliveries. From posting ferry schedules in delivery trucks to equipping commissaries with backup generators, our people understood and acted to prevent any service failure to our customers.

Chartering a plane made a declaration that we stand 100 percent behind our mission statement. Furthermore, word of it raced throughout the Domino's Pizza organization like wildfire. In 1990, with more than 600,000 annual deliveries, we experienced only 10 store closings due to lack of product—that's an overall success rate of 99.9983 percent—and even when we failed, we were only 15 to 60 minutes late!

For the president of a small company, honoring such a pledge to your customers might be as simple as loading some stock in the trunk of your own car if a delivery truck breaks down and delivering the shipment personally. You might also call a local courier service. Even taxicab companies offer delivery services.

Most other errors can be corrected:

- Poor quality products can be replaced.
- Credits for spoiled food, immediately destroyed at the store, are issued.
- Excessive charges for supplies can be rebated.

Nothing, however, can make up for the full impact of the losses in revenue and pizza customers when a store closes from a lack of supplies. If what happened with the South Carolina stores later happened to Dick Mueller, I might have lost my largest customer, and Dick was projected to soon become 10 percent of our total store market.

WHAT ELSE DO CUSTOMERS NEED?

In the Super Vision process, the better you know the needs of your customers, the better you are at recognizing patterns that point up emerging needs. When we first began, for example, we supplied almost exclusively food items. To support our customers even better, we've expanded our offerings to include equipment and supplies necessary to store operations.

Our new store equipment division got rolling with two people: Gary Josefczyk and Eileen Maisano. In the early years, stores would place orders and we'd secure equipment from suppliers to be shipped via common carrier to the new store site. As store growth at Domino's Pizza started hitting staggering levels through the mid-1980s, we discovered the need to improve our delivery system.

Problems arose from various common carriers bringing equipment from vendors all over the nation. Ovens, coolers, counter systems, and other vital pieces of equipment would be delivered at different times by different carriers. Many carriers did a great job for us, but when a key piece of equipment was damaged in transit that Domino's Pizza store could not open for business. Gary led the charge to provide an unmatched level of service to our equipment customers: centrally purchase and warehouse Domino's Pizza-specific equipment and supplies to take advantage of quantity price breaks and pass these along to customers. Further, build a transportation system that would guarantee delivery at the customer's convenience (not the common carrier's) and

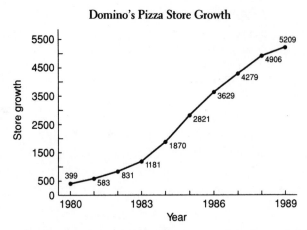

provide unloading and inspection service at the time of delivery by trained team members who could immediately resolve problems.

The system worked beautifully! Because of its success, Domino's Pizza was able to open over 1,000 stores in one year, secure in the knowledge that equipment would be delivered damage free and on time. There were dividends for us as well. Our market share on new store packages leaped from about 30 percent to over 90 percent. Damages, credits, and air freight expense dropped to less than a tenth of previous levels—including increased volumes! The customer need recognized and met by Gary and his team was "to enjoy worry-free store openings."

PROACTIVE HELP—EQUIPMENT RESOURCE CENTER

In 1985, Bill Westwood, who was working as a $3.85 an hour warehouseman in our equipment division, was finishing an equipment order for a store when an unusual opportunity to serve our customers presented itself.

Bill discovered an old oven from a store that had recently purchased a new one. He fixed the old one and sold it to a buyer outside the company for $2,000. If one oven from a customer's store was salvageable and salable, there had to be others. Thus was born the Equipment Resource Center, which now serves as a profit-making division of Distribution.

The Equipment Resource Center quickly became a major operation and has a large inventory of resale equipment because it gives us a regular channel to buy back old equipment from our customers—not only pizza ovens—while selling them a new superior model. Bingo! The successes that followed quickly led ERC to develop the slogan: "One man's trash into another man's treasure."

At the center, skilled technicians refurbish the old models, and we resell them to other DPI stores or other companies outside the Domino's family. On all items, we offer complete warranties on the workmanship and equipment, an unusual policy for used equipment. With one call to an 800 telephone number, our customers can check our latest inventory and arrange for purchase, delivery, and installation. We also provide complete technical information on the equipment we carry, including replacement parts.

With this one innovation, we've helped our customers stay on the leading edge of equipment technology by taking old equipment off their hands. While this fulfilled certain needs of our customers, it alarmed some franchisees that we were equipping "the competition" with low-cost, high-quality ovens. With involvement from our franchisees, we drafted a "mission" for ERC that serves the needs of the necessary publics. This mission calls on ERC not to sell exclusive Domino's Pizza-specified equipment to outside interests, but ovens, coolers, and so on that could be purchased easily on the market are generally available to the outside world.

When you serve a customer following the principles of Super Vision, you know when that customer needs to make an equipment upgrade. At the same time, through contacts with your suppliers, you are likely to know about new products before your customers do. You can use that knowledge to provide a service your customers may never have expected.

In every industry, every couple of years there will be something new and better to help your customers. Often, new businesses can't afford the new equipment. But they might be able to if they could easily dispose of their old equipment and get money for it.

Even small businesses can employ the same basic concept of our center. For instance, a sole proprietor may be able to match the needs of two clients, allowing one to buy new equipment and the second to purchase the used equipment.

To prepare yourself to take advantage of the deals you do run across, talk ahead of time to repair centers that handle products in your industry and find one or two that can refurbish used equipment and back it with a credible warranty.

Assuring Top Flight Customer Service

To maintain contact with your customers and stay in tune with their changing needs, its necessary to establish relationships where you are a trusted supplier and can be counted on to act in the best interest of the stores. Customers are more likely to seek quietly other sources of supply than to share plans and needs with a current supplier they don't trust or don't like.

Commissary Field Representatives

At Distribution, we created positions titled commissary field representatives to act as a single-source liaison between the commissary and the stores they service. Each commissary has at least one rep, who acts as a troubleshooter and offers problem solving and teaching at both the commissary and the stores.

The power of the position lies in every customer having the representative's name, telephone number, and beeper number. Every customer knows he or she won't have to play telephone tag, beginning with trying to explain a problem to a switchboard receptionist. Instead, whenever they have a problem, they call and ask for their designated representative. Now that's Super Vision.

Have you made it clear to every one of your customers exactly who they can call with a problem? Is it clear who the backup is if the first person can't be reached? We've established a system where every one of our customers can reach help 24 hours a day, seven days a week. People tend to take the path of least resistance to accomplish a task. You want to be sure it's easier for your customers to contact a responsive representative within your company than to call a competitor. And when they call, our reps are ready to listen. What customers want in such a relationship is an innate ability among our reps to listen to needs. Again, I recommend listening to your customers as if you had a PhD in listening.

Keys to the Store

Jim Lucas, commissary leader in Tampa, remembers when the pizza stores picked up supplies at the commissaries. "It's hard to recall now," says Jim, "but we'd have vans from the stores leaving our commissary with supplies falling out of the back. Driving home in the evening, you'd see familiar items along the road." Sometimes we forget that the most basic of innovations can vastly improve operations.

Today the commissaries visit the stores with clockwork regularity. Most of our deliveries are made after the stores are closed. Our drivers not only transport food items from the commissaries to the stores, but they also rotate the stock, check the cooler temperatures, telephones, lights, and locks, and, when necessary, mop the floors.

All the services provided by the commissary are designed to keep stores at their operational best. Store managers need only open their stores, fire up the ovens, and begin taking orders.

The integrity we've shown believing in and living our mission statement for so long has helped us develop a solid reputation with our customers. Most trust our delivery people with the keys to their store. We didn't earn that right through one single thing, but through the total package of commitment to our customers.

Usually we're the only suppliers a store owner will trust with a set of keys. That trust helps us both. First, it helps the customer because he or she doesn't have to be present for a delivery or to pay someone else to be there. Our delivery people also provide an extra set of eyes for store security.

Second, having a set of keys helps us do our job because we can make deliveries around the clock. We don't have to depend on a manager remembering to stay late for a delivery. We don't have to worry that we're keeping someone up late if a truck is running a little behind schedule. In all cases, we easily have the products in place by the time the store opens the next day.

A store manager discovered how valuable it was to trust us with the keys one day when he was detained and couldn't make it to the store in time to open. Eddie Bell, one of our delivery and service team members, was making deliveries to stores and arrived to find the store vacant and no prep work done shortly before opening time. Eddie contacted the store manager, discovered he was running critically late and wouldn't be there in time. Eddie went to the cooler and prepared all the fresh food necessary to open the store. Next, he donned an apron, opened the phones, and started taking orders on behalf of the store. When the store manager finally arrived, he started making the pizzas while Eddie tended the ovens to get through the rush. Eddie stayed until further help could arrive and even delivered pizza orders to customers.

Why would Eddie do that? It was clear to him through our mission

statement and our commitment to delivering our Package that he
needed to do everything he could to service a Domino's Pizza store—
his customer! Fortunately, Eddie was responding to a work environment where Super Vision is taught, not an environment tightly controlled by supervisors.

OUR PRICE PLEDGE

We use several methods to ensure our customers that the products they
buy from us will bring them the best overall financial return. Here are
key components of our price pledge:

- Moving down the blue line.
- Net profit rebates.
- Gross profit refunds.
- Open financial records.

Moving Down the Blue Line

We believe we have a responsibility to become more efficient and
skilled and to pass the resulting savings on to each customer. While
making a presentation to our commissary leaders, I happened to use a
blue marker to demonstrate a downward-sloping line indicating reduced costs through efficiencies. This team knew I was a fanatic about
hockey, and one asked if they were supposed to "skate" down the blue
line. It stuck (which further demonstrates the power of battle cries to
communicate company priorities) and "moving down the blue line"
came to mean improving efficiencies and reducing costs. This concept
supports our pledge to provide customers with products that give them
the best overall financial return.

Our customers know we spend every dollar they spend on us wisely.
Their money goes toward buying the best raw materials we can find,
fair compensation for our team members, a fair profit for the company, or research that will result in improved products.

Our corporate strategy is to allocate any cost savings directly back to
the customer (i.e., the franchisees and corporate-owned stores), so
they can grow, flourish, and strengthen the overall posture of our total
team.

Net Profit Rebates and Gross Profit Refunds

Our financial responsibility to our customers goes a step beyond sharing cost savings. After all our goals are met, if we're left with a profit in excess of our stated target levels, we refund the difference to our customers. Your eyes are not deceiving you.

We consider our customers to be an integral part of our corporate team. It doesn't enhance our position if our customers are struggling through tough economic times and they see us reporting outrageously high profit levels. They may naturally think, "Well, it's no mystery why I'm hurting this year. My supplier has made record profits and I can see where they got the money. . . . By overcharging me!"

Prices on products can vary seasonally, and we don't want to commit to refunding profits because we got a temporary price break on tomatoes, for example. Next quarter, we might get stung badly on another commodity. When we determine our profits annually, we also calculate any refunds that may be heading back to our customers.

Jerry Owens, our commissary leader from Pompano Beach in south Florida, led his team to such efficient operations in 1990 that the commissary was able to rebate $20,000 in net profits to its customers. "When my customers first learned that Domino's Pizza Distribution was going to give them a check because it made more than it had targeted, they thought they had died and gone to heaven. Now the stores realize that we are truly part of their team and that they benefit every time we are more efficient."

This rebate did a lot to help our company's credibility, but a program like this alone doesn't assure customers they will get the best prices. It would be easy to hide inefficiencies in income statements, pad expenses, and accelerate depreciation and not rebate any savings to customers.

Because of this, we also commit to a gross profit cap. If, at the end of the quarter, our gross profit as a percentage of sales has exceeded the cap set by our board of directors, we refund the excess back to the stores in proportion to the amount each store buys from us. Both the net profit rebate and gross profit refund must work together to assure a successful and fair rebate program.

The profit refund policy has been a valuable tool for increasing Distribution's productivity. We had one customer who adamantly insisted we offer lower prices. So we showed him the books. Although he saw that our margins were already thin, he said he had to have better pricing and that he might stop buying from us.

I didn't want to lose him, so I dropped his prices. Also, in fairness, I had to lower prices for *all* of our customers. Naturally, this reduced our overall financial performance and hurt the bonus pool. That's when I learned a powerful lesson in how well our total system could work: The team members who suffered the cuts in their bonuses found ways to improve efficiency to make up for the price cut and quickly restored their bonuses to previous levels.

Even in a small company, you can set up some sort of bonus system to your customers, possibly an announced rebate or refund similar to the airline frequent flier mileage programs. Such programs will help ensure customers stick with you despite occasional, but inevitable, blunders you're going to commit. When you slip up, they may scream, but they will be more inclined to give you a second chance because you've given them incentive to stick around. Your goal is always to be their best supplier.

Open Financial Records

Our customers are always free to visit our offices and examine our financial records. Yes, you read the last sentence correctly. Opening up your financial records may be one of the toughest programs for you to sell to executives in your company. Businesses as a rule are distrustful and tightly guard their financial secrets as privileged information.

The payoffs to doing this, however, are immense. One of our largest franchisees, Rick Flory, is the best I know at understanding the intricate details of his business and ours. We opened our books to Rick and he gave us fresh new ways to analyze our operation and we still use his suggestions.

Open books also satisfy your customers' curiosity as to how you base your prices to them. Most people will estimate your profits to be two to three times what they actually are. Letting them see they are not financing runaway profits helps them remain loyal to your company.

It can also be important for some of your customers to view your financial records and know that your company is financially sound. When they use you as a supplier, they place a part of their business security in your hands. If your company goes belly-up on them unexpectedly, it can ruin them as well. Your customers don't benefit one whit from your secrets. They can, however, benefit tremendously from knowing you are financially secure, and in the process can become even more loyal customers.

They will likely want to choose suppliers that they absolutely know will be able to keep up with their increased demands. Showing them the books may be the key to winning a large order over competitors. The access we give our customers to our financial records helps make them aware that we constantly strive to save them money and return those savings to them. We do not seek profits in excess of our stated goals.

Customers will likely want to choose suppliers they absolutely know will be able to keep up with their increased demands. Showing them the books may be the key to winning a large order over competitors. The access we give our customers to our financial records helps make them aware that we constantly strive to save them money and return those savings to them. We do not seek profits in excess of our stated goals.

YOUR MISSION FOR CUSTOMERS IS THE KEY

In employing any of the customer-focused strategies we've presented here, view them all in the long term. A properly developed mission for your customers does not focus on your bottom line of the next quarter; it focuses on ensuring that customers believe you're "the best place to shop" over the long haul.

Once you've got everybody in the company pulling toward that goal, you'll find more customers supporting your efforts in more ways than you had dreamed possible.

CHAPTER CHECKLIST

Identify your customers.

* Never lose sight of who your customers are and assure that every member of your team knows.

Thoroughly listen to and understand their needs.

* Determining your customers' needs is an on-going, never-ending process. Use the resources you have to ensure that you understand what they need from you, if you are to serve them better than anyone else.
* Figure what needs are sacred. In our industry, it's avoiding

having the customer shut down because we didn't deliver on time. In your industry, it could be something else.

Sort the needs into patterns.

- Devise some sort of research program, even if it's only a brainstorming session in which you discuss ways to better serve your customers. Report the results of your "research" to your customers and let them know how they'll benefit.
- Recognize and communicate customer needs using "battle cries" that are meaningful to your team members.

Develop a mission statement.

- You can continue to be the "best place to shop" even if you are not perfect.

Set key indicators and levels of performance.

- Set up measureable objectives and regularly ask customers how they think you're doing.
- If you discover the source of any discontent, let them know it was an exception to the long-term vision of your relationship with them, then correct the problem before they have time to find a new supplier.
- Go through a painstaking process to ensure you ask correctly worded questions to discover your customers' true feelings about your organization.

Establish an automatic reward system for top performance.

- Set up a bonus system that rewards your team for superior customer service.

Establish ongoing programs to support your mission.

- Make a delivery pledge to your customers that suits your business. Honor that pledge as well as you possibly can.

- Hold regular, in-depth reviews with your suppliers. If customers know you're getting the best products available, they will not downgrade their quality permanently because you make an occasional mistake.

- Help your customers grow in any way you can. Helping every customer achieve higher sales and incessantly streamlining your operations enables you to provide products with ever greater value.

- Identify the crucial areas of your business and develop a certification program for team members.

- Keep your customers loyal by letting them know their most critical items are handled by certified team members.

- Make it clear to every one of your customers exactly who they need to call with a problem. Make it easier for your customers to contact a responsive representative within your company than to call a competitor.

- Let your customers know where you stand financially. Give them the data they need to order from you with confidence.

- Look for ways to handle more of your customers' needs. Serve as a resource center for your customers on how to save time and labor dollars.

- Continually become more efficient and skilled, and then pass the resulting savings on to each customer.

- Provide goods that are of unlimited quality, consistent nationwide, and never falling below your published specifications and standards.

- Be open and honest with your customers: listening, treating them equally, furnishing them with necessary information and requested training, and inviting their input into your decision-making process.

- Maintain up-to-date knowledge of the latest equipment your suppliers have to offer. Use that knowledge to provide an equipment update service to your customers.

Chapter Three
What Do Our Team Members Need?

T eam members who can't think of a better company to work for."
Accomplishing this aspect of our mission has been one of the greatest
challenges I've had and the most fun. We arrived at that part of our
mission after spending significant time identifying who comprises this
group (Step 1), listening to the needs of these people (Step 2), and
seeing what patterns emerge (Step 3). We're lucky; the team members
at Domino's Pizza Distribution believe their leaders are committed to
making this the best place to work and, in turn, offer serious, construc-
tive input toward that goal.

OUR TEAM

Our team consists of dough production people, delivery and service
team members, team leaders, customer service representatives, commissary field representatives, shippers, receivers, inventory control specialists, equipment and supply sales teams, executives, home office
support teams, and many others. Within each group are characteristics
such as largest, most nit-picking, most visionary, and so on.

They're a great team and I'm proud to work with them.

IT STARTS WITH HONESTY

I've always let my team members know I will answer any question they ask honestly and completely, even if they ask about my sex life. Despite the awkwardness, if I can't answer that honestly, they'll wonder what else I've decided to keep from them. Sometimes they do ask questions that hurt, but we've learned to handle it.

If we ever get in the habit of skirting the tough questions, we will eventually fail to live up to our mission because we'll lose touch with the true needs, wants, and feelings of our public, in this case, team members.

During my first travel-filled years in Distribution, I spent considerable time in our commissaries meeting and getting to know team members. When I say getting to know, I mean more than walking through the production area shaking hands before meeting with the manager. Lunch was spent in the break room with the team members; we'd go out for beer after work; there have been dozens of card games late into the morning where the titles of "president" and "doughmaker" were forgotten and the talk was upfront and straightforward.

It wasn't until a team member was comfortable enough with me to call me a "S.O.B." (or other highly creative metaphor!) that I was sure this person would level with me and be honest about his or her needs. That type of honest, two-way relationship must be established between you and your team if you are going to fully understand their needs.

OTHER OPPORTUNITIES TO LISTEN

As we started adding commissaries and team members, Joan Curran, a member of our home office training and development team, and I traveled among the commissaries to conduct "syndags." The syndag was created by Ichak Adizes and is one of the greatest tools I've found for eliciting information from groups. The process is effective: a trained facilitator leads a group through a methodology where "pips" (potential improvement points) are generated. These pips must be presented in positive language and can address any aspect of the organization.

As a particular syndag was winding down, I pushed the group with the same statement I used in the Canadian franchisee meeting: "OK, we're about through here. If you've put everything you've got out on the table, that's fine. But if you haven't, then after you leave here you can't talk about it anymore. This is your time to clear the air."

As we went around the room a final time, a member of the warehouse team said that with the recent reduction in overtime hours he wasn't sure he'd earn enough to feed his family. I was floored. We're not talking about not having enough money to take a trip, upgrade a car, buy a boat—we're talking about people and their families. This severely affected my understanding of team member needs. I have never forgotten this. I am reminded daily that I lead "people" not "workers" by using a razor given to me by Joe Petty from our Kentucky commissary as a thank you for spending time and efforts like these syndags with my team.

ONGOING OUTLETS TO BE HEARD

We established a monthly, confidential survey to assure that team members would retain a voice in the direction of the company. Our format and questions have always been simple and pointed; we want to know how our people feel. Typical questions include:

- What are the three best things about working here?
- What are the three worst things about working here?

We appreciate team members who level with us. To the latter question, we have received such down-to-earth responses as:

- My team leader is a jerk.
- Too much overtime—I don't get to see my family.
- Home office is still requesting information from us and asking us to attend meetings without much notice or explanation.
- . . . nonavailability of people in home office—I speak more with recorded messages than humans.
- . . . not having more of Domino's literature published in Spanish, making it difficult to explain to a new team member the company's goals and expectations.

With a continuing stream of candid, timely responses such as these, we have come to understand what our team members need from the company. The key is to get the bathroom talk out in the open. You can be assured your employees are talking about their disappointment in the halls, by the copier, and in the bathroom. Use every creative method you can to encourage them to be candid with you. You might think we loathe receiving such feedback, and I admit we are sometimes stung by some of the comments, but ultimately, they make life easier for the executive team because we find out precisely what stands in the way of being the best place to work. If your goal is truly to create an environment where everyone is happy, you can view these comments as opportunities.

SORTING IT OUT

Our team members make it clear to us what they need through surveys, one-on-one conversations, and team meetings. We've been able to sort these needs into patterns (Step 3) and have found three principal areas: the team members at Distribution need us to be leaders in the areas of providing family atmosphere, tools, and rewards. Collectively, we use the battle cry "the Present" to philosophically describe what we offer our team members:

• Family Atmosphere.   We will strive to have team members feel the trust, respect, and sense of security needed to believe that their overall happiness is of importance to their team leader. We will provide opportunities that allow team members to speak openly to reduce their frustration and obtain support.

• Tools.   We will provide team members with those things necessary to help them grow as a team member and as people. Above and beyond job training, we provide financial assistance for educational and counseling programs that help team members lead better personal lives.

• Rewards.   We will provide benefits and freedoms to team members in direct proportion to their contributions in helping our company grow and prosper.

We further communicate these patterns to our entire company in a

Public	Groups	Major Needs/Pattern
Distribution team members	Corporate executives	"The Present" Family atmosphere Tools
	Team members	Rewards
Our mission statement:	Team members who can't think of a better company to work for.	

concise, easily understood mission statement (Step 4): "Team members who can't think of a better company to work for."

We have a system in place to monitor, from our team member's perspective, how effective we are in providing the component of the Present (Steps 5 and 6). We also refer to the survey for team members as the ISS (ideal service survey). We tie the individual bonus of every leader of the company to the results from that survey (Step 7). Further, the entire bonus pool is tied to these results creating a double whammy for the people responsible for providing family atmosphere, tools, and rewards: the team leaders.

TIE PERFORMANCE TO BONUS

As mentioned above, how well we perform as a company fulfilling our team members' needs is scored and tied to our bonus plan (Step 7). Because of this, leading-edge programs as well as simple daily practices have been developed throughout Distribution to provide the necessary family atmosphere, tools, and rewards needed by our team members. It hasn't always been initiated by the leadership of the company. That stands to reason: who knows better what can satisfy a need than the person or persons with the need!

REWARD BASED ON MERIT FOR ALL

Far too many employees work in an environment where their highest reward is a paycheck and no punishment. If there is no system within a company for its team members to share in the rewards of prosperity, then the management has no right to wonder why team members lack motivation.

Top company executives seem to get ever bigger and better perks. Also, they often receive large bonuses and extravagant golden para-

Key Indicators for Team Members

Team Members' Identified Needs	Crisis	Expected	Exceptional	Measurement Method
Overall satisfaction with Distribution				
Is Distribution the best place to work?	30% no	10–15% no	<10% no	Monthly ideal service survey
Family atmosphere				
Do you have fun on your job?	30% no	10–15% no	<10% no	Monthly ISS
Do you feel secure about your future with Distribution?	25% no	8–12% no	<5% no	Monthly ISS
Is your work area safe?	5% no	2–4% no	<1% no	Monthly ISS
Does your team leader practice the Golden Rule?	20% no	8–12% no	<5% no	Monthly ISS
Tools				
Do you have the tools you need to do your job?	20% no	8–12% no	<5% no	Monthly ISS
Do you have the training you need to do your job?	20% no	8–12% no	<5% no	Monthly ISS
Rewards				
Considering wage, benefits, and bonus, are you compensated fairly?	30% no	15–20% no	<12% no	Monthly ISS
Do you receive recognition when you perform at exceptional levels?	25% no	10–15% no	<8% no	Annual summer survey
Leadership				
How long since your last one-on-one planning session with your team leader?	Average 4 months	Average 6–8 weeks	Average <6 weeks	Monthly ISS
Do you trust the leadership of Distribution?	20% no	10–12% no	<8% no	Annual summer survey

chutes to reward them even if they fail at their job. Meanwhile, team members often have little or nothing to look forward to.

We believe that when people are given a clear vision of responsibility, a clarity of priorities, and quantifiable levels of performance (crisis, expected, and exceptional), they will succeed on their own merit. When team members are free to operate under their natural self-motivation to do a good job, then, more often than not, they will excel.

When the successes do come, team members deserve to share in the financial prosperity that rolls into the company as a result of their extra efforts.

Annual Bonuses Destroy Energy and Fairness. When a reward system operates through a mechanism as mundane as an annual Christmas bonus, it fails to tap team members' full creative powers. No reward system is equitable if everyone gets a share of it based on his or her pay or a holiday event.

I once worked in a meat-packing plant that had a policy of giving away a ham to every employee at Christmas. They each were allowed to handpick the best ham they could find, and the bonus hams were run through special processing to turn them into a premium-quality cut of meat. It was a big event, and everyone looked forward to it every year.

One Christmas, the company was experiencing some financial difficulty and decided to forgo the customary free Christmas ham. The reaction from the employees was devastating. Everyone gave up on the company. Within two years, it was bankrupt and out of business. As the final day at work approached, 3 of the 65 people who worked for me said, "I knew the company was doomed when we didn't get our hams."

Since then, I've been adamantly opposed to any "bonus" tied to a calendar event. Knowing how important it is to a company to have team members holding a positive vision for the future, I cannot afford to allow my team members to believe the company is doomed if we miss an established bonus. Such negative visions among your team members can quickly become self-fulfilling prophecies. We're in business to perform, and bonuses have to be tied strictly to how we meet our goals.

Therefore, anyone who has knocked himself or herself out all year to help the company only to see the laggard or brownnose in the next office get a larger Christmas bonus because of higher seniority is not likely to see your company as the best place to work. In every company, there will be those team members who will merely squeak by and those who daily will outhustle even baseball's stolen-base king Ricky Henderson.

We have constructed an equitable bonus system (described in Part III) that gives team members an ongoing mechanism for rewards. A portion of the corporate profits is set aside for distribution to every team member who helped us obtain our financial success. The fairness of our system is one of its strongest keys for success. We use specific tools for calculating how each team member merits in comparison to his or her contemporaries.

STAR PERFORMERS DESERVE ADULATION

Of the 1,600 team members in Distribution, approximately 1,200 hold positions that many people would label as blue-collar jobs. To me, "blue collar" implies someone with no interest in the company beyond a regular paycheck. With that definition, we don't have a single blue-collar worker in Distribution.

The lowest-paid jobs in a company are often regarded lightly by its leaders. We regard all team members throughout Distribution as professionals because the company can gain or lose substantial sums of money as a result of their performance. At Distribution, our lowest-paid team members are the cleanup crews. Commissary leaders cannot take the cleanup crews lightly because the health department can close a commissary if the cleanup crew fails to perform well and our corporate record for store closings could be marred. If you can truly regard members of your public as nonessential, then remove them from your list otherwise treat them all like stars in your show.

Over and above our regular bonus programs, we have other programs that seek out our best performers at every job function in the company and honor them as professional athletes or celebrities are honored. Competitions are held daily throughout all our commissaries to qualify team members who become eligible to compete in the Domino's Pizza Distribution olympics. Once identified through their daily performance, candidates compete regionally, and the winners of the regional competitions then advance to our annual national competition (see Chapter 14).

The Distribution olympics holds competitions in such events as doughmaking, delivery and service, vegetable slicing, even accounting. The national winners receive cash and other awards and the opportunity to act as a company representative in their area of expertise. We've enjoyed the tremendous energy that radiates from these competitions.

MAKING IT HAPPEN

"The Present" is supported by several specific component programs to turn the vision into reality. Some of those will be covered in later chapters so you can see how to implement them in your business. For now, we will discuss overlaying team member support elements that let team members know we acknowledge and seek to meet their needs and that provide examples of all team members pitching in to make this the best place to work.

A CONSTANT FOCUS ON TEAM MEMBER NEEDS

To be consistent with our seven-step system, we continually need to examine and stay in tune with team member needs. To do so, we have built a multistep system that allows team members to express their needs in a manner most comfortable to them. Every four weeks, team members receive a confidential survey to complete, can participate in a group meeting at their facility that has their needs as the forefront of the agenda, and have an opportunity for a one-on-one job planning and review (JPR) session (the focus of Chapter 11). Further, team members can turn to prepaid confidential counseling and a "grief relief" system. People express themselves differently and we try to anticipate this and provide communication vehicles for them. In addition to the confidential survey above, we employ several other vehicles:

Huddle

Each division holds monthly "huddles" at which team members can provide input and ask questions. The meetings are headed by a team leader, but not the team leader directly responsible for the operating unit. This outside leader acts as a facilitator who will help create an unbiased, productive, and positive exchange of communication.

Team members get continual reminders that we are serious about our commitment to provide them with the best place they can think of to work. We encourage them to be completely open with team leaders in these meetings. They know their communication can—and often does—go all the way to "the top."

Team members also know their team leaders have realistic performance expectations that acknowledge the reality of errors and shortcomings in daily life. That understanding, combined with their belief that we truly want to make Domino's a little bit better every day, leads people to trust that we would rather fix a reported problem than place the blame for it.

No Waiting for Annual Reviews

Rather than making team members wait for annual performance reviews to see if the company even recognizes what they've done, we offer our job planning and review (JPR) system where each team member can conduct a self-evaluation every four to six weeks. During these sessions, team members discuss personal missions, roles, needs, their performance, and subsequent action plans with their team leader (the focus of Chapter 11). The team member sets the agenda for his or her own session. This unlocks the creativity, talent, and drive of each team member in ways that more restrictive, structured corporations do not experience.

Team Member Assistance

It became clear in the mid-1980s to then commissary leader Ken McPherson that if we were really trying to be the best place to work, we needed to offer support to our team members in all aspects of their life. We were growing at a breakneck pace, and many team members were subject to stress and could potentially burnout. Ken, acting as the champion of his idea, researched and established a team member assistance program where every member of our team would have confidential professional counseling available to them.

This counseling is prepaid and available to help team members with issues such as family problems, credit advice, or managing stress. We also depend on the counselors to direct recovery programs of people detected as having substance abuse problems and posing a threat to the rest of our team.

Grief Relief

Sometimes the survey, huddle, and JPR systems fail. It is key that if communication or trust breaks down to the point that normal channels (such as the monthly meetings) are ineffective, there has to be a backup. Carla Wilson, a member of our home office team, ran with the idea of a "grief relief" system to address this need. Each team member has an 800 telephone number of a designated grief relief representative in the home office. This representative listens and tries to see that every team member's concerns are recognized and resolved.

We've designed the program to keep our communications open. The grief relief representatives are empowered to investigate problems and remove roadblocks to understanding.

No company is too small to have a similar system for its team members. Even if you're operating a small company, you can have this two-step program. First, we give all team members a monthly opportunity to give us feedback on what they think about working for us. Second, in case the normal system is insufficient, they have the assurance that their grievances will be heard through a crisis channel and that the person they talk to about the problem has the tools to resolve the issue.

THE RESULTS AND ONGOING EFFORTS

We strive to nurture an environment where team members grow along with the company, both financially and personally. I believe the rewarding experience we have with our team members stems from our mission as it relates to them: ". . . team members who can't think of a better company to work for," and who believe that because they work with us their lives are "going to get better."

We have team members challenge what is wrong, innovate to make jobs better, and reach decisions based on the mission statement. They have to have input into making the company a place they brag about. This approach works for us, it works for our team members, and it works for companies we advise.

Just like your team members, ours evaluate their company through feedback they hear from friends and neighbors and the general attitude toward the company in the community. We want them to frequently hear praise and be proud to accept credit when they do, but you've got to have a way to find out what they think about the company. As a rule, top executives should play their hand in full view of team members throughout the organization to gain trust and elicit the fullest possible participation.

TEAM MEMBERS UPHOLD THE VISION FOR ONE ANOTHER

Every team member in the field and at the home office is acutely aware of Distribution's vision for team members. Does that mean that since it's a corporate vision, team members need not participate in it? That they simply do their jobs and let the company take care of the vision? Not according to what I see.

Our commissary in South Carolina hired two team members who were hearing-impaired. Several other team members who worked with the hearing-impaired members enrolled, on their own, in a sign-language course. In some companies, there might have been an attitude of, "Why in the hell are they hiring somebody for me to work with every day who can't even hear?"

Instead, our people showed their allegiance to the company mission that strives for "team members who can't think of a better place to work" by acquiring the skills that would enable new team members to directly experience the vision for team members.

Those enrolling in the course said they didn't have to think twice about doing it because if they hadn't, the new team members could easily have thought that somewhere else—where their fellow team members cared enough to learn to sign—would be a better place to work. This is a clear case of Super Vision working magnificently. Those two hearing-impaired team members in South Carolina believe Distribution is the best place for them to work. While this story is typical of dozens of others, I still find it gratifying when team members strive to maintain the corporate mission for other team members.

BALANCE PREVAILS

Chuck Gill, our former general manager of commissary operations, approached me one day with what seemed like a lose-lose scenario and a challenge to our mission for our team members. He had learned that some of our customers wanted deliveries Christmas Day.

With the mission obviously in mind, he asked, "How can we have these customers think we're their best place to shop and at the same time have the team members who have to work on Christmas Day think this is the best place to work?"

Chuck had already asked the appropriate questions of the people on both sides of the dilemma. He had checked to see if any team members were interested in working on Christmas and had found none. He also asked the customers if they could accept a larger delivery a little earlier, and they said, "No, we must have it on Christmas Day."

This was one situation where for a short period at least we couldn't please both parties. We want our team members to be home on Christmas with their families, yet we want to serve our customers. Remember, we consider it a disaster when one of our customers closes because it runs out of our products.

Some companies would have little trouble pleasing the customer in this case. They would simply order some team members to come in on Christmas and fulfill the requested delivery. We also had to fill the order in this case, because the customer pays our bills, but our team handles the orders.

Tough Decisions. We cannot afford to have disgruntled team members when our mission statement says we want them to see Domino's Pizza as the best place they can work. Clearly, however, every Christmas morning, we were going to have some folks able to think of plenty of places they would rather work. The key to recovery from this dilemma was to look at the mission statement long term. So we discussed some possibilities that you, too, could use. The issue wasn't that we valued one public (customers) over another (team members), it was, instead, an issue that the needs of both were not easily resolved.

Because of this dilemma, we chose for the customers, not because we discounted the needs of our team, but because we had more opportunities to make up for the unfairness with our team. Think about it: we deliver to our customers only twice a week, but we interact with our team members daily. We had a better chance to recover from this disappointment with our team members. And that's what we tried to do.

We believed that if commissary leaders had to force people to work, they would owe those people some special attention to restore their temporarily marred image of life in the Domino's family. The commissary leaders could dress up as Santa Claus and visit the team members' homes, taking them a Christmas dinner and some gifts for the kids.

When you do make a decision that undermines others' belief in your mission you have toward them, you must help them to see where they are keeping the overall mission statement alive and that they will be rewarded for their extra efforts. Also, if team members believe you are fair the other 364 days of the year, one "glitch" won't undermine the belief that this is the best place they can work.

NO CUMBERSOME POLICY MANUALS

We've dispensed with the antiquated notion of trying to produce a policies and procedures manual that attempts to define how team members would proceed in every instance. Kathi Seglund, part of our communications team, recalls that in the mid-1980s the company faced many new challenges.

"People in the field kept asking for policies, so they wouldn't have to make decisions," Kathi says. "At that time, Don Vlcek was especially interested in some of Tom Peters' philosophies. We decided to scrap our policies and procedures manual, which had grown to be 10 inches thick!

"To reinforce reliance on the mission statement, a few of us from the home office went to the Michigan commissary, placed a manual in a fireproof metal container, and ceremoniously burned it in front of everyone. In the weeks that followed, everyone in the company began shredding or stomping on their manuals until none were left anywhere."

The manual had simply gotten in the way of our mission for employees: ". . . team members who can't think of a better company to work for."

UNOFFICIAL LIFETIME EMPLOYMENT

At my first executive team member meeting in 1978, I was the new kid on the block. My predecessor said he would do me a favor and get rid of all the people he didn't believe would have a future under me so that I wouldn't have to come in and be the bad guy by immediately firing some people.

One of the managers he fired had run the Michigan commissary, the home office commissary. At this first meeting, I noticed many of the other executives were spending a lot of time discussing ways they could find a job somewhere else in the company for the guy who had been fired.

I was curious because I had been told of all his weaknesses and they were considerable. He had trouble with people, he couldn't seem to make a profit, he frequently fell behind on production, and quality was slack. When I asked why they wanted to save this guy, Bob Cotman and Helen McNulty told me that because we were planning to grow fast, we needed all the good people we could get. They believed that sometimes good people get put into positions they can't handle and this manager might be such a case. Why not try him elsewhere?

Since the early days of my career in the meat-packing industry, I've always seen job security as a leading concern of team members. Domino's Pizza Distribution is no exception. As president, however, I wanted to make a bold statement to my team to address this concern. I wanted to tell my team members that they would never have to worry about losing their job. Our attorneys, Mel Muskovitz and Ed Pear, nearly flipped! They rightfully warned against blanket guarantees that could expose us to unnecessary litigation. With their help, however, we kept the statement's emotion without the legal headaches: as long as team members perform at expected or exceptional levels and we have the business, we will keep them.

We can't guarantee job security, but most team members will be able to remain with us as long as they wish. We don't fire people because they fail to excel. Team members can work for us for years and remain secure with the knowledge that they have a job as long as their performance does not permanently drop into the crisis zone.

In the cases where we may eliminate a position, team members have our assurance that we will provide other internal employment or assistance in obtaining external employment.

Providing job security can be a serious and potentially costly problem for any company. The survival of the company, especially small ones, may sometimes depend on letting some people go. Nonetheless, having team members who live under the fear of being laid off can be disempowering to your company's mission. For one, those people could easily think of better places to work and probably are actively seeking them.

This hurts you as well as your team members. Still, there are ways to uphold policies of near guaranteed long-term employment even in a small company in all but the most dire of circumstances. You can adopt another of our programs:

Use Consultants and Outside Services.   When we need a highly specialized skill on one short-term project, we prefer to get the help of outside consultants rather than create new positions that we know will end soon.

Our philosophy has long been, "When in doubt, farm it out." It's contributed immeasurably to our ability to protect the job security of those team members we have accepted as permanent.

Whenever possible, however, we keep all work internal. The workload within a large corporation will never be perfectly even throughout. Some departments will be swamped while others have slack time. You can use this natural variation to move people around to help those who are in a temporary crunch. It's not fair to team members to spend money on consultants when you could reassign some duties internally and keep the money in the bonus pool. Plus, the reassignment is an opportunity for a team member to develop skills beyond his or her current ones.

We don't use temporaries for long-term assignments. When I discover a breach like this, I go crazy! In a family atmosphere, temporaries are an insult to people we consider family members. We don't invite strangers into our family any more than you would invite a total stranger to stay in your house for a few days. You've got to preserve the sanctity of the family as much as possible.

A GROWING COMPANY HELPS MEET NEEDS

We all know we can count on inflation, it appears to be about the only constant in our economy. If your company's volume remains stagnant, you cannot offer ever-increasing pay to team members without eventually pricing yourself out of the market. To keep compensation ahead of inflation, you've got a responsibility to your team members to increase your sales volume. We regard company growth as crucial to retaining happy team members.

Quite frankly, we want our team members to do "better than the Joneses." That has been my concern since hearing that warehouse team member's concerns about feeding his family. When a company has a profit-based bonus system that grows faster annually than the inflation rate, then team members can count on pay increases that outpace inflation. One study recently revealed that the average worker in America has lost 15 percent in net purchasing power over the past 12 years because wages haven't kept up with inflation. Over the past 12 years, our average team member compensation has increased every year at a rate greater than inflation. Focusing on growth has allowed us to do this, while also increasing profits at a similar pace.

COMMUNICATIONS AND COMMUNICATIONS TOOLS

We provide some of the most advanced two-way communication systems available and make sure that both team members and team leaders know the appropriate method for obtaining or inputting information. To ensure that we have open communication lines, we also employ or have employed a variety of tools, such as:

- 007 Reports—generated daily as regional managers report updates and requests from the field to the home office. Responses from the home office to the person making the request are guaranteed by noon the following day.

- WDPD (simulated radio station)—a monthly audiotape that shares news, company priorities, success stories, and plain old good music.

- The *Innovator*—a monthly publication for team members that shares innovations and top agenda items and identifies which facilities are meeting company objectives.

These reports and communications tools (the focus of Part IV) help to ensure that the company is operations-driven and not driven by administrative bureaucracy. Some of our communications systems may not seem so advanced. The innovations are not in the invention, however, but in the implementation.

For instance, as we'll elaborate in Chapter 13, suggestions from the field to the home office are guaranteed a response by noon the next day! Few things will stifle creative input from your team members more than having their suggestions answered weeks or months later, especially when the expressed need is no longer an issue.

FIVE AREAS FOR PERSONAL BALANCE

Much of our spectacular, long-term growth comes from a corporate recognition that there is more to our team members' lives than their jobs. Everyone has dreams in life. If we can't help team members with their dreams, we'll never fulfill the vision of our mission statement for team members.

Tom Monaghan identified five areas of each team member's life that need to be addressed for that individual to be a well-balanced member of society: spiritual, physical, mental, social, and financial. He placed the financial need last because he has discovered that if the first four are fulfilled in a person's life, the last one takes care of itself.

We've developed many programs to address these needs for our family of team members. Here are a few examples:

• Spiritual. Among other activities, we respect all religious holidays and try to provide necessary time to team members to celebrate in the manner of their choosing with their families.

• Physical: We include articles on health and fitness in each issue of our publications. Some facilities have access to health clubs, and we sponsor weight-loss and stop-smoking programs. You'll find several of our warehouses equipped with basketball hoops or floor hockey sticks.

• Mental: Educational Reimbursement Programs. When our team members attends a management seminar, college course, or other vehicle to further their education, they can gain reimbursement from Distribution.

• Social. Beyond the team member assistance program, several of our facilities sponsor fund-raising activities for local charities or our National Partner's foundation, established to help team members in dire financial need due to personal tragedy.

• Financial: Individual Performance Bonus Programs. Covered in-depth in Chapter 10, our program is directly linked to team members' contribution to our efforts and is never based on seniority, previous awards, or percentage of base pay. We have not missed a bonus payment yet due to Distribution losing money.

We constantly analyze our wage and benefit package searching for ways we can do more for our team members than be the highest-paying company in town. We believe it's more important to channel resources to provide for all five needs so that team members are happy and successful in all aspects of their lives.

We will never view these programs as optional. They're not simply nice things to do for team members when times are good. These programs reflect our commitment to the Golden Rule. Therefore, the tougher the times, the more committed we will become to the integrity of these programs.

When other companies may be looking for ways to save money by cutting costs on employee programs, we will be enjoying greater-than-ever efficiency gains as the effects of these programs flow naturally back to us.

OUR BOTTOM LINE

Every four weeks, when each team member is polled in our confidential survey that asks, "Considering everything, is Domino's Pizza Distribution the best place for you to work?" we find that we continually meet our mission for team members. Our commitment to our team members is the right thing to do, but even if our team member programs were to be viewed as cold-blooded business decisions, we know with certainty that they would handsomely pay off, enough to satisfy the most tightfisted bean counter.

I wouldn't work one day in a company where an abusive style of employee relations produced inordinate prosperity for a handful at the top while everyone else's job was in jeopardy. At Distribution, we've found that by sticking to the principles of Super Vision and continually meeting team members' needs, there is room for everyone in a company to prosper.

CHAPTER CHECKLIST

Identify your publics and inventory their needs.

- Solicit candid, timely feedback from team members and you'll never need to wonder what to do to improve morale among team members.
- Seek honest input that will challenge you to maintain your vision for them.

Sort the needs into patterns.

- In every decision, take into account that your team members are going to be with you every day. If you have to displease them, help them see where they are keeping the overall mission statement alive, but do something positive to make it up to them.

- Take on the responsibility to protect the job security of every team member you accept as permanent. Adopt the philosophy of "when in doubt, farm it out."

- Acknowledge that there is more to your team members' lives than their jobs. Everyone has dreams. Address their spiritual, physical, mental, social, and financial needs.

Develop a mission statement.

- Maintain the integrity of your mission statement in the face of apparent conflicts by taking the long-term view and go with the best answer in that context.

Set key indicators and levels of performance.

- Tie the bonuses of the company's leadership to the measured feelings of the team members.

Establish an automatic reward system for top performance.

- For team members to remain happy and productive, offer rewards to reinforce outstanding performance.

- Tie your bonus system to the calculated performance of the company and each individual instead of using seniority. No reward system is equitable if everyone gets a share of it based on his or her pay.

- Construct an equitable bonus system that provides an ongoing mechanism for rewards to every team member who helps you obtain your financial success.

- CEOs should give a small thank you gift to every team member when the company achieves special milestones.

- Over and above your regular bonus programs, install other programs that identify your best performers at each specific job function and honor them.

Establish ongoing programs to support your mission.

- For team members to remain happy and productive, create a family atmosphere and give them the tools to do their job.

- Encourage them to challenge what is wrong, innovate to make jobs better, and reach decisions based on your mission statement. Nurture an environment where your team members can grow.

- Keep team members totally informed of company affairs, polling them on decisions in the works.

- Play your hand in full view of team members. Trust elicits the fullest participation.

- If an unfavorable announcement or news of a forthcoming unpopular decision is made, offer a complete explanation as to why this course of action needs to be taken now.

- Give all team members a forum for communications that has an open channel straight to "the top." Provide a multistep system that includes frequent regular meetings and a special grief relief channel if the normal system fails to address an issue to the team member's satisfaction.

Chapter Four
What Do Our Communities Need?

One of the first things Tom Monaghan told me when I came on board was to remember to help the communities wherever we operate a commissary or other facility. Nevertheless, this was the last group of my publics that I identified as such. I know now that they are as important as any other.

We have a responsibility to uphold all laws and to be as much a part of the community as possible. When we serve the needs of the community and gain its respect, it improves the corporation's success.

If we were to violate food quality regulations or if our delivery teams had poor safety record, our sales would suffer because people would stay away from Domino's Pizza once such transgressions hit the newspapers. The final consumers who drive our business are the individuals in the community whose image of Domino's brings them back as repeat customers in the stores.

Upholding the law is not a new corporate strategy. We comply fully with all federal, state, and local health and safety laws and regulations. However, we believe that some of the efforts we put forth to fulfill our legal obligations are uncommon.

TAKING EXTRA EFFORT TO LISTEN

Listening and assessing the needs of the communities in which we do business is by far the most inconvenient of all our publics. We routinely interact with our team members and customers, our suppliers are eager to come in and talk, and our parent company makes its needs quite clear through performance requirements and financial goals. We use the grouping "community" to represent a vast array of municipalities, government agencies, local inspectors, and the general public, to name a few. Therefore, we must make extra efforts to discover their needs and invite their input.

A PLACE TO START

Our goal is to visit the mayor's office annually in each town and ask, "Do you know we are in town? Are we good for your town?"

The quest to be perceived as a valuable member of a community is not based on corporate platitude, but on local team leaders' realizations that they will flourish in an environment that appreciates them and supports their business.

When Distribution sought to establish a commissary in Tallahassee, Florida, for example, the team leaders contacted the local chamber of commerce and the mayor's office. While these groups were accustomed to meeting with new businesses in town, they weren't prepared for what they heard from Domino's Pizza Distribution.

We explained that whenever a new store or commissary is opened, we regard the local people, especially the mayor, the council, and the chamber of commerce as newcomers into the Domino's Pizza family. We accept them as partners in our business, and we expect them to have as much interest in our growth and prosperity as we do in theirs.

We briefed Mayor Dorothy Inman and Chamber President Bob Bone about the development of all our new facilities, and we included them and the community in various aspects of our installation, seeking their advice and expertise.

Their response could not have been better! Through their help, we secured property in a city-owned industrial park at a fraction of the cost of similar real estate acquired for other commissaries. Further, both the mayor and chamber president made us feel welcome.

Once the installation was complete, the mayor reported to our home office, "We have never had a company move in and make us feel like we were the company's customer. Many companies move in with good intentions, but you were the first that asked us point-blank: What can we do to be a full participant in this community?" The mayor added that she liked "being a part of the decision-making team at Domino's." We were so excited about our welcome we honored Mr. Bone at our national awards ceremony and presented an award to Mayor Inman in Tallahassee.

The Distribution philosophy is "we don't want to operate knowing that some communities don't like our company being in their town." Our goal is to have every mayor unconditionally say, "Yes, we want you in our community." We take the same approach with state and federal government agencies and also with every other organization we touch.

GETTING THEIR FEEDBACK

To channel what might be a steady stream of unrelated input, Distribution carefully gathers the bulk of its community-relations information during our annual summer survey. The survey provides a comprehensive look at how Domino's presence is perceived in respective communities and where there is room for improvement (see Chapter 9). We may vary the questions on the survey from year to year, but the purpose remains the same: to gather input and assess what communities need from us.

Our partners in the community know we will contact them regularly for their feedback. When the results of the survey are tabulated, we will let them know how we will address the concerns they shared and the contributions they offered.

This still leaves room for ongoing input, of course. For instance, we've got a standing offer with every community to keep us informed about the performance of any of our team members while on the job. If one of our huge delivery trucks is ever seen speeding, for example, we will make inquiries and take appropriate action in cooperation with local authorities. We've even taken this one step further. On several occasions, members of the state trucking regulatory agencies, such as Michigan State Police or federal Department of Transportation agents, have been invited to inspect our vehicles and judge our Olympic events.

IT'S MORE THAN TALK

Talk of community involvement and social responsibility circulate through the halls of most major domestic corporations. Many times the true agenda of such talk is the corporate bottom line. At Domino's Pizza Distribution, community involvement is part and parcel to Super Vision. It is a way of life.

We know we affect the communities in which we have commissaries; clearly they are one of our most visible publics. We see community involvement as a natural responsibility for our company and regard it as the appropriate posture for any business in any community.

We've been able to recognize key patterns (Step 3) of needs communities have from us. Collectively, we think of these as being a responsible neighbor. We do not devise massive public relations inititatives; rather, we act according to the Golden Rule: "Do unto others as you would have them do unto you."

- Put back more than we take.

- Be a leader in the community.

- Be safe, friendly representatives of Domino's Pizza.

- Be an unquestionable friend of the environment.

Our concise, clear mission point addressing these patterns (Step 4) is to have "Community (government) that considers us a fine example of what business should be."

Most companies assess their community participation by keeping score of contributions to local charities and occasionally lending key executives to serve on charitable, civic, and community boards. Instead of participating in think tanks that muse over what might be done in a community, we take a hands-on approach, believing more in action than talk. We've found that when we get busy with action, the problems tend to disappear and talk is no longer necessary. We ask communities to evaluate us on our performance through the survey mentioned above and also by looking at incidents (positive and negative) involving our team members (steps 5 and 6).

Needs of Community

Public	Groups	Major Needs/Pattern
Community	Citizens Business leaders Local government Police Regulatory agencies (DOT, OSHA, etc.)	"Responsible Neighbor" Put back more than we take Be leader in the community Be safe, friendly representatives of Domino's Pizza Be an unquestionable friend of the environment
Our mission statement:	Community (government) that considers us a fine example of what business should be.	

ENCOURAGING AND REWARDING COMMUNITY INVOLVEMENT

In reinforcing the Super Vision philosophy of Distribution, we celebrate all team members who go above and beyond the usual responsibility of a being a good citizen (Step 7). We're diligent about recognizing those who have helped save lives, donated their time to charities, and participated in other community events. To show our pride, we present ethics awards to those who have shown exceptional community involvement.

We also promote team member community involvement through a variety of organized local activities held by our team members. They have sponsored local sports teams and events, contributed to local charities and drives, and provided food and meeting space.

Our team members go beyond merely making their facilities available. They work closely with the local communities to share Domino's methods of success. To that end, we've set up a speaker's bureau that we use as a forum to share our philosophies with local businesses.

Our team leaders in Distribution work with colleges, universities, and businesses throughout the country through our Innovation Network. In countless special programs, they teach innovation, corporate communication, entrepreneurship, and the Domino's system of distribution.

Key Indicators for Community

Community's Identified Needs	Crisis	Expected	Exceptional	Measurement Method
Overall satisfaction with distribution				
Are you glad we are in your town?	>10% no	3–6% no	<3% no	Summer survey
Put back more than we take				
Do we try to source from local vendors?	No local sourcing	Several products	As much as possible	Vendor records
Do our people participate in community volunteer activities?	No participation	2–4 groups supported	>5 groups supported	Survey team members
Be a leader in the community				
Do you view Domino's Pizza Distribution as a leader in your community?	30% no	10–15% no	<10% no	Summer survey
Does Distribution comply with state and federal laws?	Any violation	0 violations	0 violations / 2 years	Federal DOT reports, state, local police, regulatory agencies
Be safe, friendly representatives of Domino's Pizza				
Are you aware of our safe-driving programs?	60% no	40–50% no	<30% no	Summer survey
Do our trucks operate safely in your town?	>20% no	8–12% no	<1% no	Summer survey
Tracking accident and incident reports	3 / annually	0 / annually	0 / 2 years	Police and accident reports
Be an unquestionable friend of the environment				
Recycling programs	No programs	3/4 of possible trash recycled	All possible trash recycled	Commissary records
No environmentally unsafe acts	Any unsafe act	0 unsafe acts	0 unsafe acts/2 years	Commissary, EPA records

David Materne, head of the Materne division, which includes sales to new stores, the Equipment Resource Center, emporium, and retail operations and corporate licensing, has prepared a comprehensive paper and video presentation on the nature of innovation. He shares this inspiring message as often as possible.

Overall, community involvement programs such as these have brought us more win-win situations than we ever imagined when we made the commitment to share ourselves openly. Any size business can offer business expertise to others in the community. The key difference between mere mediocrity in community affairs and profound success is ensuring that the help you offer is always your best effort and not corporate bromides employed for quick-hit image brushups.

Your best tactic over the long term is to work with every member of your community as a valuable member of your public and essential to your success. The result will be government agencies that wish every company acted as you do.

TAKING THE PAIN OUT OF COMPLIANCE

There's a reason for the existence of every government agency. When you regard them as members of your public, take on a deeper role with them. Find out their overall charter, their needs, what makes their job enjoyable, and what makes it miserable.

It may seem that in the short term you're spending a lot of time learning about government agencies that many people hate to deal with. However, they exist, and if you fail to abide by the regulations and someone gets hurt or you are found guilty of damaging the environment, the short-term expense of compliance will prove to be small compared to the larger costs for noncompliance. Various local, state, and federal regulations call for providing a clean, safe environment at our commissaries. We welcome inspections by the Occupational Safety and Health Administration (OSHA), asking for input that will help us create the safest and cleanest workplaces possible. Our level of cleanliness is a marvel to behold—you could eat off the floor in any of our commissaries.

Hair Nets in Place?   At all times, all visitors to the food-processing portions of our commissaries have to wear a hair net. This includes Tom Monaghan, Dave Black, president of Domino's Pizza, Inc., me, any members of the executive staff, and any visitor from any other company or from the community. To be frank, the hair nets make most people look silly. But looking silly is a small price to pay to avoid the possibility of even one hair getting into our food.

We also equip our team members with the finest gear available. When one commissary discovers a new or innovative way to raise its level of health and safety, we immediately pass that information on throughout the company. Team members wouldn't believe Distribution is the best place for them to work if we failed to provide a safe and healthful workplace.

I could go on and on about the innovations we've instituted, many originally put forth by team members. Whether it's special nonslip flooring, flame-resistant garments, or an improved alarm system, we are constantly on the lookout for new ways to make the operating environment cleaner, safer, and a more enjoyable place to work.

CREATING A SAFE DRIVING ENVIRONMENT

We don't want our safe-driving programs to be limited to helping local authorities take corrective action. Here again, we use a preemptive strategy. Our driving program is part of our pledge to the community. At Distribution, "all team members, prior to performing in any position, will satisfy all certification or licensing required by the company or by government."

Our national director of transportation, Gary Kelly, has developed a radically new approach to recruiting delivery and service team members. The need for the program became clear when we noticed a shortage of qualified truck-driving applicants. Our response was to do what we do best—promote from within.

Our new program, called Trucking 101, began with a corps of our best drivers. We put them through a special training program to become driver trainers. These certified driver trainers then teach and coach Domino's-qualified team members to obtain a commercial driver's license (CDL) and become driving team members.

Rather than putting an untested team member behind the wheel of a large truck, we're now able to select driver candidates who we already know share the vision of our mission statement. Our course includes a professionally produced audiocassette package based on the CDL applicant's study kit. The study kit was developed by the professional tractor-trailer instructors of American Roadcraft in cooperation with the training experts at the University of Maryland's Center for Safety Education.

When used together, the cassettes and the study kit provide each of our driver-candidate team members all the information they need to pass the exam. The package also covers the information necessary for obtaining special classifications on the CDL for hauling hazardous materials and transporting passengers.

This targeted course makes passing the CDL exam easier for our candidates. It also ensures we have the best chance to uphold the law as a company and to fulfill our vision of having communities consider us a fine example of what a business should be.

A natural follow-up to our driver-safety consciousness is our cooperation with recent drug and alcohol testing regulations. Our commitment to safety goes well beyond our driving program. We require drug and alcohol testing for all team members who are in any safety-sensitive position, as well as for those in positions where the health and safety of fellow team members or the community is in danger.

We also support the community with drug and alcohol abuse awareness by cooperating with Mothers Against Drunk Driving (MADD). Never believing that our responsibility is to simply make cash corporate contributions, we get the entire Domino's family involved.

As a result of these vigorous ongoing activities in 1989, Domino's Distribution drivers earned the U.S. Department of Transportation's highest possible safety rating.

TEAM MEMBERS WITH COMMUNITY AWARENESS

Early in 1988, our delivery and service team members volunteered to solicit pledges from individuals both inside and outside the company to sponsor drivers for their safe-driving accomplishments. Truck drivers from across the country tracked their accident-free miles and collected pledges of more than $13,000 during the first year they participated in the program.

Recognizing that the state and local police are usually the first to assist when our drivers have a problem, the drivers donated all collected contributions to local police and fire widows' and orphans' funds. Our drivers then used their contacts with other drivers to influence their companies to join Domino's in the safe-driving pledge programs.

We're constantly surprised and pleased at the unexpected ways in which our overall mission statement is manifest in visible action. This is another case where our team members have adopted the visions of our mission statement and have taken it upon themselves to fulfill it in their communities.

Maintaining all our facilities and equipment in top condition also helps Domino's be considered as a pillar of the community. For example, our trucks are washed and serviced on a regimented schedule. We believe this reflects well on our position within the community and in our commitment to the community.

While many other companies maintain their facilities with excellence, we believe that at Domino's the commitment comes from within every team member. They've made us partners with the community in ways that touch the lives of the local people more deeply than anything the executive team could have envisioned. The spontaneity of our community outreach could never have been dictated from the executive level. We can't thank our team members enough for their contributions to the company's goal of becoming a positive force in the community and respecting the people and property of each community in which we're involved.

THE ENVIRONMENT CAN'T WAIT

Our parent company created a special committee on the President's Council to increase the company's emphasis on environmental matters and hired Larry Hull, an environmental specialist, to launch the program.

Larry immediately established three goals for our company:

- To conduct a self-audit to see where we stood.

- To develop and enhance our positive environmental impacts by minimizing or eliminating the corporation's negative environmental impacts.

- To communicate our attitudes, actions, and beliefs both internally and externally to the extent that the name Domino's Pizza becomes synonymous with environmental protection and enhancement.

In keeping with the vision of our mission statement to have the parent company be proud, we consider such environmental concern to be a permanent concern. Larry Hull has worked with other companies on the highest level to help us achieve our environmental goals. For example, one of the first things he did was to influence major companies, such as Dow Chemical, Coca-Cola, Weyerhaeuser, and Consolidated Aluminum, to form alliances to develop environmentally sound alternatives to our shipping, packaging, and solid-waste issues.

These alliances have proven fruitful in improving the environmental friendliness of our packaging while decreasing the amount of consumable materials we had been using.

While your business may not be large enough to approach manufacturers to lobby for new environmentally sound products, you may find that unnecessary. Distribution and other companies that share our vision of the planet have already had a major impact on the availability of recyclable products.

Use every product and procedure that you can to aid in preserving the environment and let the community know of your commitment. As a business leader, your actions can multiply throughout the community. Your achievements may help someone else see the necessity for helping out. You have a real chance to make a difference in the world, even if you're a small company.

THE HOW-TO'S OF PARTICIPATION

You don't need a resident expert to become active in environmental issues. Your community most likely has one or more recycling programs under development or in place. Through your regular contacts with local community leaders you can let them know you want to help.

If you're searching for a major way to get involved with environmental affairs, contact the environmental coalition known as CERES. Becoming a member of CERES, as we have, will help your company make a public commitment to operate within the framework of 10 environmental rules known as the Valdez principles, so named following the Exxon tanker oil spill. In joining CERES, we have pledged to uphold and abide by the following guidelines:

• Protect our earth, by eliminating and minimizing pollution discharges.

- Protect our soils, water, and forests through the conservation of renewable resources.
- Dispose of waste wisely, striving to minimize the creation of waste.
- Strive to conserve energy throughout our operations, using safe energy sources.
- Use safe technology and operating procedures to minimize environmental, health, and safety risks.
- Sell products and services that are safe for both consumer and environment.
- Take responsibility for damage if we cause any to the environment.
- Make public disclosure if our operations cause environmental harm or pose health hazards.
- Responsibility for environmental effectiveness rests with the board of directors and company president.
- Conduct an annual evaluation to chart our progress in implementing these principles.

CERES has a structured membership fee, starting at $100 for companies with annual revenues less than $5 million. For more information or a copy of the latest *CERES Guide to the Valdez Principles*, write to CERES, 711 Atlantic Avenue, Boston, MA 02111, or call 617-451-0927, fax 617-482-6179.

PUTTING PRINCIPLES INTO PRACTICE

I own stock in about 15 other corporations, which means I get that many annual reports and voting proxies. Within the past year, five of these companies voted on a proposal for the company to adopt the Valdez principles. In every instance, the corporate position was to vote "no" on the proposal. And, sadly, it has always been voted down. I can't understand why, because no corporation need fear these priniciples unless it is not dedicated to protecting the environment. The reasons for voting down the Valdez principles generally were because the corporation had a better plan. Valdez is the toughest set of principles

I've ever seen. What could be better? Would these companies place profits in front of the environment? I don't know, and I hope not. I only know that if they did adopt the Valdez principles, we all could rest more easily.

Even when voted in, hanging a plaque of the Valdez principles on your wall does not create an environmental program. You'll have to use them as a checklist for turning your company's vision for the community into responsible action. Here's a partial list of some of the past and current initiatives we've implemented to hold up our end of the agreement to be partners with community in protecting and improving the environment:

• Cardboard Recycling. All of our boxes are now made of recycled cardboard and Distribution recycles 97 percent of the cardboard waste we generate. Further, where other recycling opportunities are not available, we will use our trucks to pick up cardboard the stores have collected, as well as from pizza customers, for recycling. In some locations, a single store might not be able to recycle its waste economically, but the large-scale nature of the Distribution commissary system allows us to help individual stores to easily participate.

• Office Waste Recycling. Within the company offices, we set up a system of double trash cans at every desk. We have now scheduled pickup of the cans on alternate days. The key to success in the program is that the alternating pickups did not result in increased trash collection costs.

• Ozone Preservation. We have achieved dramatic reductions—approaching elimination—of R-12 freon refrigerant in commissary and store cooling systems. We are now widely using R-22 refrigerant, which is less harmful to the ozone. Further, we have recovery systems in place to recycle much of the freon we use.

• Environmentally Responsible Supplies. The Distribution equipment and supplies catalog now offers a wide range of environmentally sound equipment for purchase and use by franchisees in local stores. One example is the new, high-efficiency coolers we've added that use a precooler to produce a dramatic reduction in energy use. Special "Earth Partner" fluorescent light fixtures that allow the removal of half the bulbs, with little or no loss in light output.

• Honoring Team Member Participants. In conjunction with the parent company, we've created a program to identify individual team members, stores, and commissaries that implement successful environmental strategies. We've flown in and honored team members with national awards for their efforts in such undertakings as recycling, Adopt-A-Highway programs, team member carpooling, and responsible community activities.

• A Special Award for Top Achievers. In keeping with our companywide policy to recognize our top achievers, we've created an annual award, the Distribution Environmental Award of the Year to honor special efforts in commissaries and stores. Some of the innovations that have evolved from this program are:

• In-store recycling of cardboard, aluminum.

• Plastic wrapping sent to florists for further use.

• Junk mail becomes notepads.

• Plastic vegetable tubs go to nursing homes for re-use.

• Pizza parties held at schools to promote recycling consciousness.

• Telephone book collection programs.

• Adopt-A-Highway program participation.

DEVELOP YOUR OWN UNIQUE RECYCLING PROGRAMS

We recognize that supporting our environmental partnership with local communities requires going beyond our past successes and the more obvious recycling programs. To reach beyond the obvious, we've developed some innovative strategies.

For example, we're constantly searching for opportunities to convert our dough wastes at our commissaries to alternative uses, thereby avoiding its disposal as solid waste. One of the uncommon uses we've found for dough wastes is as a high-energy food supplement for farm animals.

Another way we help is to view all our facilities in the context of their total involvement in community activities. For example, where it fills a gap in community collection facilities, our commissaries will open their parking lots on weekends so members of the local community can bring us their recyclable products.

Since we've got the collection mechanisms in place, it makes sense that we share them as fully as possible with the community. A program like this can be a great win-win situation for your company, as well. Not only do you get to participate in environmentally responsible activities, but you also help others do the same.

A CHALLENGE TO OTHER CORPORATIONS

Domino's Pizza started the first corporate chapter of Ducks Unlimited in the organization's 53-year history. With the help of Ducks Unlimited state official Fred Hingst, volunteers from Distribution, the parent company, and other members of the Domino's Pizza family (including our bankers!) have organized and created one of the leading chapters in Michigan. Recognized as "1990 Rookie Chapter of the Year" in Michigan, this chapter went from 3 sponsors to over 150 in three years. How did it do it? By acknowledging and responding to the needs of the membership, sponsors, and the Ducks Unlimited state and national organizations. Sound familiar? This group took the seven-step method and created a chapter where sponsors enjoy over twice the regular benefits found in other chapters and records for the most money raised for wetlands reclamation projects are in sight.

Ducks Unlimited was chosen by this group for its efficiency at getting monies to the projects, not the coffers of the organization to cover administrative overhead. In fact, no other environmental organization tops Ducks Unlimited in getting the largest percent of your donation to the actual project (*Money*, December 1990). Here's the challenge: select an environmental charity and start your own corporate chapter. Also, let me know about it through the survey in the back of the book or contact me for information about our chapter.

INTERPLAY OF THE MISSION

One of your best resources for environmental responsibility is team members. With the vision we have to be the best place our team members can think of to work, they know they have nothing to fear by reporting environmental problems to team leaders. Rather than face the threat of being fired as whistle-blowers, Domino's team members stand to be recognized and rewarded for reporting ways we can be more efficient in the use of the planet's resources.

There's the interplay between visions of our mission statement again. The real key to having your community consider you a fine example of what business should be is in having team members who share your overall vision.

CHAPTER CHECKLIST

Identify your public and inventory their needs.

- Don't consider government health and safety inspection agencies as threats to your team; learn what their needs are. And I don't mean merely to cooperate with inspectors; everyone does that because it's required by law.

- Think of the people in those agencies as your neighbors and fellow community members. Once you've established a good working relationship with the people in government agencies, you may find them giving you the opportunity to become partners with them in enhancing the overall safety and health of your shared community.

- Visit the mayor's office annually and ask, "Do you know we are in town? Are we good for your town?"

- Conduct regular surveys that give you a comprehensive look at how your presence is perceived in the community and where there's room for improvement. Get back to respondents as to how you will address the concerns they shared and the contributions they offered.

Sort the needs into patterns.

- Acknowledge you will more easily flourish in an environment that wants and appreciates you and your business.

- Welcome input from your team members. A real key to having effective community involvement is having team members who share your overall vision.

Develop a mission statement.

- Strive to have your community consider your company to be a fine example of what a business should be.

Set key indicators and levels of performance.

- View compliance with laws and regulations as a common company goal rather than a shackle to your profitability.
- Pledge to the community that all team members, before performing in any position, will satisfy certification or licensing required by the company or by government. Then back it up with positive action plans.
- Require drug and alcohol testing for all team members who are in any safety-sensitive position, as well as for those in positions where the health and safety of fellow team members or the community are at risk.

Establish an automatic reward system for top performance.

- Celebrate all team members who have gone above and beyond the usual responsibility of a citizen. Recognize those who have helped save lives and donated their time to charities and to other community events.
- Present ethics awards to those who have shown exceptional community involvement.

Establish ongoing programs to support your mission.

- Abstain from viewing community involvement as a vehicle to higher profits. It's a natural responsibility for your company. Make it a way of life.
- Support local community fund-raising efforts by getting the entire extended company family involved. You won't become a pillar of the community by sitting in your office and writing checks.
- Maintain all your facilities and equipment in top condition. This will reflect well on your position within the community and demonstrate your commitment to the community.

- Work closely with local communities to share your methods of success. Share your philosophies with other local businesses, schools, colleges, and universities.

- Conquer mediocrity in community affairs by offering only your best efforts.

- Recognize that environmental protection is the only responsible position a company can take.

- Join CERES to help your company make a public commitment to operate within the framework of the 10 Valdez principles.

- Go beyond your past successes and the more obvious recycling programs; develop new and innovative environmental strategies.

Chapter Five
What Does Our Parent Company Need?

We list our parent company as one of our publics. By "parent" we include Tom Monaghan, the owner, Domino's Pizza, Inc.; the Domino's Pizza board of directors; stockholders; and our own board. If discovering the needs of the communities is the most inconvenient, determining what our parent company needs is the most convenient. It tells us.

We try to stay in tune with the needs of our parent company. Each year, when systemwide performance objectives are set, Distribution has been in the unique position of approaching this process from a "what can we do to help" standpoint rather than hearing "what we must do."

Almost invariably, the response is: "Take care of the franchisees and produce even higher levels of product quality and hit record efficiencies." This message has been constant since I've been at Domino's Pizza. First from Tom Monaghan, then Dick Mueller, through Dave Black and Mike Orcutt to the current head of operations, Kevin Williams: take care of the franchisees, produce even higher levels of quality, and hit record efficiencies.

And this message makes sense. Franchisees and pizza store managers tell us on surveys and in person that they appreciate the strong relationship we have with them and they believe we are making continual strides on product quality. The ultimate challenge, therefore, is to always be more efficient in everything we do. We view ourselves in the financial middle of three key groups: franchisees who want lower prices, team members who want more rewards, and a parent company that wants higher profits.

With these three key needs defined essentially as "patterns," we were able to easily articulate the parent company's needs in our mission: "Parent company proud to have us on its team."

From the need list above, we then apply key indicators in our quest to make the parent company proud to have us as part of its team. Our contribution to overall profits, for example, can be monitored through annual and quarterly reports. Our desire to provide the best possible food products to the Domino's Pizza stores can be tabulated through our annual survey, interim customer surveys, and mystery customer reports (see Chapter 10).

REWARDING PERFORMANCE

Increasing efficiency perhaps is the easiest thing for us to automatically reward. As Distribution lowers operating expenses, we can lower prices to our customers. As customers experience lower prices, we get increased market share and sales volumes. These increases feed our bonus system, and there is more money available for monthly bonuses.

THE PROOF IS A MATTER OF RECORD

Everything discussed so far in this book probably sounds good to you. Many of our unusual approaches to running an organization, serving our customers, and caring for our team members make good business sense, and you'll probably try some. However, I'll bet you want to know the answer to the question, "Have they contributed to improved financial performance?" Our success at Distribution allowed the parent company to qualify for more bank loans that enabled it to open more corporate stores. This also increased interest among potential franchisees, resulting in more franchise stores as well.

The whole process feeds on itself because with a greater number of stores, we were able to realize savings through greater economy of scale and increase profits more, which led to the parent's ability to open yet

Needs of Parent Company

Public	Groups	Major Needs/Pattern
Parent company	Tom Monaghan Domino's Pizza, Inc. (DPI) DPI Board of Directors Distribution Board of Directors Stockholders	Distribution contributes to overall corporate profits Support the franchisees Distribution provides the best possible food products to Domino's Pizza stores Distribution is an excellent representative of the Domino's corporate image Uphold Tom Monaghan's views on working and living according to the Golden Rule
Our mission statement:	Parent company proud to have us as part of its team.	

more stores. Central purchasing and central production of fresh dough products ensure that consistent product is available to each store, no matter how new it is to our system.

Tom Monaghan told me point-blank, "Without commissary profits, we would not have been able to get loans to buy or build company stores." His acknowledgment of our successes has been constant. For example, when Tom bought the Detroit Tigers baseball team, the team began the next year, 1984, with a fabulous string of victories, amassing a record of 35 wins and only 5 losses. The local press was absorbed with curiosity about the guy who had just bought the team. At a meeting with bankers, with all the focus on Tom, he introduced me as, "The guy who generated the profits and enabled me to buy the Tigers." That was one of the greatest fringe benefits I've ever received from any job.

Allow me to toss out a couple of numbers and let you be the judge of our financial performance. Over an 11-year period, starting from when Distribution was established as a separate entity, we have limited the price increase to Domino's Pizza stores to 1.9 percent. That's not annually. That's over 11 years. During the same period, national prices on pizza supplies and ingredients rose 33 percent, and the consumer price index rose 89 percent.

Key Indicators for Parent Company

Parent Company's Identified Need	Crisis	Expected	Exceptional	Measurement Method
Be proud to have Distribution as part of its team				
Survey of communities: are you glad Distribution is in your community?	10% no	3–6% no	<3% no	Community surveys
Positive impressions of Distribution	Negative press	Uphold DPI public image standards	Contribute to DPI public image	Media reports
Distribution contributes to overall corporate profits				
Percent variance from profit goals	Under profit goals	Meeting profit goals	Exceeding profit goals	DPI Annual Report Accounting reports
Distribution provides the best possible food products to Domino's Pizza stores				
Survey of stores: Does Distribution provide the highest quality items?	>10% no	3–5% no	<3% no	Franchise customer surveys
Survey of pizza eaters: Did the pizza taste fresh and was it of good quality?	>10% no	3–5% no	<3% no	Mystery customer surveys
Distribution is an excellent representative of the Domino's corporate image				
Survey of stores: Do our team members (a) embarrass you; (b) support the DPI standards; or (c) exceed the DPI standards?	(a) Embarrass	(b) Support	(c) Exceed	Store surveys
Efficiencies				
Net reductions in annual operating expenses	No reduction	____ %	____ %	Accounting reports

Also, during the 1980s, Domino's Pizza, Inc., grew an average of 45 percent annually. During the same period, Distribution grew an average of 75 percent annually. When Domino's consisted of 144 stores, we were supplying 62 percent of them. Today, with more than 5,300 stores worldwide, we continually capture about 95 percent of the market (remember, franchise stores remain free to buy products from any source they choose).

Overall, we've grown well over 65 percent faster than our parent corporation. Meeting the parent's needs has served both Distribution and the parent company well. We still have a lot of room for improvement, but at the least, Domino's Pizza, Inc., is proud to have us as a member of its team.

OTHER WAYS TO MAKE THEM PROUD

Our pledge to our parent company is to provide resources and support when it is for the good of the overall organization. You already know about how our drivers make late-night deliveries and leave the stores in top shape for the next day's operation. We go beyond that to support our parent company. Distribution team members will provide on-the-spot training on request, particularly when it comes to handling dough.

We will work in the stores, and we will support the stores by helping them with door hanging (distributing those fliers you see on your doorknob suggesting you call Domino's Pizza). We keep our promises, large and small, both with the stores and with headquarters.

Our system works because it's an open, two-way street between us and the parent company. The focus is always on solving problems in support of our mission for the parent company rather than on finding out who is responsible for a problem or why it occurred, not that we're uninterested in why it occurred.

For instance, when Domino's Pizza needed to distribute training materials to new stores as they opened, we included the materials with our standard new store packages.

A particular decision may seem odd when viewed by itself, but our parent company has the map and compass of our mission so it always knows where we're pointed. The support we have given it has been returned to us many times over through its support of us. If the DPI people get wind of something that initially sounds like somebody at

Distribution has gone nuts, their first reaction is to remember we do everything to support the overall vision for all five areas of our own mission statement (see Chapter 7).

STRENGTHENING THE TIES INTERNALLY

Making the parent proud to have us as part of the team is enhanced by a custom that has taken hold in recent years. Dave Black, president of Domino's Pizza, Inc., thought it would make good sense to take a picture of our home office staff to send to all field and regional offices. He wanted to photograph them wearing the familiar red and blue Domino's uniform.

Tom Monaghan's wife, Marge, was on hand for the photo session. Marge has always had a strong influence in the company. Every fourth Friday, she walks through the building and personally hands out bonus checks to more than 400 team members. When she saw Dave taking the uniform photo, she asked, "You are going to do this for more than just one day, aren't you?"

Following Marge's remark about the uniform idea, it caught on throughout DPI and Distribution that you could wear the red and blue uniform if you were not going to wear your traditional office garb— suit and tie or dress. Today, many home office staff in the parent and at Distribution routinely wear the uniform at work, particularly on bonus days. It helps remind all of us that it is the people in the field who make the ultimate sale.

The gesture also helps convey a continuing image to people in the field that home office people care. Any time field or regional staff members, or anyone else, visit headquarters, they gain an active, visible reminder that we're committed to supporting fellow team members throughout the company.

SHARING OUR GOALS, PLEDGING OUR PERFORMANCE

A Program for Quality.   Our performance pledge includes our quality assurance program that gives the parent company additional assurance hard-won product improvements will benefit the company overall. As discussed in the previous chapter, it is our responsibility to ensure that all our products are produced and distributed to meet the quality, sanitation, health, and safety levels set by the parent company in cooperation with government requirements and customer needs.

Because we fully cooperate with all inspections, testing, and auditing requests to prepare complete, accurate, and truthful documentation, this takes a great burden off the parent. We conduct "dough audits" just as many companies conduct internal financial audits.

Sharing the Risks of Innovation.   The parent company helps us to be innovative with its attitude toward those people who take risks. DPI does not react negatively to failures unless they are repetitive, careless, or major. That support of our team members has permitted us to create a positive atmosphere in which our team members can take risks.

At Distribution, there is practically no such thing as a failed experiment. When team members fail at something innovative, they know the home office will want to know all about it, primarily for what can be learned. Conversely, when an innovation results in a productivity improvement or a cost saving, the team members know they will be rewarded through one of our incentive programs.

Above All, Ethics.   Domino's Pizza, Inc., stands for ethical treatment of everyone the company touches. To support this vision of corporate ethics, we adopted the three-part ethics checklist from the book, *The Power of Ethical Management*, by Ken Blanchard and Norman Vincent Peale. Its basis is a pledge to the parent that we will consciously abide by the Golden Rule in every decision we make. Here's the checklist we use:

• Is It Legal?   Will we violate either civil law or company policy? And we don't stop there. At times, laws and company policy may not relate closely. In those cases where something might be legal, yet remain questionable, we continue with the next two questions.

• Is It Balanced?   Will anyone win by causing others to lose big in the long term or short term? Regardless of legality, we ask whether a decision is fair to all involved.

• How Will It Make Me Feel about Myself?   Will I feel proud of my decision? The best guidance to answering this question comes from asking yourself how you would feel if your decision were published on the front page of the newspaper. Would you frame that clipping or want to leave town for a few weeks?

STRIVING TO UPHOLD THE PARENT'S IMAGE

For most people, "Domino's Pizza" almost instantly brings to mind a store delivery driver in the familiar red and blue uniform. When most people hear of Domino's Pizza Distribution, they immediately think of the parent, not us. Ever mindful that what we do will inextricably be associated with the parent, we are committed to reflecting a positive image of the parent company to the general public.

Therefore, we adopt the same strict dress code necessary for our retail food outlets: no beards, haircuts above the collar, strict corporate dress requirements, full adoption of the uniform policy (if you wear the pizza store uniform, wear it correctly!). These standards are in place for everyone from the pizza delivery person to the doughmaker to the executive team—it wouldn't be fair to have double standards. As a side note, we've just awarded our DPI advertising account to Grey Advertising of New York. The head of the creative efforts on the account, Steve Novick, decided to cut his shoulder-length hair (a style nearly every creative director I've ever met chooses) in line with our standards! We didn't ask him to do that; it was his decision based on noticing the importance of standards to our culture.

The best and brightest image we can make, other than maintaining excellent community relations, is through our drivers. Our drivers are truly key players of Distribution. Without safe, reliable drivers, it wouldn't matter what kind of products we produced for our customers. Nothing works if the goods don't get from the commissary to the individual stores.

The Towel Drive.   Current events have prompted our team members to enhance the parent's image in still other ways. Soon after the Exxon Valdez oil spill, environmentalists put out an emergency call for towels to help the rescue team clean animals stuck in the mire of the spill. It was impossible to clean the towels and reuse them fast enough, so a massive supply of towels was needed.

When we heard about this, we decided we had to help. The concept was simple and superb. Our delivery service, in reverse, could also function as a pickup service. Distribution began collecting towels from local franchise stores after our regular deliveries and returning them to central locations where they could be sent to Alaska. We encouraged DPI and its stores to ask their customers to donate old towels to the Domino's Pizza deliverer when the pizza arrived. The local drivers delivered pizza to homes and returned towels to the stores. The commissary drivers delivered products to the stores and returned towels to the commissaries. We rapidly accumulated truckloads at the commissaries and then used our own trucks to drive them to Alaska. As each Distribution truck arrived in Alaska with the towels, we knew the parent was proud to have us as part of its team.

Aluminum Can Recycling. The principle of reversing the pickup process for the towel collection drive has been adopted to support the parent's quest to practice recycling nationwide. Everyone knows that when people eat pizza, they also consume soft drinks or beer in bottles or in aluminum cans.

One of our franchisees, Jim Hatfield of London, Kentucky, with support from franchisees Jeff Litman of Denver, Mike Chiodo of Chicago, and Brian Dennis of Houston, introduced a unique recycling program. Thanks to their pioneering efforts, we now supply our franchisees with special boxes for collecting aluminum cans. The franchisees give the boxes to their customers. The boxes have holes on top perfectly sized for aluminum cans and they have a line to indicate when they contain 100 cans.

When a pizza customer has collected 100 cans, he or she calls the local Domino's Pizza store, orders a pizza, and tells the order taker he or she has a full can recycling box. The customer then gets a free topping for that pizza order, and the driver picks up the cans and returns them to the store. The collection boxes provide an easy method for consumers to recycle.

To further enhance participation in this program, we offer a can-pressing machine to the stores. The machines compress 100 cans at a time, so an entire load of cans is quickly compressed by store personnel and stacked up like wood for the commissary truck to pick up after the delivery.

In areas where can deposits are required by law, cans are often worth 10 cents each. Therefore, 100 cans would be worth $10. We're now developing a program whereby pizza buyers will be able to trade in their cans for a "free" pizza, and we'll arrange for our customers—

the stores—to get paid for the deposits we collect when we turn in the recycled cans.

We're providing a service to individual consumers by giving them an easy way to responsibly dispose of their aluminum cans. We're providing a service to the environment, and we're supporting the national image of Domino's Pizza, Inc. We also help the store, since many consumers will order a Domino's pizza because of the recycling service that is included.

ASSISTING THE PARENT IN MATTERS OF SECURITY

In late 1989, we linked both our mission for our customers and our parent company to enhance store security. The parent company announced its commitment to make store employees the safest in the nation, through a series of innovative security training and compliance programs. For example, we use a positive reinforcement system whereby supervisors can issue tickets to team members when they see them upholding security procedures especially well.

DPI's protective services director, Brad Bonnell, summed up the mission of his department by saying, "It's our job to teach and lead the drivers, managers, and supervisors to make them our security and safety agents in the field." Under a program designed by Brad, nearly 300 DPI store supervisors, as well as Distribution drivers, attended a special security school. The school held intensive, daylong seminars focusing on reducing losses by identifying potential problems before they occurred.

Participants studied cases of actual security incidents to identify options for minimizing the number and severity of internal and external incidents. DPI security supervisors and Distribution drivers were trained to be "detectives," checking store records and conducting audits of store security measures.

Working closely with the new security program, we were able to support both our customers and the parent company by upgrading the security checks our drivers performed when they made late-night deliveries. In addition to bringing in the products the store has ordered, our drivers use the knowledge gained by the parent company's security school to enhance the safety of our customers' stores.

CHAPTER CHECKLIST

Identify your publics and inventory their needs.

- Recognize your obligations to your parent: the owner, the board of directors, shareholders, other divisions.

Sort the needs into patterns.

- The key areas where you can strive to support your parent company through your mission statement vision include: helping its customers, improving quality, and becoming more efficient.

Develop a mission statement.

- If you have a parent company or similar relationship, include in your mission statement a vision to have your parent company proud to have you as a member of its team.
- Focus on solving problems in support of the mission statement rather than on finding out who is responsible for the problem or why it occurred.

Set key indicators and levels of performance.

- Work with your parent company to get a clear understanding of how your organization will be judged.

Establish an automatic reward system for top performance.

- Establish a bonus system that allows everyone to benefit: customers, team members, and the parent company.

Establish ongoing programs to support your mission.

- Listen to your parent's priorities, ask how they relate to you, and develop programs that support them before the parent asks.

- Regard failed experiments as contributions to overall understanding.

- Before engaging in any activity, ask four questions: Is it legal? Is it balanced? How will it make me feel about myself? Is it safe?

- Consider all team members to be in positions of trust and conduct themselves accordingly.

- Be particularly sensitive to the many situations, on and off the job, where a conflict of interest or even a perception of such a conflict could originate.

- Look for ways to make additional use of existing resources, such as having your delivery people pick up recyclable goods.

Chapter Six

What Do Our Suppliers Need?

The public we know as "suppliers" includes everyone who provides the high-quality raw materials to us that we provide to our pizza stores. We don't, however, stop there. All who provide services to us, such as consultants Gabe Hall & Associates, or machines or trucks for our use, such as Ryder Truck Leasing, are part of the Domino's Pizza family. We know our success servicing our customers is contingent on their performance and their willingness to help us be our best.

That is why it is critical that we know and are responsive to the needs of our suppliers. Suppliers, however, tend to be the most shy when it comes to letting you know how they feel. Suppose you mistreat a supplier. If it is an isolated incident and you are a large volume account, the supplier often overlooks the incident for fear of losing your business. As someone dependent on that supplier, however, I can't afford to risk a product or service failure because one of its people wouldn't go the extra mile for us because he or she held a grudge against my company. We need our suppliers and we need to respond to their needs.

ESTABLISHING THE BONDS WITH SUPPLIERS

I came to Distribution from a meat-processing company that had gone out of business, so I looked forward to the spectacular growth I saw in Domino's future. I was excited about my first day on the job and went straight in to Tom Monaghan's office expecting to be warmly greeted.

To welcome me to work, Tom didn't even shake my hand; instead he handed over the latest profit and loss statement that showed a loss of $400,000 over the past eight months and said, "Here's your first job, Don. Straighten it out."

I spent the first week or so analyzing potential profit opportunities and noticed many glaring items that fell in the category of "quick fixes." It became clear that we could break even within 15 months and become cash positive shortly thereafter (this was contingent on a brief moratorium on building commissaries—a move that Tom disagreed with and nearly fired me for!). That meant we could start taking cash discounts within 24 months.

One of the first things I noted was that we were 60 days in arrears in payments to our suppliers. I knew their support would be crucial to our success, and we were unlikely to get it when we weren't paying them on time. Several suppliers were actually considering placing us on a cash-on-delivery basis, but I turned to them with a bold move.

I went to the president of one supplier, John Russo of Sorrento Cheese, and asked for a price break, saying, "If we spend one more dollar than we should, we can never regain it—it's gone from the Domino's family forever." I acknowledged our tardiness to him and explained there was plenty of money floating around the system to pay them all, but it was currently being wasted.

I told John that if we could get lower prices, we'd become current in our payments sooner, and once we were financially healthy, he would get paid on time. John denied my request for lower prices (I wasn't surprised). So I asked John for a cash discount if I paid my bills before the due date. John laughed and I'm sure he was thinking, "Sure, right! I just hope this bozo pays his outstanding bills. He'll never be able to pay early!" John offered the discount believing he had nothing to lose.

The gamble worked. Within nine months we were taking discounts. This was so successful John asked me if we could change the agreement—he was surprised we would be able to take so many discounts.

PAYING BILLS MORE THAN ON TIME

Our commitment to fairness has crossed over into every area in which we deal with our suppliers. Recently, another of our major cheese suppliers was experiencing cash flow problems and having trouble meeting short-term debt. This was a great concern, considering that we purchase more than 80 million pounds of cheese annually. If a major cheese supplier went out of business, it could wreak havoc on us and upset many of the visions in our mission statement.

When the supplier asked for financial relief by our speeding payments to him, we expedited payments to sustain this supplier. I then asked key executives to see if all cheese suppliers were experiencing difficulties or if this was an isolated case. They quickly discovered it was a national problem caused by a combination of high milk prices and low cheese demand, resulting in low cheese prices as raw materials expense was climbing.

All our cheese suppliers were facing financial uncertainty, although only the one company had asked for prompt payment. At the time, we purchased more than $15 million worth of cheese per month. To be fair and equitable with all suppliers and to ensure a continuing supply of cheese, we adopted a practice of paying for cheese the minute the invoices came in the door.

I recalled a lesson learned from my father, Don Vlcek, Sr. When I headed operations for the meat-packing plant, he was the controller for the same operation. It was common, as with most companies, that when a salesperson uncovered a potential new large account, the salesperson was met with joy. The president of the company saw increases in sales and profits. The salesperson saw increased commissions. The head of operations, me, saw increased volumes and more profits. Everyone in the plant saw increased wages and overtime hours. My dad, however, was the one to see reality. "Their money is no good," he had to proclaim on several occasions after researching the potential client. "We're not here to do charity—they are notorious for past dues and late payments!"

Everyone's excitement over the new business would fade. We knew we didn't want to do business with slow payers. Today, as head of a firm that buys goods from meat packers for redistribution to my customers, I know not to get that reputation. I understand this need of suppliers from both the vendor and customer standpoint.

ZERO PAYABLES PROGRAM

Recalling our commitment to fairness to everyone who is touched by Distribution, we adopted an expedited payment plan for all suppliers. From there, we pledged to take an active role in the financial security of each of our suppliers. For obvious reasons, we call the program "zero payables." It is unthinkable to allow bills to become past due or delay payment.

By speeding up our average payment by more than a week, company financiers determined we would forgo $500,000 a year in interest. But we viewed the lost interest earnings as a sound investment in our future. It is more important to build extremely strong, favorable relations with cheese suppliers than to squeeze out every dollar of profit every quarter.

While most firms strive to extend payment terms, we are unique by seeking the opposite. It's a loud, clear message of partnership to our suppliers that has given us returns such as:

• Innovative Technology.   Suppliers frequently come to us first with their newest products. Developing new technology often puts a company in a cash crunch. Our suppliers know the fastest way out of that crunch is to sell to Domino's first because we will pay the invoice immediately.

• Quality and Service.   We never have to worry about suffering a degradation in quality or service because of concerns over payment. Our suppliers always hustle to get the highest quality products for us because it will produce a quick infusion of cash.

• Service "Above and Beyond."   One of the most important benefits from zero payables is that most of our suppliers have responded to our special requests with exceptional service.

Automatic Rewards for Treating Suppliers Well.   We include zero payables as part of our bonus calculation. If we are not paying our bills on time, each person in Distribution feels it in his or her bonus. By the same token, we can realize greater bonuses by doing what's right—paying our bills on time.

Understandably, many suppliers vigorously compete for the economic privilege and honor of supplying Domino's Pizza Distribution. The more business they get from us, the higher their cash flow.

Perhaps you can't go to zero payables, but you can adopt a policy to treat all suppliers in a fair and even manner. Because of the cash requirements associated with a pending employee stock ownership plan (ESOP), we've slowed our payments to paying on time. Our suppliers understand, and we still have the reputation of being one of the best bill payers in the industry. Regardless, you can also keep suppliers acutely informed as to when you will be paying their invoices. Particularly in an uncertain economy, the partnerships you forge with your suppliers will serve as wells from which to draw when necessary.

DETECTING AND SORTING NEEDS

We have learned that our supplier's needs are very similar to our own: We address these needs in our mission statement, saying: "Suppliers excited enough to call us their favorite account."

We believe we have to develop a loyal supplier base to fulfill our long-term needs by providing unique opportunities for them and promoting an atmosphere of exceptional fairness. We want to be the favorite account of each of our suppliers and to benefit from the innovation and advice each supplier has to offer.

Our approach to suppliers, which is now being emulated by other companies, is to treat each supplier as part of our team, indeed as part of our company. As such, we encourage them to express their beliefs and feelings about us in many of the same ways we encourage our team members to do so. Why not? Suppliers are crucial to our ability

Needs of Distribution Suppliers

Public	Groups	Major Needs/Pattern
Distribution suppliers	Raw goods vendors Consultants Lease companies Training firms	Honesty and ethical behavior Upfront relations and open communication Paying bills on time Confidence that we want long-standing relationships
Our mission statement:	Suppliers excited enough to call us their favorite account.	

Key Indicators for Distribution Suppliers

Suppliers' Identified Needs	Crisis	Expected	Exceptional	Measurement Method
Overall satisfaction with Distribution				
Is Distribution your favorite account?	>20% no	8–12% no	<5% no	Summer survey
Honesty and ethical behavior				
Is Distribution ethical in its business transactions?	>5% no	1–3% no	<1% no	Summer survey
Have you ever been coerced to spend money you didn't want to by Distribution?	>5% no	1–3% no	<1% no	Summer survey
Upfront relations and open communication				
Does Distribution keep you informed about its plans?	80% yes	90% yes	>94% yes	Summer survey
Paying bills on time				
Are we at zero payables?	Any past due	All bills paid on time	All bills on time and could be paid earlier	Accounting records
Confidence that we want long-standing relationships				
Are you confident about your future as a distribution supplier?	>20% no	10–12% no	<8% no	Summer survey

to supply. With that in mind, we established key indicators to measure our behavior with our suppliers (Step 5).

OPEN AND HONEST

All our dealings with suppliers are above the table. We share our plans with them, so they know what to expect from us in terms of future business. By listening to their feedback and never using threats, we've made it clear that we see fairness as being more important than financial gain.

Each supplier is given a copy of our mission statement. We make it plain to suppliers that we place a priority on awarding business to vendors that respect the philosophies, values, and attitudes reflected in the goals established by our mission.

OUR PLEDGE TO SUPPLIERS

No "marriage" relationship will last long without honesty and trust between the partners. One important facet of a solid, trusting relationship is an agreement of confidentiality. All of our suppliers have our pledge not to disclose to others their pricing data, nor any information or techniques they consider to be confidential.

We always regard our relationships with suppliers with the long-term view, even if we've just started working together. To that end, we've established a three-point program of cooperation with each supplier:

- We visit each other's facilities regularly and openly share our joint resources.

- We have committed to seeking their feedback frequently to learn how we can attain a reputation as a "number one customer" with them.

- We have vowed to never use threats, manipulation, or coercion in our negotiations with any supplier.

MOVING THROUGH THE SUPPLY CHAIN

We have experienced annual growth rates as high as 102 percent—we should be so lucky every year. Rapid growth, however, can cause problems for our suppliers. For example, as our cheese suppliers became adept at supplying us with 50 million pounds of cheese annually, our need increased to 70 million. We could expand our number of suppliers, but that requires new tasks and responsibilities, and we are committed to giving our current suppliers a chance to grow with us.

Our growth in this case resulted in a problem for our suppliers because the increase of 20 million pounds of cheese translated into an increase of 200 million gallons of milk. Many of our cheese suppliers had difficulty finding suppliers for the extra milk. They had trouble persuading farmers to "beef up" their milk herd to produce the needed increase.

The farmers, in turn, faced enormous expenses in expanding their herds and building new facilities to handle the larger herds and milk output. They were concerned about what would happen if the demand from us dropped, causing the cheese suppliers to stop buying the increased volume of milk.

Farmer's Appreciation Day.   Jim Zimmerman, one of our Wisconsin cheese suppliers, came to us with a new cheese formula that significantly reduced costs while maintaining all quality standards. We knew his new cheese would be a boon in lower prices to our customers, so we decided to increase our purchases from Jim. His increased business was going to put a big strain on the farmers who supplied him from the Blanchardsville, Wisconsin, area. They were concerned about our long-term intentions.

Reviewing our mission statement enabled us to quickly come up with a way to help our suppliers settle the farmers' fears. Since the farmers were not directly our customers, they didn't know how strong a long-term commitment we make to all suppliers. To demonstrate our commitment, we set up an appreciation day for the people who supplied milk to Jim Zimmerman.

We flew our executive team into Blanchardsville in a helicopter along with Jim Northrup, former Detroit Tigers baseball star, and hosted a parade using the cheese supplier's trucks, some of our delivery trucks, some pizza delivery cars from Wisconsin franchisees Merle and Colleen Butterick, who came dressed in Domino's delivery uniforms, plus horses and carriages.

We paraded down Main Street handing out Domino's promotional items from the carriages. This entire event was held before there were any full-time public relations people on our staff. We didn't retain PR people because it wasn't done for publicity—we weren't interested in a staged media event. Besides, the local people already knew our name well enough.

We simply went to Wisconsin to tell the local people about our visions for growth, which turned out to be integral to their growth as well. What they didn't know—and they learned that weekend—was that they were important to us. We used the parade as our opportunity to thank people who were contributing to our growth and to let them know we regarded them as a valuable link in our growth chain.

After the parade, we had a barbecue with some of the townspeople. The Chamber of Commerce kicked in to help defray costs, and local residents brought potluck dishes. During the picnic, we made our helicopter available to give farmers and their families an aerial view of their farms.

After the picnic, we had a friendly baseball game with the local people. Jim Northrup signed autographs. The day ended with a special ceremony for the family of one of the farmers who had perished when a tornado struck his farm. The executive and office teams from Ann Arbor had taken up a collection on behalf of this family. During the ceremony, we presented his family with a check from donations we had collected in the town.

Helping our suppliers when they need it the most has been a hallmark of our business strategy and it has served us well. We were warmly received that day in Wisconsin and built a strong and lasting relationship with the farmers. They now had security while bearing the costs of expanding to handle our needs.

ABOVE BOARD AND FAIR

One of the things I have always been proud of is never having my decisions to do business with a supplier be influenced by gifts or gratuities. By initiating a "no gratuities" policy within Distribution, we've been able to take the pressure off our team members who, in a moment of weakness, might be influenced wrongfully.

With some of my long-term vendors it became almost a game. An executive recruiter with Roth Young, Jerry Matlon, made an agreement with the hostess at a restaurant and actually presented his American Express card to her in advance of the meal just so he could buy me lunch. When the end of the meal came, and the completed charge slip was presented to him for his signature, I was mad. Jerry laughed and said it was the first time in five years of doing business with me that he picked up the check and that no matter what I said, he was going to revel in it. I looked at Jerry and said, "OK, you win. Just because I've been caught for the first time in my life, let me see the charge slip with your name on it." He fell for it. I tore up the slip and immediately tendered cash for the meal!

This pledge is honored by all team members, each of whom has agreed to never accept any gifts or gratuities or any form of compensation from any supplier, no matter how small. Even when a supplier attempts to coerce a team member into accepting a gratuity, the team member has to refuse.

In extreme cases, where one can't refuse a forced gratuity, a team member needs to quickly report the incident to his or her team leader and work together to reciprocate by giving the supplier something of equal value, removing any lingering "debts." If the forced gratuity is some sort of perishable food item, our team members usually will donate the food to charity and send the supplier a letter informing them what was done with the item.

At one point, we invited our suppliers to participate in our national awards celebration. This turned into a learning situation for us. Most of our executives believed the suppliers should pay their own share. Each meal would be a huge, costly event with hundreds of people coming to eat. I disagreed with having the suppliers sponsor the meals, but I was outnumbered and didn't have the conviction on the issue that I do now. We did ask our suppliers to cover the cost of a meal.

Once our board of directors met the suppliers face to face and more fully understood their role as members of the Domino's team, they immediately wrote checks to every supplier in attendance, fully rebating the expenses they had incurred.

At the banquet, we all clearly saw that suppliers should be treated as our guests, as being part of our team. We would never have asked our team members to pay, and there was no reason to treat the suppliers any differently. Since then, it has been a consistent policy throughout the extended Domino's family that everyone receives team member treatment.

CONNECTING WITH OUR SUPPLIERS

In the early 1980s, I flew to California for a meeting with one of our suppliers, Tri-Valley Growers. Its sales representative, Sue Zentmeyer, picked me up at the airport to drive me to the meeting. On the way, we passed our commissary in that area and I asked Sue if she would mind stopping for a quick visit. They were not expecting me, but I wanted to say hi to everyone anyway.

I walked into the middle of a disaster. The dough machine had broken, causing major problems in keeping stores supplied. People had been on the job for 14 hours trying to get the machine repaired and were stripped down to their T-shirts, covered with sweat and grease.

In the middle of this crisis, the sauce supplier, Sue's company, had missed a delivery, further complicating the problems. The commissary manager had been forced to have his drivers pick up the sauce at the warehouse and deliver it directly to stores. This extra burden was the last thing they needed that day, and everyone in the commissary had to work overtime to keep up.

Sue couldn't believe what she witnessed. She was appalled and embarrassed that these people were suffering because of a problem with her company. She immediately got on the phone and got the deliveries made.

Afterward she told me, "Don, I've sold you millions of cases of sauce, yet I've never been in a commissary. It's different now that I've seen how hard these people work and how much my company can affect their day. You should have your suppliers visit the commissaries."

SWAT Camp. Involving our suppliers in our operations spawned an idea that would pay big dividends for us. Jerry Graf, Carol Weaver, Jim Caldwell, and Carol Keller, Distribution's purchasing team, built a program that we call our SWAT camp (Suppliers Working Actively Together). At the SWAT camps, we get our supplier companies together and the weekend becomes an event. We balance meeting time with informal fun, including trips to Detroit Tiger baseball games.

Our executive team meets personally with executives from our supply companies and explains what our company's goals are for the coming year. We get their input and ensure that we share the same vision of growth. The openness of the meetings has helped us brainstorm with suppliers to find ways to obtain mutual success. We even see suppliers, many of whom are direct competitors, comparing notes to see how they can collectively contribute to our company's success!

LOYALTY WITH A CAPITAL L

In supporting more than 5,500 pizza stores worldwide, we have delivered a lot of pizza-making equipment to those stores. One of our major oven suppliers was experiencing money trouble. When we heard it was experiencing a financial problem, we wanted to help.

The problem occurred when the company began building up its stock in anticipation of an influx of large orders from many of its biggest customers. As a result, it spent a lot of money and became strapped for cash while increasing and storing its inventory. Domino's was among the largest of those key customers.

The president of this supplier went to his customers to explain the jam the company was in and to ask for financial relief. Although our zero payables program was in place, our orders had slowed, leaving the company with excess inventory and strapped for cash. The company asked us to pay, in advance, for orders yet to be delivered.

We realized we had to do something dramatic to help it out because we were one of the prime reasons it was in a financial bind. To support the company as a member of our team, we gave it an unprecedented $2 million check, which immediately relieved its financial stress.

The Plot Thickens.   Years later, this same supplier developed the technology that would revolutionize store operations. Where do you think this company turned first for orders for the new oven? You probably guessed it. With one new product, it could give us a major competitive advantage in the pizza-delivery wars.

Helping this supplier with the mega-check so solidified our relationship that it had no reservations about approaching us first.

The ovenmaker's board of directors asked the president why he brought this product to Domino's Pizza, not a bigger or faster growing customer?

His response was simply, "When I was in financial trouble, Domino's Pizza Distribution went over and above its commitment to me, and enabled us to stay in business. I believe in honoring the loyalty factor in that."

HELP YOUR SUPPLIERS TO SELL MORE

Not everyone is financially able to place a large order for a new product and pay for it immediately. However, there is much you can do with your suppliers to enhance your relationship so you will get the inside track on new technology, as we did with the new ovens.

The key to increasing your sales and thrilling your suppliers is a three-step process. First, you learn the complete line of products from your suppliers. Next, study the needs of your customers. Finally, apply some creative thinking to find ways to match your suppliers' products with your customers' needs.

You probably can find some of your suppliers' products that your customers didn't even know they needed. The prospects for doing this have never been greater. The majority of manufacturers are beginning to update their traditional product lines with new, energy-efficient replacements.

Here are some brief sketches of a couple deals we put together that anyone can do:

• Energy-Efficient Products.   One of your suppliers will likely now have the new fluorescent exit signs in its inventory. They're hard to sell because few people even think about their exit signs. If your customers knew the fluorescent ones existed and they pay for themselves in energy savings, you could unload a warehouse full of exit signs for your supplier.

The ones we found were an exact replacement for standard incandescent signs that minimized installation costs and brought a prompt payback to our customers.

• Recycled Products.   We made a lot of progress in this area and you can, too. You can survey customers for the products they use and then query your suppliers for replacements that are recyclable or that are made from recycled products.

• Environmentally Responsible Equipment.   We discovered a manufacturer of food coolers that used R-22 refrigerant instead of the standard R-12 that depletes the planet's ozone layer. You could make a deal with your customers to buy your supplier's new equipment, by showing your customers how they could benefit through a promotional campaign telling the public the environmentally responsible stand they've taken.

Some companies committed to helping the environment have suffered from cash flow problems in getting the new products out the door. When you begin to put together such deals as these, your customers may well remember you as their best account.

We developed another program that is similar in its basic nature to the one outlined above. Our Equipment Resource Center also makes us a favorite with many of our suppliers. When our equipment suppliers add new technology to their line, their salespeople often encounter resistance from customers because of the investment they've got tied up in their existing equipment. Financing the new purchase may be too great a financial burden.

However, since our suppliers know we give our customers an outlet to dispose of their older equipment easily and at a fair price, we've become a hit with them. Anything we can do to improve sales for our suppliers moves us up their list of favorite customers.

ORDER WHEN YOUR SUPPLIERS NEED YOU THE MOST

Your suppliers also will love you if you tell them of your purchase plans far in advance. If you know you've got a big order planned soon, don't spring it at the last minute. The advance knowledge you pass on will help your suppliers make wiser purchases themselves, which ultimately saves you and your customers money.

Ask your suppliers what their worst months are. If August is always a dead month, then promise to make a large purchase that month. If you've got the warehouse storage facilities, then you could make your largest purchases in August. Besides a price break, during suppliers' slack periods, you'll get better service than at peak times.

Also, you can query your suppliers from time to time to see if they have discontinued stock. They may have it right now, stashed in a warehouse wondering what to do with it. If you've got some extra space in your store, you could reach terms with the supplier to offer it at bargain prices to your customers.

Even without spare floor space in your store, you may be able to feature the suppliers goods in a catalog or newsletter to your customers. Whole businesses have been spawned off this idea alone. You probably get the DAK catalog, for instance, featuring discontinued, high-tech, specialty electronics equipment.

TAP COMMUNITY PRIDE

We consider professional associations part of our supplier family. To support the efforts of a California-based agricultural association, we issued a press release recently that read as follows:

> *California Connection Helps Domino's Pizza Deliver*
>
> *California's sunshine and perfect climate have made the state the sole supplier for tomatoes used in Domino's pizza sauce.*
>
> *Last year, Domino's stores around the country used 2,500,000 cases of pizza sauce. Each case contains more than 91 pounds of tomatoes for a whopping total of 228,600,000 pounds of California-grown tomatoes!*
>
> *The tomato-based pizza sauce also is packed in the state. Produce buyers for the world's largest pizza delivery company have contracted to purchase nearly 265,000,000 pounds of California tomatoes in 1990.*
>
> *The Domino's-California Connection doesn't end with the tomato. All domestic olives used by Domino's Pizza were grown in California and hundreds of California stores use vegetables from farms around the state.*
>
> *Additionally, 15 percent of the cheese used by Domino's, a total of 23,000,000 pounds, comes from California.*

Remember, our mission for suppliers is to have them be "excited enough to call us their favorite account." Few things stir emotions like state, regional, or local pride. When that press release was published, we got a lot of nice calls from our California suppliers.

Our parting advice here is recognize your suppliers' core needs and meet them, while continually searching for new ways to get suppliers excited about you and to have them consider you their favorite customer. Then, enjoy the rewards that will naturally flow your way.

CHAPTER CHECKLIST

Identify your public and inventory their needs.

- Listen to their feedback, implement the requests they give you, and never use threats. Make it clear that you see fairness as being more important than financial gain.

Sort the needs into patterns.

- Treat each supplier as part of your team. Consider your relationship with suppliers as "a marriage" to be honored with openness, fairness, and honesty.
- Never accept any gifts or gratuities or any form of compensation from any supplier, no matter how small. If one is forced on you, reciprocate with a gift of equal value or donate it to charity and immediately notify the supplier what you did with the gift.
- If you have the means, adopt a zero payables policy.

Develop a mission statement.

- Strive to be the favorite account of each of your suppliers and to benefit from the innovation and advice each supplier has to offer.
- Share your mission statement with suppliers and let all of them know you give priority to awarding business to vendors who respect the philosophies, values, and attitudes reflected in your company's mission statement.

Set key indicators and levels of performance.

- Let your suppliers rate your performance—make sure it can be done without fear of losing your business.

Establish an automatic reward system for top performance.

- Hold a supplier appreciation day. Let them see your appreciation of their efforts to support your mission.

Establish ongoing programs to support your mission.

- Develop a loyal supplier base to fulfill your long-term needs by providing unique opportunities for them and promoting an atmosphere of exceptional fairness.

- Make a pledge of confidentiality to all suppliers. Vow not to disclose to others their pricing data or any information or techniques they consider confidential.

- Be alert to help your suppliers when they need it most.

- Help both your customers and your suppliers by thinking newly of your role between them. You are in a unique position in your industry to put together deals that neither your suppliers nor your customers may see without your expertise.

- Tap the power of state, regional, or local pride to get suppliers excited about you.

- Smooth out the cash flow peaks and valleys for your suppliers by placing your largest orders in their slowest months.

Chapter Seven
A Sense of Mission

I referred to our mission statement in Chapter 1 as a vital part of the Super Vision process and cited components of our mission statement in the previous five chapters on addressing the needs of your publics. Step 4 in the Super Vision process, after sorting the identified need within each group into major patterns, is to write a concise, detailed wording of each of those needs patterns into a mission statement.

Most successful companies have a mission—a stated reason they are in business. The more heartfelt a mission is, the better focused everyone can become and remain. Curiously, not all companies articulate their mission and make it widely known to all members of the organization. Too often, the mission resides only in the head of the founder, CEO, or other leader. The most important role of a leader in any organization is to articulate the organization's mission, share it with team members, and elicit their support.

Distribution didn't always have a mission statement. In the early years, this hurt us considerably. Good people with talent and drive were working at cross-purposes with one another. As president of Distribution, I frequently found myself having to say to team members, "Excuse me, but you're heading in a different direction than the rest of the company." I always felt uneasy reining in an employee because I understood the importance of not containing the power and drive of individuals. Still, we couldn't have people heading in different directions.

In the mid-1980s, it became clear that we needed to adopt a formal, more balanced approach to fulfill our obligation, so I told the other executive team members what I thought the company could become. I explained that we needed to reach a consensus on the mission of Distribution. Further, once we reached a consensus, we would then need to embark on a perpetual quest to ensure that each team member within the company understood and personally accepted our mission statement.

Eventually, Distribution adopted its mission statement from a variety of sources, and it continues to evolve. We've been making decisions according to our mission statement for the past seven years, but the process of developing the mission statement was anything but smooth.

GETTING IT ON PAPER

At first, few members of the executive staff were enthusiastic about discussing a mission statement. Thus, I was "free" to develop the first draft on my own and submit it to the executive team for revision. Putting it on paper was a larger challenge than I had imagined.

Each time it seemed like everything fit, I would look back over the draft and ask myself, "OK, does it take into account our successes and failures?" Did it address issues that most frequently upset our customers—the thousands of Domino's Pizza stores? What had they screamed the loudest over when we failed to satisfy their most pressing wants and needs?

What's Missing from Many Mission Statements.   Many companies make the mistake of failing to take a complete inventory of everyone who is touched by the company—their publics. It's easy to develop a mission statement about yourself, about your own team or your own product, but there's much more to your success than these internal elements.

For our mission statement to be effective, I believed it had to encompass the critical elements of our business. Most importantly, the mission statement needed to be worded so as to empower every team member to be able to handle the challenges he or she might encounter. The key to Super Vision would rest with every team member hav-

ing the tools and freedom to do on-the-spot thinking and creative problem solving.

Writing the mission statement was an emotional roller coaster for
me, because with draft after draft, I knew it wasn't complete yet. When
I recognized that the mission statement was a continual climb up a
staircase, not something to be carved in stone, finishing the draft became a little easier. I spent several late nights in a row, once working
until eight the next morning, to draft the mission statement.

During the day, I shared what I had written with other executive
team members to gauge their enthusiasm. There was little zeal for the
overall idea, but they gave me terrific feedback for refining my drafts.

SAILING TO NOWHERE

I believed I had finally completed a good draft of our mission statement, but enthusiasm from the executive team remained absent. I
decided I needed a slow-paced setting, away from the distractions of
their daily duties, so I chartered a sailboat in Frankfort, Michigan. In
such a setting, I would make a formal presentation to fine-tune the
mission statement, see if there was any enthusiasm from the executives
to support it, and see if working on it would help them do their jobs.

Once we were all on board, we told the captain, "We don't care
where you go; we don't want scenery. This may sound crazy, but we're
actually going to work. We want peace and quiet. When we think
we're halfway done, we'll tell you and you can turn around and come
back."

As the seven of us got under way, my heart sank. Everyone was
wearing sunglasses and talking about how they'd prefer to be golfing or
relaxing. I was counting on reading their eyes and body language to
gauge the reactions to my presentation. With all the shades on, you
couldn't tell whether they were paying attention, rolling their eyes in
disgust, or sleeping.

Before reading the first draft, I explained the development process,
telling them how the statement needed to include a mission for everyone we touched and how it needed to be easily readable, clear, and
understandable for all levels of education. Then I read my latest version of the Domino's Pizza Distribution mission statement.

Their reactions remained bland. There were many suggestions at
first about how to change it, although most suggestions sought to move
from the bold to the mundane, employing well-known phrases like

"customer satisfaction." Every company says it wants to achieve "customer satisfaction."

We needed something remarkable, like "being the best place to shop," and we needed to ensure that the mission statement demanded thoughtful answers. How much can you learn by asking a customer, "Are you satisfied?"

"Do you think we're the best place for you to shop?" would cause customers to ponder the question. Their answers would give us practical information and guidance as we moved forward.

FROM PAPER TO POLICY

Chuck Haffey took the lead in overcoming the inertia. Lynn Pallot chipped in, and we soon began improving the statement, keeping in mind the notion of including every person the company touched. Before long, almost everyone in the group was contributing powerful enhancements. As we continued sailing, the quest for a bolder, more inclusive mission statement began to take hold. What unfolded was the sense that our mission would include our goal of being the best in the world at what we do.

During what proved to be a four-hour cruise, we examined the meaning and possible interpretations of every potential word contained in the mission statement—e.g., should it be "should" or "could"? Our purpose was to produce a statement that someone without a high school education could readily understand. As the captain plied the waters, we plied the words, modifying and refining the statement among ourselves.

When it seemed complete, we moved to the all-important question that each member of the executive team had to answer for individually—"Can you support this? Can you support a mission realizing that it means we have to head down a path of doing a complete job with every human being we touch in our business?"

Supporting the mission statement would be a challenge. It contained apparent contradictions; we essentially were promising our customers lower prices, our employees greater compensation, our suppliers increased business, and our parent corporation improved profits. As crazy as it seems when looking back, everyone on board that day committed wholeheartedly to the statement that emerged.

When we got off the boat, the captain said he was so impressed at what he'd heard and that he would try a Domino's Pizza the next time he had a chance!

TAKING IT TO THE STREETS

Back in the office, confident that we had produced a statement that everyone in the company could understand and support, the executive team set about to communicate the mission statement on all levels. Here again is our never-to-be-reached goal inscribed on a plaque:

> *The Domino's Pizza Distribution Mission Statement*
> *Through continuous innovation and living the Golden Rule, we*
> *will attain:*

- Customers' belief that we're the best place to shop for their needs.

- Team members who can't think of a better company to work for.

- Community (government) that considers us a fine example of what business should be.

- Parent company proud to have us as part of their team.

- Suppliers excited enough to call us their favorite account.

> *. . . resulting in constant improvement in those key operational*
> *areas so vital for our success.*

The plaque hangs openly throughout corporate headquarters and at our commissaries. The statement is also printed on the back of business cards of Distribution team members, primarily so they will refer to it on a daily basis and let it be a guidepost for their thoughts and actions. The mission statement does not say we will raise sales, increase profits, increase output, or the like. These outputs are the natural results of following the tenets of our mission statement.

CRAFTING YOUR MISSION STATEMENT

Your company may not have the resources or desire to charter a 40-foot sailboat for a day to develop your mission statement. You can still make the day as memorable as possible, however. Something as simple as having everyone show up at a local park in blue jeans and sweatshirts for a fried-chicken picnic is sufficient to set the stage for a creative day. (Heck, you could even call Domino s Pizza; we'd be glad to deliver to Shelter #6 at your nearest park!)

The best setting for such a meeting is not in the boardroom office with everyone in regular business attire. One significant factor behind getting away is to eliminate outside distractions, especially telephones. It may be better to begin the session with some playtime. After all, relaxation is not a distraction if used appropriately, and it can serve as an icebreaker to lighten the tone.

There's a well-known quotation here at Distribution passed on from Rita Long, a longtime supplier of training and good advice, who said, "If you always do what you always did, you'll always get what you always got!" Your mission statement probably also needs to be a bold departure from the norm, so let its conception unfold in a new environment.

The Golden Rule—More Than Altruism. Our mission statement begins with the opening, "Through continuous innovation and living the Golden Rule, we will attain. . . ." Distribution affects the lives of millions of people. To stand proud of our efforts, we need to go beyond self-fulfillment. "Do unto others as you would have them do unto you." This creed provides an atmosphere of mutual respect and support among all parts of the Domino's Pizza family.

Both the company and each team member have a responsibility to apply the Golden Rule before making any decision. Are we successful at doing this at all times with everyone around the clock? Of course not, but we continually strive to be. In turn, our team members treat us and every human being they touch according to the same creed. Distribution expects the entire team to act fairly and ethically toward every person and company with whom we interact.

WHAT THE MISSION MEANS TO TEAM MEMBERS

We expect our team members to creatively handle their jobs, look for better ways to do their jobs, and challenge systems that aren't all they could be. We believe everyone has a responsibility to become more skilled and efficient and as our corporate efficiency improves, we pass the savings to our customers.

Particularly for team members who cannot envision their role for themselves, we attempt to impart the message with our mission statement: "Here is how big our dream is. Here is how profitable it will be. Here is what your share will be, and here is how we will check your progress." Each team member works closely with his or her team leader—we do not say "boss"—to carry out the principles for which Distribution stands.

Working with their leaders, each team member works out a personal plan to contribute to the Distribution mission. Leaders give each team member the space and resources to reach those individually set goals.

Rather than making team members wait for annual performance reviews to see if the company even recognizes what they've done, we offer a system where each team member can review his or her performance every four to six weeks through a self-evaluation, while planning for future growth. During such reviews, the team member has as much input into the evaluation as the team leader. This frees the creativity, talent, and drive of each team member in ways that more restrictive, structured corporations fail to foster.

When two or more people debate whether a particular action is consistent with the company's overall mission, the company and the team members win. We know Super Vision is working well when a team member does something and another says, "That's not in line with the mission." What better way to reinforce and uphold the corporation mission?

A GOOD MISSION STATEMENT MAKES
LEADERSHIP EASIER

When constructed, introduced, and applied properly, the mission statement can lighten your leadership burden. To understand what people need from a leader, let me first list some things people don't need from a leader:

- They don't need someone watching every move from over their shoulder.

- They don't need a leader who thinks they're lazy freeloaders who will take advantage of every opportunity to slack off.

- They don't need a leader who thinks he's done them a favor by giving them a paycheck every two weeks.

- They don't need to have their highest form of thanks be not getting fired this week.

Too many corporations implement leadership policies that provide just about everything an "employee" needs from a "boss." They provide little of what a creative, innovative team member needs from a team leader. Tom Monaghan separated Domino's from the crowd by taking the stand, "If you treat your people just well enough that they won't quit, you'll get employees who work just hard enough they won't get fired."

Developing your own mission statement will be easier when you understand that true leaders only need to provide four basic things for the people they lead:

- A sense of purpose—company mission and the individual's role.

- Priorities—expected level of performance.

- How performance will be calculated—the "grading" scale, or "what will be on the test."

- What will be the results of their performance—rewards and corrections.

To keep things simple (and because Tom Monaghan also owns the Detroit Tigers baseball team), we've developed a baseball analogy for the four points above that seems to help people understand them better.

We've laid out the four points in a chart with three columns. The first column shows each of the four points listed above, the second shows their relationship to Major League Baseball, and the last shows common errors many companies make instead.

There's a fourth column to this chart, titled "Hand Tools," but we'll save that column for the next chapter. It relates to the measures we use to ensure optimal team member and company performance.

Trust the good in Everyone.   Many leaders from other companies express concern that they cannot trust people to adopt their mission. They fear their "employees" want to rip them off and get away with whatever they can when they're not being watched. To those concerns, I answer that we believe, with extremely few exceptions, that every human being has a natural yearning to be creative, be innovative, and do a good job. Frank Meeks, one of our most successful franchisees who operates in the Washington D.C. area, has been ex-

What People Need from a Leader

What People Need from a Leader	Major League Baseball Analogy	What To Avoid
Sense of purpose (Company mission versus the individual's role)	Define the game (playing field, rules of game, ground rules, foul lines)	Many companies don't have a mission statement (or, it's flowery, incomplete, or average people cannot relate to it)
Priorities (expected levels of performance)	League standings (league leaders, attendance, pennant race, World Series)	A series of plans, objectives, chores (often billed as priorities, yet not linked to mission)
How will performance be calculated (the "grading" scale, or "what will be on the test")	Statistics (batting averages, RBIs, ERAs, fielding percentages, stolen bases, home runs)	Nonspecific goals (not put at the individual level or defined vaguely with no key indicators)
What will be the results of their performance (rewards and corrections)	Trophies, awards, Cy Young honors, MVP, all-star status	Focusing on the negative (often it's easy to find out what will get you fired, but not what will get you promoted)

tremely successful in part because of his ability to tap that natural yearning among his team members.

Frank understands the needs and motivations of his store team. Not a month goes by without his issuing a challenge to his team to break records and earn incentives. Frank is perhaps the best person I know when it comes to understanding and using "battle cries" to communicate and motivate. His Domino's Pizza Team Washington even produced a rap video that starts with "Domino's Pizza Team Washington, selling more pizzas, having more fun. . . ."

Running a company by Super Vision taps that innate desire to excel because it requires you to trust people and permit them to do their best. The trust you send out returns to you through innovations you may never have found yourself.

Unfortunately, parents and teachers often do a good job of teaching us not to be innovators by placing controls on our actions and stifling our natural proclivities. When we get into the working world, our managers, raised on the same basic philosophies, continue to quash the natural creativity in each of us. In practice, following our mission statement and making it known to every person touched by our company has proved that our basic beliefs are correct—i.e., nearly everyone deserves to be trusted. We do not assume our team members are looking for a place to wile away the hours.

By focusing your mission objective for your team members on them and how they feel about you, you will naturally create a trusting atmosphere for them to display their highest good. They will reward you as well as our team has rewarded us.

CONTINUAL REFINEMENT

Our mission statement is continually balanced against the changing environment in which we operate. Over the years, we've discovered that periodically revising the mission statement is a powerful exercise for our company. If your mission statement already is widely circulated, known, and accepted, imagine the impression you'll make on your team members when you issue a revision.

When your people see that a new line has been added to the company's mission statement, they'll think, "This must be important to have prompted a change in the mission statement." However, you have to be careful not to revise it too often, because you'll dilute its value. If people believe it may soon change, they may ignore some segment, hoping it will be cut in the next revision.

CHAPTER CHECKLIST

- Make your mission statement a simple set of guidelines for decision making at all levels. All successful companies or organizations exist for a reason—including yours. The more heartfelt your mission is, the better focused your staff will become and remain.

- Arrange a memorable setting for the presentation of your rough draft mission statement.

- Don't be discouraged by a bland reception initially to your vision of creating a mission statement for your company.

- Avoid using platitudes, like "strive for customer satisfaction." Use bolder more captivating language, such as "being the best place to shop."

- Reflect on the meaning of every potential word contained in your mission statement. Your goal is to produce a statement that someone without a high school education can readily understand and follow.

- Incorporate the Golden Rule in your mission statement, or at least write it with that principle in mind. Keep asking yourself how you want to be treated.

- With your statement, include a component for your customers, team members, community, and suppliers, and any other public in your sphere of operations.

- Address in your mission statement those areas in which your customers are the most upset. Vow to satisfy their most pressing wants and needs.

- Design your mission statement as if you had a magic wand and could satisfy every human being you touch—state what you would give them if you had unlimited power.

- Make your mission statement reflect those big key wins in your past so you can continue to experience them and have their incidence increase.

- Embark on a never-ending quest to ensure that each team member within the company understands and personally accepts the mission statement.

- Don't worry that everything possible is included in your mission statement. Each step has to be taken individually before you can reach the next, but there will always be more steps; you can never stop striving to be better.

- Print your mission statement on the back of all business cards, so that all team members as well as outsiders have a continual reminder of it.

- You'll know your mission statement is working when two people or more debate whether a particular action is consistent with your overall mission.

- Give your team members the tools to do their best and then stay out of their way. With few exceptions, every human being has a natural yearning to be creative, be innovative, and do a good job. The trust you send out returns to you.

PART

III

Tools for Measuring Performance

For Domino's Pizza Distribution, the vital key to making Super Vision work has been our mission statement. The vision we created with it for our customers, our team members, the community, our parent company, and our suppliers has enabled us to tap the power that has fueled our drive toward growth.

In the next five chapters, we'll explore Steps 5 through 7 of the Super Vision process, which include transferring needs/patterns into key indicators, comparing actual performance to the desired level, and building in a reward and corrective action system based on the performance as measured by key indicators.

Chapter 8 details how we determine how well we meet our publics' needs based on three levels of performance—crisis, expected, or exceptional—used in the formation of key indicators. You were exposed to this process in Chapter 1 when I used the seven-step Super Vision process on the single project level. When I equated 15,000 books sold in the first year as *expected* performance, the number 15,000 became a key indicator. Let's see how to put numbers to work for you to measure performance and establish accountability.

Chapter Eight
Exceptional, Expected, Crisis

Once your machine—your business—is gassed up and running, you need to know its mechanical limitations. No machine is or can be infinitely powerful or perfectly suited to its intended task 100 percent of the time. Most of the time, the machine will perform as expected; sometimes it will surprise you and do something exceptional; and sometimes it will break down and force you to make a pit stop to get it fixed.

As a business leader, if you run your company so close to the edge that you have to rely on exceptional performance to win, you may end up hitting the wall. If you never bring a pit crew to the race, you'll surely be shut down by a crisis one day.

For years, I knew this intuitively, but there was nothing in place in the company that acknowledged it as reality. What I wanted to see in place was an established system that would succeed on a balanced, everyday performance, take full advantage of occasional bursts of exceptional performance, and have a great pit crew to make speedy repairs if something broke.

That day in Canada when I refereed the conflict between the franchisee and the area supervisor (Chapter 1) regarding sales levels, I knew we had a strategy for winning.

Levels of Performance

| Crisis | Expected | Exceptional |

DEFINING ACTION BY THE NUMBERS

Thereafter, we saw we needed to develop a set of numbers that would serve as a floor. If anyone dropped below that floor, we would declare a crisis and put everybody in the pits until we returned to acceptable performance.

The crisis level was to mean there would be no excuse for remaining below it. It's the business equivalent of needing a top-notch pit-crew mechanic to get you back in the race. Nothing else matters until you're at least back on the track. When the expected level was reached, there would be an acknowledgment of those team members involved. They would be *recognized* for what they had accomplished, but they would not be *rewarded*. Pulling out of a crisis would be reward enough.

Ending a crisis would put us in the *expected* range. Once the expected level was attained, we would avoid occurrences like the one in Canada. It would no longer be only a team leader's job to let someone know what was expected of him or her. The target numbers would be made public throughout the company. Anyone could look up the three numbers that applied to his or her area(s) of the company.

David Gausden would *know* what level of sales stores comparable to his were attaining in that market. However, if he was content in the expected zone (i.e., running comfortably in the middle of the pack), he could "sleep" there eternally and we shouldn't criticize him for not producing higher figures.

To conclude the racing analogy, it's the way we feel when the Domino's Pizza car was running at the Indy 500. We all *expect* the car to finish the race and place respectably. When Al Unser, Jr., brought us a second-place finish like he did in his spectacular duel with Emerson Fittipaldi in 1989, we congratulated him and the Doug Shearson racing team on a great second-place finish. We're not going to fire Al or his crew for not finishing first.

If we'd won the race, that would have been truly *exceptional*, and we'd have all had a wild celebration. Everyone would have received more than they expected in terms of rewards and pats on the back— that's when you pop the champagne corks. However, if the car had experienced a mechanical *crisis* during the race, the entire crew would have gone on red alert to get it fixed and back in the race.

If it had been forced out of the race, the entire crew would have put every effort into eliminating whatever caused the breakdown. Nothing else matters if you're not even on the track. We've all had this same three-level concept in operation for decades in many areas of our lives.

At Distribution, we formally define the three levels as follows:

- *Exceptional* is performance that deserves special recognition and makes you want to throw a party.

- *Expected* is performance at a level sufficient to accomplish company goals. This is also termed the *Sleep Zone*, meaning that if a team leader has team members performing at the expected level, then the leader has no reason to be concerned and hence can "sleep" comfortably.

- *Crisis* performance always requires urgent action, and makes you want to grab everyone and say, "Come on, we've got some work to do, now!"

The Baseball Model. Another area where the exceptional, expected, and crisis rating system works is baseball. Every Major League Baseball player knows his "crisis" numbers—the dreaded stats that can get him a trip back down to a small-town farm team.

He also knows the numbers that can bring him back to "the show"—once relegated from the Major Leagues back down to a farm club, most ball players will bust their rears to get off the crisis list.

Finally, you can rest assured that every Major League player also knows the numbers that will produce bonuses. They're constantly aware of bonuses that are tied to such things as hitting so many home runs, or stealing a certain number of bases, or being named to the All-Star team.

LETTING PEOPLE CHOOSE THEIR LEVEL OF PERFORMANCE

This concept works with nearly any area within any company, and any size business can set up a three-level system such as ours. Nevertheless, instead of providing a multilevel performance system, almost all companies have a singular performance goal throughout their operations.

Their employees are usually expected to meet a single set of guidelines in their work. Below the established standards, they can expect to be fired. Above that, they're safe. It's often that simple. There are a couple of serious shortcomings with such a simplistic setup.

The worst part of normal performance criteria is that people are sometimes fired for *not* excelling. Conversely, nearly everyone knows that somewhere in the grand scheme of the company there is a performance level that will get a person promoted. Normally, it is not clearly stated and well-known to everyone.

Also, not everyone is going to excel. There's room in any company for lots of people who want to be average. That's fine, as long as you show them what is acceptable as average, versus the floor of the crisis level. Every person in every department within our company and yours needs to know that if performance dips below that floor, a crisis is at hand. They also need to know you will act.

Once the crisis has passed, most people will want to take off the battle gear and shift into a more sustainable work level. When they do, acknowledge the rally efforts they put in and allow them to "go to sleep" if they are content to do so.

Finally, to keep goal-focused, people also like to be able to see a target that will push them to the point of excellence. We've all got that natural human instinct to excel. Within the Domino's Pizza family, we've found few people who consistently remain in the expected zone. We've got such an enticing system of rewards and bonuses that nearly everyone strives for the exceptional level.

MAKE ROOM FOR AVERAGE

We suggest clearly establishing the crisis level and having everyone understand that alarms will go off and their world will turn upside down if their work area drops to a crisis level. But *do not* fire people for having a crisis. Instead, create an atmosphere in which they will sound the alarm themselves and scream for your help when they see a crisis.

Once the situation returns to the normal range, acknowledge the energy that everyone involved put into overcoming the crisis and move on. One good technique for acknowledging those who helped pull out of a crisis is to write about what happened in your company newsletter afterward. While it gives the "battle weary" a nod of thanks, it more importantly lets other team members know a crisis occurred and why.

From the article, they see what caused the crisis and how the team members in that department dug their way out of it. You'll want to spread the word far and wide every time a crisis occurs, openly sharing the details of what happened with all team members, team leaders, and the parent company.

Once the crisis is passed and you've responded to their help, leave them alone—i.e., let your normal be your normal. Remember, we trust the human instinct to naturally get better: people will naturally move from expected to exceptional, if it is clear to them what the awards will be.

Every team member every day also will know the numbers that will move him or her into the exceptional category and gain special recognition. The energy of your mission statement will draw people to seek the exceptional level for themselves. When they hit it, ring the bells as loudly as you would for a crisis alarm.

ON THE TEAM MEMBER LEVEL

When a team member and his or her leader meet for a job planning and review session, they develop individual performance objectives and assign points for specific results. An exceptional performance occurs when the team member exceeds corporate requirements of the job and achieves a score of 125, where 100 equals expected performance.

In general, expected performance occurs when the team member achieves a score of 80 to 105. A crisis occurs when the team member scores 60 or less. For example, suppose one component of a team member's role was to call 100 customers weekly. If that team member only made 50–60 of these calls, clearly that is crisis performance and requires immediate attention by the team leader to protect the objectives of the company. If that team member were able to call 120–130 customers weekly and didn't allow other job functions to slip, that would deserve praise—it is exceptional performance.

With a clearly defined three-level system of exceptional, expected, and crisis, all team members know at all times their expected range of performance. In fact, team members may remain in the expected range for years and be fairly compensated and treated. The expected level is what they're paid to achieve. There's no special recognition for it because it's their job. To those folks I simply say, "Thanks for doing your job. God bless you. Keep doing it."

ON THE COMPANYWIDE LEVEL

Thinking about your various operations or departments in terms of crisis, expected, and exception has benefits for the overall health of your company. When I first became president, our overall profitability was poor and it was easy to discover which commissaries were in crisis: they were posting loses. Our commissary in North Carolina was posting a 3 percent loss every month, and, by examining their income statement, I knew we could find some waste. The easiest way to do this, I discovered, was to compare the North Carolina income statement against one of my top performing, that is, exceptional, commissaries. I turned to Kelley Hannan's operation in Zanesville, Ohio. Kelley has always run a tight ship for us and I couldn't think of a better commissary to use.

All at once, it jumped out of the income statements. For the daily cleaning and sanitation of our production room and equipment we use quite a few cleaning towels. The line item cost for North Carolina was 3.2 percent of sales while Kelley's cost was .3 percent of sales. I called Kelley and asked how he did it. It was as simple as washing, drying, and reusing the towels up to four times instead of discarding the towels after every use as North Carolina was doing. I got back on the phone and told the commissary leader in North Carolina to call Kelley. North Carolina became profitable.

By identifying our exceptional performers and encouraging our crisis and expected performers to contact them for advice, a "cross-pollenation" of innovation and good business practices occurs. People naturally want to improve and if they have access to exceptional ideas and, in the case of the towels, common sense, they will improve.

BUILDING EVERYTHING IN THREE LEVELS

All of the measurement tools to be discussed in the next four chapters are constructed to include the exceptional, expected, and crisis performance rating system. When we tabulate the results of our summer survey, for example, the raw percentage answers are interpreted according to those three established ranges.

In advance, we may theorize that if, say, 70 percent of the responding communities answer "yes" to the question, "Are we good for your community?" then we've achieved an expected performance. If 85 percent say "yes," that's exceptional and we celebrate that performance, and if 60 percent say "yes," that's a crisis and we are required to take action to resolve the issue.

Initially, we make a subjective assessment as to what constitutes exceptional, and so forth, just like I did when I assessed book sales. As we use the rating system over successive periods, we get better in determining how to interpret future scores because we have historical data for reference.

The key to quick and easy interpretations is in how you set up your levels. Nearly every area of operations will have a different set of numbers. Some of the numbers will be based on satisfied responses and some on dissatisfied responses. We've got some expected ranges as high as 95 percent. In some areas, expected is as low as only 80 percent, while in others, 85 percent would be a crisis. Exceptional can be 90 percent or as high as 98 percent.

Initially, you'll have to decide your own numbers, which ideally will be based on your own company's mission. In Chapters 9 and 10, you will see how we've set up ours in specific areas of operation.

THE CHALLENGE OF LEADERSHIP

Chapter 7 presented a chart titled, "What People Need from a Leader." Now that you are familiar with our mission and our vision and have had some exposure to our three-pronged performance rating system, we are ready to examine a revised version of the chart.

On page 144 is a variation of the chart with a new third column. This column indicates our specific programs that answer what people need from a leader.

The rest of Part III on measurement tools will cover the programs shown in the right-hand column: summer survey, national performance indicators and key indicators, job planning and review sessions, individual performance indicators, and blueprints. We'll cover how to build company and individual performance goals and how to implement rating and reward systems based on these three levels of performance. We'll discuss how to locate problems within individual performances before they create problems at the national performance level.

By following the Super Vision process to track individual areas of the company, we're able to stave off problems before they become overwhelming. It's nearly impossible to reach a tragic crisis point for our company overall. That's because, like airline crashes, corporate tragedies are rarely the result of any one massive failure.

What People Need from a Leader (Reprise)

What People Need from a Leader	Major League Baseball Analogy	Specific Domino's Program
Sense of purpose (company mission versus the individual's role)	Define the game (playing field, rules of game, ground rules, foul lines)	Mission statement, the Golden Rule, coaching, and blueprints
Priorities (expected levels of performance)	League standings (team and personal averages, pennant race, World Series)	NPOs/key indicators and IPOs
How will performance be calculated (the "grading" scale, or "what will be on the test")	Statistics (batting averages, RBIs, ERAs, fielding percentages, stolen bases, home runs)	Summer survey and exceptional, expected, and crisis performance ratings
What will be the results of their performance (rewards and corrections)	Contract (guarantees, performance bonuses, release clauses)	Reward systems

Disasters are usually the culmination of several small failures coming together at precisely the wrong time or in the wrong combination. Our constant tracking of every area in the company on the three-level system allows us to squelch every crisis while it is still manageable and hasn't affected the company's overall mission.

In companies with annual reviews of team member performance, a team member could perform at exceptional levels for an entire year before anyone takes time to commend him or her. By then, this person may become so disenchanted that he or she decides it isn't worth working that hard without appreciation and becomes content to do only what is necessary—that is a crisis.

MAKE SEPARATE GOALS FOR EVERY AREA

In any company, even in a good year, there are some problem areas somewhere in the company. Your team will know as well as you—possibly better—where those problem areas are, who did a good job, and who nearly wrecked it for everyone.

Few things will stifle innovation and creativity in a company as will a reward system that's generic and rewards everyone evenly based on overall company performance. You can easily waste the power of bonuses. The team members who deserved a bonus won't appreciate it fully, and the ones who didn't will laugh all the way to the bank.

When you track exceptional, expected, and crisis performance of individuals separately and reward team members specifically, you'll create a true incentive system that is more effective than a bonus system.

CHAPTER CHECKLIST

- Never run your company so close to the edge that you have to rely on exceptional performance to stay in the race—you may end up hitting the wall.

- Let your team leaders know that expected performance is perfectly acceptable from the people they lead.

- Inform your team members that no one will ever be fired for not being exceptional. Allow team members the space to be average.

- Establish expected performance standards separately for every area of operations.

- Identify the crisis level and spell out what will be done if it's reached. Lay out the rewards that will come to those who turn in an exceptional performance.

- Share every crisis experience with the entire company. You'll help prevent future occurrences of the same thing and acknowledge those who pitched in to help.

- Celebrate the victories of your exceptional performers with the entire company. Write about them in the newspaper, and make heroes of them.

- Avoid annoying your top performers by rewarding everyone evenly for overall company performance.

- Turn your old bonus system into an innovative reward system by showing your top performers that they will be recognized and rewarded for their exceptional work.

- Rate the performance of your team members monthly to stave off problems early before one person's crisis spreads to others and affects the overall performance of the company.

Chapter Nine
Summer Survey

We balance our objectives for each new business year beginning in the previous summer, with a tool I've referred to as our *"Summer" or Annual Survey*. The summer survey is important for Distribution and its team members because it enables the executive team to listen to what the team members and our other publics have to tell us about our performance. The executive team then uses this feedback to build on the company's established strengths and tend to its identified needs.

Offering team members the opportunity to have a direct impact on corporate policy is unique in today's business world. Yet, it's an every-day occurrence at Distribution because we realize people are the back-bone of our company.

The team members who quietly accomplish the mission of Distribution on a daily basis and who deal directly with our customers are, without question, our greatest asset. In recognition of their capabilities and extensive capacity for innovation, we tap our team members as an important source of information in determining company policy.

Because we consider our extended family part of the team as well, we survey them. After years of refinement, the summer survey has become a thorough, balanced audit that also monitors how well we're serving our customers, communities, parent company, and suppliers.

We then read and compile the information gathered in our annual summer survey and use it to establish the appropriate corporate goals for the following year.

Among store managers, for example, in 1990 several hundred responded to the comprehensive, multipart survey that sought their opinion on dozens of topics, including our products, proposed products, and changes in equipment.

They were also asked if the proposed national premium advertising on TV would help sales and about new packaging design, new ingredients, and other key areas affecting their ability to be successful. Among our customers, we also surveyed nonmanagers and key store team members.

We regard their input as crucial to making Super Vision work. We're continually searching for ways to increase the response rate to our surveys. Follow-up surveys conducted during the rest of the year are reduced to a single sheet of paper.

IDENTIFYING KEY ISSUES

In assembling a summer survey, we view the document as a shopping list of what we want to accomplish overall. The list includes questions on all the new goals we've thought of for the coming year. The information received from these surveys is entered into the Distribution computer network so it can generate a variety of reporting options to help the executive team identify key issues for the coming year. The results of the survey help us cull from our initial list of potential goals a more manageable number and ultimately help us select our key indicators for Distribution as a whole.

Reports are generated for each of our five publics targeted by the survey—customers, team members, parent company, community, and suppliers. Within the context of our established key indicators, later we use the information from our team members on the surveys to build national performance objectives (NPOs).

Below are two examples of the types of reports we compile from the surveys. We've selected the results from our community leaders' and suppliers' surveys. We've included two to show the differences in how we structure the questions and tailor the response options.

In the first example, these survey questions went out to 150 city mayors, city council members, and local Chamber of Commerce offices. Of that total, 55 responses were returned and tabulated to produce the report on community:

1989 Summer Survey Report from Community

(1) Are you aware that Domino's Pizza Distribution Corp. has a commissary in your town/community/county?
    Yes—74.5%   No—25.5%   Don't Know—0.0%

(2) Do you find that the commissary has a positive image in your community?
    Yes—49.0%   No—5.9%   Don't Know—45.1%

(3) From what you know of our company, do you consider Domino's Pizza Distribution Corp. to be an ethical company?
    Yes—70.9%   No—7.3%   Don't Know—21.8%

(4) From what you know of our company, do you consider us a fine example of what a business should be?
    Yes—60.4%   No—11.3%   Don't Know—28.3%

(5) Are you aware that our commissary has a safety program to promote safe driving habits?
    Yes—21.8%   No—63.6%   Don't Know—14.6%

In the next example, the data represent the tabulation of 55 surveys returned out of 86 sent to all suppliers. For easier reviewing, we've marked the percentage of dissatisfied responses to the questions with asterisks.

Notice that both of these surveys contain few questions, with easily chosen answers. We designed them that way because of who will an-

1989 Summer Survey Report from Suppliers

(1) Does Distribution conduct business in an ethical (fair) way?
    Yes—94.6%   Maybe—3.6%   *No—1.8%

(2) Have you ever felt compelled to spend money you didn't need to spend at Domino's request?
    *Yes—16.4%   Maybe—10.9%   No—72.7%

(3) Are you able to find out things you need to know?
    Yes—72.7%   Maybe—25.5%   *No—1.8%

(4) Do you think we're one of your fastest-paying customers?
    Yes—87.3%   Maybe—9.1%   *No—3.6%

(5) Do you feel at risk of losing our future business through no fault of your own?
    *Yes—10.9%   Maybe—29.1%   No—60.0%

(6) Have you been treated fairly by Distribution?
    Yes—90.0%   Maybe—7.3%   *No—1.8%

(7) Considering everything, are you excited enough about working with our company to call us your favorite account?
    Yes—70.9%   Maybe—29.1%   *No—0.0%

swer them—very busy people who do not relish filling out surveys, even when they know the information could directly benefit them. In general, for people you survey outside the company, it's best to keep the length of the survey as short as possible.

For our own team members, and often for our customers, we use longer surveys providing for more detailed answers because we know that they'll give it to us.

ALLOWING FOR CRISIS, EXPECTED, AND EXCEPTIONAL PERFORMANCE

Our summer survey is our major application for the three-level performance rating system. The tabulated percentages from the multiple-choice questions are always interpreted in the context of exceptional, expected, and crisis performance. For example, on the question, "Do you think we're your fastest paying customer?" our interpretation, based on previous years, could prompt us to conclude in advance of the current results that 20 percent "no" responses is a crisis, 5–10 percent is expected, and 2 percent is exceptional. We also take our "gut" feelings into account: crisis can be described as a level at which we'd be ashamed of our performance, expected would leave us basically satisfied and exceptional would move us to celebrate.

When your survey reports are interpreted with those three ratings in mind, you'll get a clear picture of how to set future goals for the company. You will also be better positioned to use your reports to find key indicators and to build the next year's national performance objectives.

By definition, any area that shows a crisis level on a summer survey report will get the "all-hands-on-deck" treatment to end the crisis. However, even if you solve the crisis quickly, the area may still deserve inclusion on your list of NPOs for the following year.

QUESTION CONTENT

To make sure our surveys reflect what we most want them to include, we draw up a pro forma of the finished product before we start; in this case, we do it in outline format. Here's the outline for our 1990 summer survey we used to develop our 1991 NPOs. Some of the terms presented here may be unfamiliar to you, but you'll still get the idea of how we planned the survey.

A set of well-written survey questions can do more than merely generate numbers to plug into a computer system. We want the raw

Summer Survey: 1990 Blueprint

I. Types of Questions
   A. To get information
   B. To confirm or verify information we already think we know
   C. To inform or educate (hidden, subtle)
   D. To investigate opinions (potential controversy)
   E. Don't duplicate questions we ask in other surveys

II. Types of Answers
   A. Yes/no
   B. Scale of 1 to 10
   C. Brief comments (free form)
   D. Best 5, worst 5 things
   E. Better or worse than before
   F. Multiple choice

III. 1990 Issues
   A. *Customers (franchisees, store managers, both)*
      • Value of CFRs compared to FCs
      • Willingness to accept a new way of pricing like "competitive pricing" (change gross profit refund system)
      • Distribution selling to other companies—but not other pizza companies
      • Awareness of Solar Dough progress
      • Selling Solar Dough products that aren't used by Domino's through other channels
      • Number of deliveries
      • Pre-attached box toppers from commissary
      • Additional services that the commissary could provide
      • Need for store computers/inform that computers are coming from DPI
      • National premium on TV to increase pie sales
      • Things needed to do more carryout business
      • Need for new uniform
   B. *Suppliers*
      • Ethics, Golden Rule for surveys to suppliers, community
   C. *Team Members (Olympic champs, all others)*
      • Benefits most valued by team members
      • Workbench
      • Ability to give input that will be used to make decisions
      • Safety
   D. *Parent Company*
      • Ethics, Golden Rule for surveys to suppliers, community
   E. *Community*
      • Ethics, Golden Rule for surveys to suppliers, community
      • Safety

numbers information, but we also want information that tells us how well we're supporting our mission.

Questions with a Double Payoff. Another goal for the types of questions we employ is to subtly inform or educate our publics. You can convey a lot of information by asking the right questions.

For example, one question on the supplier survey asks, "Considering everything, are you *excited* enough about working with our company to call us your favorite account?" You recognize those words, straight from our vision for suppliers. It's unlikely that any of your suppliers are asked that question by their other customers. Its presence in the survey reminds them of your mission statement.

Similarly, in the survey of community leaders, we asked, "From what you know of our company, do you consider us a fine example of what a business should be?" Not only does that question help us determine if we're fulfilling our mission statement, but it also reminds the community leaders of our vision for them.

The last question on the community survey asked, "Are you aware that our commissary has a safety program to promote safe driving habits?" Naturally, that question told us how many community leaders knew of our program at that time. But what would their answers have been if we'd asked the same question the next day? That's what we mean by making your questions count double. Respondents would not have known the details of our program, but after completing our survey, they would have at least been aware of its existence.

Especially with community officials and suppliers, you won't get to ask many questions, so make the ones you include count double by providing a two-way street for information flow—to your company and to the people you're surveying.

LONG-TERM COMPARISON—THE KEY TO SURVEY POWER

The percentage-type answers generated by your Yes/No/Maybe questions gain in potency when the results from two or more years are compared. Such comparisons can reveal trends, identify future trouble spots, expose persistent problems, and confirm the effects of your current programs.

An example of this potency showed up between our 1989 and 1990 summer surveys. On the question that asked about awareness of our commissary safety program to promote safe driving habits among our truck drivers, in 1989, only 21.8 percent were aware we had such a program.

As a group, our driver team members were proud of the driving safety record they had built over the years. But the results of this survey showed them that nearly 80 percent of our community leaders knew nothing of their accomplishments.

During 1990, our drivers assumed major commitments to participate in driver safety programs through the community. They joined a
campaign initiated by Mothers Against Drunk Driving, in which participants tied red ribbons on antennas or mirrors to display their support for MADD's efforts. Meanwhile, they extended their extraordinary driving record into another year.

That was the year our drivers earned the top safety rating from the
U.S. Department of Transportation. The percentage of local community leaders who knew of our safe driving programs for commissary
drivers, as reflected on the 1990 summer survey, nearly doubled to 39
percent.

To help our drivers gain further recognition, our 1990 summer survey also included a new question that asked, "Did you know Distribution received the top rating on safety and compliance from the U.S.
Department of Transportation?" While 96 percent of respondents said
"no," how do you think the responses to that question looked in the
1991 summer survey? You're right—the number of "yes" responses
shot up dramatically to over 50 percent.

Merely by asking the right question, we've spread the word about
their accomplishments.

Identifying National Performance Objectives.   The comparison
of statistics from one year to the next can often show you which goals
as a company to target for the following year. We usually find one or
two goals (NPOs) each year that we would not have thought of including if the need had not jumped out from the comparison of summer
surveys.

MULTIPLE-CHOICE QUESTION CONTENT FOR TEAM MEMBERS

As you might guess, we also make the questions in our team member
surveys do double duty. With team members, in addition to creating a
two-way street for information flow, we open an avenue for expressing
opinions. The deepest feelings of team members can be discerned
through open-ended essay-type questions as opposed to the yes/no/
maybe questions we use for others.

Even multiple-choice questions, however, can be written to give
you a good picture of how team members are feeling. Here's an example of a recent team member summer survey, including the responses:

Team Member Summer Survey (NA = ₍no answer)

(1) I feel a sense of achievement in my work.
Yes—58%   No—8%   Maybe—33%   NA—1%

(2) I get the amount of recognition I deserve for my day-to-day job performance.
Yes—32%   No—29%   Maybe—38%   NA—1%

(3) I usually like the kind of work I do.
Yes—76%   No—2%   Maybe—21%   NA—1%

(4) I feel I am given enough responsibility.
Yes—71%   No—12%   Maybe—16%   NA—1%

(5) I have opportunities for advancement.
Yes—48%   No—34%   Maybe—17%   NA—2%

(6) I am able to grow.
Yes—54%   No—24%   Maybe—20%   NA—2%

(7) I usually understand and agree with company policy and administration.
Yes—47%   No—11%   Maybe—42%   NA—1%

(8) I usually feel good about the leadership of my team leader.
Yes—55%   No—16%   Maybe—28%   NA—1%

(9) I usually have a good relationship with my team leader.
Yes—72%   No—10%   Maybe—17%   NA—1%

(10) I have good working conditions overall.
Yes—72%   No—7%   Maybe—20%   NA—1%

(11) My compensation is fair for the work I do.
Yes—45%   No—33%   Maybe—21%   NA—1%

(12) I usually have a good relationship with my fellow team members.
Yes—89%   No—1%   Maybe—10%   NA—1%

(13) I feel good about my personal life.
Yes—75%   No—7%   Maybe—16%   NA—2%

(14) I get the status and respect I deserve from others.
Yes—54%   No—9%   Maybe—36%   NA—1%

(15) I feel secure about my job.
Yes—62%   No—15%   Maybe—22%   NA—1%

(16) I do a good job.
Yes—96%   No—0%   Maybe—3%   NA—1%

(17) I receive enough information about what is going on in the company.
Yes—48%   No—20%   Maybe—31%   NA—2%

(18) Distribution's overall benefits package meets the needs of myself and my family.
Yes—69%   No—12%   Maybe—18%   NA—2%

(19) Are your huddles/team/plant meetings useful?
Yes—36%   No—22%   Maybe—39%   NA—3%

Team Member Summer Survey (*continued*)

(20) Has Distribution provided more tools for your career development this year than last?
      Yes—54%   No—40%   Maybe—6%   NA—0%

(21) Do Distribution's atmosphere and reward systems encourage you to find better ways to improve quality and efficiency?
      Yes—66%   No—31%   Maybe—4%   NA—0%

Recall our vision for team members: "team members who can't think of a better company to work for." Most of the questions on our survey directly tell us whether we're meeting our vision in that area—something you'd expect us to track.

There also are some subtle conclusions to be derived as well from these questions.

We want to cultivate the best possible atmosphere for our team members to be creative and innovative. Testing our success in that area is another objective of our team member survey. Questions such as, "I feel I am given enough responsibility," "I am able to grow," "I receive enough information about what is going on in the company," and "Are your huddles/team/plant meetings useful," are all subtle indicators that give us specifics about the atmosphere in which our team members feel they operate.

We also use those questions as additional verification to responses to the last question on our survey, "Do Distribution's atmosphere and reward systems encourage you to find better ways to improve quality and efficiency?" This is among the most important information you track on your team member surveys.

No executive team can preside over an innovative company without team members operating in an atmosphere that encourages innovation. You won't succeed by innovating solely in the corporate boardroom. When you've got an optimal number of people in your company working on innovation, you'll excel beyond anything you've previously expected.

Well-crafted surveys will help you learn whether you're tapping the innovative resources of your team members.

RATING SCALES

Professional survey people will probably disagree with me, but I believe that rating scales need to be designed from the perspective of the survey taker, not to fit a specified statistician's model. People often do not understand 1–5 or 1–7 scales. Our concern is with the *feelings* of the survey taker. Everyone knows what a perfect "10" is and knows that a "90" or above is an "A." If you build a survey that can be easily taken by a subject, you'll have greater access to their gut-level feelings on issues.

ESSAY QUESTION CONTENT FOR TEAM MEMBERS

Open-ended essay questions limited by focus or by asking the subject to list "the three best" or "the three worst" often yield startling insights, and the fully tabulated compilation of essay responses on hundreds of team member surveys provides us with a powerful and privileged look into what is going on in the minds of our team members.

We ask them to list the three best things and the three worst things about their job, then we read every single one of them. The first time the executive team met to review these, we used Ed Moody's log cabin deep in the woods near Frankfort, Michigan. Around the bonfire, I asked everyone to begin reading the 250 surveys we had collected without taking notes, but instead, to listen to the words of our team members and let them sink in. With three complaints per survey, that meant we would read 750 complaints!

After about 40 minutes, several executives asked if we could stop because they were cold (it was November in northern Michigan!) and were reading the same complaints repeatedly. Collectively, their attitude was, "Okay, Don, we get the picture."

"No, we've got to read every single survey. These people took the time to write about their feelings; they deserve to be read. If you're tired of reading the same thing over and over, think how tired they are of seeing it every day. If we don't correct these problems now, we'll have to sit here at the same time next year and read the same complaints again."

As darkness fell, everyone was cold, shivering, and getting frustrated.

Their frustration wasn't due to participating in the process, but rather, because our team members couldn't call our company the "best place to work." The frustration turned to anger and then, resolve. Our executives made the decision to ensure that our team had the proper tools, family atmosphere, and rewards they needed.

Of course, it wasn't all bad, either. We also got hundreds of compliments on how well some of our programs were working. Many of these candid responses help us develop innovative programs that affect the quality of life for all team members. When we institute a new program spawned by team member input, we know it will have a better chance of being accepted.

Essay questions enable us to probe controversial issues in two ways. First, we include essay questions that directly address current issues we know to be sensitive. Second, we include items we see as having the potential for controversy when introduced. The team member survey can give us advance warnings that help us tailor new programs or concepts to align better with their visions.

Here is a set of open-ended essay questions from a team member survey, along with a sampling of the answers we received:

Team Member Survey Questions

1. **List three areas in which your Team Leader excels:**
    Golden Rule, company knowledge, good listening skills, computer skills, innovative ideas, experience, fun, vision, credentials, organizational skills, fairness.

The italicized responses tell us we're going in the right direction toward building an innovative company that fulfills the vision of our mission statement for team members. The other areas are those where we're happy to see excellence, but we can't use them as direct tests of how we're doing our job.

2. **List three areas in which your Team Leader could be better trained:**
    Distribution procedures, needs to learn to keep personal problems at home, decision making, assertiveness, positive reinforcement, he gives lousy JPRs, fairness, organizing self, not showing favoritism.

The italicized answers from this question reveal areas in which our team leaders need work to help our team members think Distribution is the best place for them to work. The other answers reveal areas we might consider emphasizing in our newsletter, on our computer network, or even when establishing a seminar or training series.

3. **Needs that you are NOT getting from your Team Leader.**
    Decision making, more praise, he's great, ideas, mutual respect, responsiveness

without dictating, he should be fired, I want a team leader who cares about the job—not her personal life, a chance for advancement.

We got a short list of answers to this question, which told us we were doing well at meeting our mission statement vision for team members. As you can see, a sprinkling of the answers to this question seeking critical information was actually positive input.

The italicized answers show us areas where we can help our team leaders make Distribution a better place for team members to work; from them we might be able to create a video or cassette program to ensure that our team leaders share our vision for team members.

4. **What three priorities should the executive team address immediately to make the company the best place to work?**
   Stop gouging suppliers, hire team leaders who are leaders—not dictators, the executives should live the Golden Rule, consistency, don't burn us out by forced understaffing, stop changing direction, better minority opportunity.

This is a question many management teams would not ask their team members. But look at the powerful insight we got out of it from even these few responses. The first three clearly told us we've got team members who don't believe we live by the Golden Rule, even to the point that someone has witnessed what they believe to be us gouging a supplier!

Information like that demands to be checked out immediately. If there's any supplier gouging going on, we're falling down on three visions of our mission statement. One, we're not living the Golden Rule; two, that supplier is not going to consider us its favorite account; and three, the team member who sees it won't believe we're the best place to work, and may even be embarrassed to work for Domino's.

You've got nothing to lose and everything to gain by asking the questions to which you might not want to read the answers.

The truth is that we might have found out most of this information one way or another. Without the survey, it might have been the other, which would be when we lost the supplier or a valuable team member.

5. **If you could add one benefit, what would it be?**

This was an easy question for us. They don't all have to be the tough ones. Among the answers, we found only two relating to direct compensation and those asked for an annual bonus and an annual pay increase. Most of the others addressed pension benefits. Since we're not going to institute any sort of benefit program tied to the calendar, that left us with a good place to target future compensation increases.

6. **Why are you in favor of an ESOP?**
   and

7. **Why are you NOT in favor of an ESOP?**

There is little benefit in shying away from controversial questions. At a time when there had been much discussion of a sale or buyout of the parent company, we knew the subject weighed heavily on the minds of team members.

Such concerns can take a heavy toll on productivity and team morale. Low morale can dampen relations between team members and customers, causing them to no longer see us as their best place to shop.

If you've got a controversy brewing in the company, don't keep it locked up behind the doors of the boardroom. I can assure you, someway, somehow, your team is already talking about it in the hallways and bathrooms. Many companies keep secrets because they fear publicity could affect the value of the company. Realize that the value you are trying to protect may be dropping precipitously due to dissatisfied team members, suppliers, and customers, while you're trying to iron out a major business decision.

8. **If you could change one thing about the company that would help us better serve our customers, what would it be?**
    Get CFRs out of the commissaries and into the stores where they can provide hands-on training as to proper product management.

We culled this answer from pages of detailed answers on how we could better help our customers. It was representative of many that addressed the same issue. Answers like that offer great benefits to the executive team.

First, they let you see ways to help customers and to expand the company. Moreover, answers like that—and there were many similar to it on different areas of our company—will let you know your company has innovative team members who are interested in upholding your mission statement.

OLYMPIC ANSWERS FROM OLYMPIC CHAMPS

The multitude of programs we've created to enhance innovation frequently work in concert with each other, making the whole more powerful than the sum of its parts. In the area of team member surveys, this amalgamation proved dynamic when we began a specially targeted survey of our olympic champions.

Since the olympics program has identified the top team member in every field within the company, as you'll discover in greater detail in Chapter 14, it made perfect sense that their input would be especially valuable to us. With only 15–20 olympic champions in the company each year, the executive team is able to carefully consider the answers from each one.

We created a simple form asking our olympic champions the question, "If I were a member of the executive team, I would . . . ." The results were assembled into a two-page report consisting of a paragraph from each champion.

The report we get from the olympic champion survey is but one example of the synergy we experience from the interplay between our programs for team members. An executive team would be wise to listen carefully to what the top team member in each field would do if he or she were to become an executive. Here are a couple of examples of responses from olympic champs:

- I would concentrate the company's efforts on increasing the levels of quality and service and place price third. I believe the commissaries are sacrificing levels of safety, quality, service, and team member development in order to reduce onions by a nickel a pound or sauce by 3 cents per case. Then, I would help the franchisees to buy into this belief that quality makes repeat customers, not price.

- Do an appraisal of all production equipment in the company. From this, I would schedule repairs that would ensure its ability to be equal to its book value or its needed value. This appraisal should be done on a regular basis and if the equipment is not maintained, it will be charged back to the commissary leader.

Both of those answers relate directly to our mission statement and our overall system of rewards based on performance. Gaining insights like that from our team members is a result of Super Vision, which encourages innovative thinking.

These two answers are only a sampling, but they illustrate the value of a summer survey—or its equivalent—in any innovative company. Actively look for ways to tap the innovative ideas of your team members, and then use those ideas to improve your performance in light of the company mission.

CHAPTER CHECKLIST

- Treat your team members as an important source of information and innovation.

- Tap what the team members are saying about the company they work for with a summer survey. Then use their feedback to build on the company's established strengths and tend to its identified needs.

- Make your summer survey a complete audit, incorporating input from every group that your company touches.

- Interpret your summer survey using the three-level performance scale of exceptional, expected, and crisis. Deal with any crisis areas immediately, then consider including them in next year's objectives.

- Compile the information gathered and use it to establish appropriate corporate goals for the following year.

- Design your survey to maximize the response rate. Use single-page survey questionnaires, if possible.

- Make your survey questions perform double duty. Structure them so that even if the answer is "no," the question will inform or educate the respondent.

- Tailor all questions to the context of your overall mission statement and that of your specific vision for each respondent answering a survey.

- Include one question that directly seeks responses about how you are doing with your mission. This will also serve as a reminder to respondents of your mission.

- Retain your survey results and use it for year-to-year comparisons. Search for repetitive weaknesses, trends you might catch before a problem becomes critical, and evidence that confirms your current programs are working.

- Include the tough questions. Ask the ones for which you're afraid to hear the answers.

- Ensure your survey respondents anonymity.

- Never use the results of surveys as a tool to mete out

punishment. Your executive team needs to welcome the publication of the results.

- Use open-ended, essay-type questions for your team members, to read what they have to say from the heart.

- Test any potential controversies that may be ongoing or on the company's horizon.

- Single out your top performers for a special survey. Tap their outstanding knowledge of your company by asking them, "If I were on the executive team, I would . . . ."

Chapter Ten

National Performance Objectives/Key Indicators

In this chapter, we'll explore how we arrive at national performance objectives and key indicators of performance from the data we receive from our publics. These numbers are then used to establish companywide, group, and individual accountability, and all performance is compared to desired levels, Step 6 of the Super Vision process.

Short-term profits are the most easily measured performance indicators in a company. Perhaps this is why it's become standard practice in many American businesses to focus on the next quarter's bottom line. However, many other performance indicators also are crucial to a company's long-term success. Usually companies are satisfied simply when profit goals are met, because everything else is more of a challenge to quantify.

At Distribution, we employ different indicators to gauge our success. While some are particular to our business, most are of high utility in any business. Through years of refinement, our system, which tracks many areas within the company, has made it possible to measure all performance areas as easily as most companies measure only their profits.

The scale we've established for measuring our overall corporate progress is called *key indicators*. The key indicators measure our national performance objectives (NPOs). What is unique about these indicators is that they help us keep an ongoing score on our performance all year and in plain view of all our team members. A Towers/Perrin study discovered that in 1990, 54 percent of America's hourly workers did not know if their company hit their stated performance goals. If people don't know how well they are doing as a company, how can they improve? As we tie our performance to an automatic bonus system you can bet our team members are aware of every level of performance posted in the NPOs!

Our NPOs and a targeted crisis, expected, and exceptional performance level of each objective are determined each fall by the executive team after tabulating, analyzing, and discussing the results from that year's summer survey and by incorporating other information as well, such as our more frequent sampling of stores and team members.

This produces a roster of focus areas to which we then commit the entire company for the following year. However involved that sounds to you initially, it works.

As part of our national performance objectives for 1992, among other questions, Distribution will closely monitor how satisfied our customers (the pizza stores) are with our dough product. Your company will have its own indicators, as unique to your business as satisfaction on dough quality is to our business. Many of our NPOs, however, as well as the key indicators with which we measure them, are common to nearly any company.

ESTABLISH YOUR "DO OR DIE" AREAS

We have six areas of business where "we must do or die." In each of these areas, our goal is "do" whatever it takes to be the best in our industry. We call these our "vital areas." The theory is that even if we don't meet that goal, we'll be so good our customers will easily consider us as the best place to shop.

One of our key areas, for example, is to avoid store closings, even for as little as 10 minutes. At Distribution, some of our commissary team leaders in northern areas have arranged for delivery by snowmobiles when needed. In others, leaders have identified sources of helicopter or charter plane services, just in case. Leaders in storm-prone areas, such as commissaries in coastal regions—where they operate with the ever-present possibility of storm disruption and power loss— have access to backup generators to preserve their perishables.

As you identify your vital areas—however many you may target—

think of them as being the ones where you have to be ready for all contingencies. Your leaders, in their quest to achieve Super Vision, will be expected to anticipate what could happen to undermine your success in those critical areas and then plan for problems.

The Vital Areas. My mission as president of Distribution is to ensure that the company strives to be the industry leader in the six areas we've identified as vital, while not being regarded as lacking in anything else we do. If any of these areas fall into crisis, it affects nearly every aspect of our company. If we strive to be the industry leader, falling just short will still mean we're performing at adequate levels. Our six vital areas include:

- *Total operating expenses*—The clearest need from our parent company is to be more efficient every day, lower expenses and prices to the stores and increase profits.

- *Centrally produced fresh dough product*—No one beats our level of centrally produced quality dough.

- *Zero payables to all suppliers*—We pay our bills faster than anyone else.

- *Treat our team members so well, no other company can come close to our pro-people accomplishments*—We are committed to treating our team members better than any other organization in the areas of tools, family atmosphere, and rewards.

- *No store closings due to a lack of supplies*—We only had 10 in 1990 out of more than 600,000 deliveries. Those that did close ranged from 15 minutes to an hour. Some year soon we're going to get it to zero.

- *Golden Rule*—We will maintain the highest levels of ethical behavior in everything we do.

It's an ambitious goal to strive to be the industry leader, but if we are and no one knows about it, the impact is diminished. With a company of our size, to me that means being nationally known.

Our programs help ensure we can make claims on the level of national excellence and back them up. Without our system of summer surveys, national performance objectives, and incentives for team members, we couldn't identify appropriate areas to emphasize, nor motivate our team members to fulfill them, nor measure the ones we choose.

THE POWER OF NATIONAL PERFORMANCE OBJECTIVES

While we have 6 "do or die" areas, I can come up with about 300 areas where our performance needs to be top-notch. You can probably do the same in your company. But if you try to emphasize 300 areas, you'll dissipate your focus. Your team members can't maintain focus on that many topics and you can't easily keep track of more than a few anyway.

Our approach is to stick to our six "do or die" areas (which evolve over time) and add up to four more that reveal themselves through the results of our summer surveys. By restricting ourselves to a maximum of 10 areas, our corporate objectives began to truly receive national attention within our company.

So, each year our list of 10 NPOs changes somewhat. We'll retain some of the revolving four items from the previous year, drop some, and add others. Some items may make the list only once. We believe NPOs are ineffective if they represent only the pipe dreams or "gut feel" of the executive team. But sometimes "gut" is all we have, and we'll stick with it. Whether based on reliable knowledge or instinct, they all have to support the overall mission statement.

A BALANCED PERFORMANCE

Because our NPOs deal with much more than profits, we avoid getting lost in the mire of chasing the bottom line on the income statement. Such a narrow emphasis often can hurt company performance in other areas.

If we were to put all our focus on producing a profit, then we would be able to tie our bonus system only to profits. When a team member is faced with a quick decision in the field that might affect profits, he or she is likely to be driven by thoughts of a bonus check. Under such a scenario, we could have a team member making a decision that increases revenue or cuts a cost temporarily but hurts our long-term relationship with a customer or supplier.

If team members' rewards are based on a broad spectrum of company NPOs, then they will make a different decision because they can see their bonus points will come from many areas. One decision might take a little out of the profit pool but pump up the bonus points elsewhere and, hence, "even out."

Sometimes we've had a set of annual NPOs that did not even include a sales figure. If your company turns in expected performance in most key areas and exceptional performance in some, you will be profitable.

The Mission Always Prevails.   Whenever doubt exists about what to do in a given situation, team members learn to relate the situation to the mission statement. They'll usually find the answer there. Our list of NPOs encompasses the visions of our mission statement.

By tracking many areas of the company's performance and tying the monthly bonus of every team member to it, we've been able to banish a cliché from our company. You no longer hear people say, "That's not my job." There is simply no such thing at Distribution; everyone's performance drives the bonus system.

QUALITY COMES FROM TEAM MEMBERS . . .
WHO TRACK THEIR PROGRESS

The quality that comes out of your company is the result of the quality that goes into it. The real source of that quality comes from each team member and not "the corporation."

Your customer is the sole judge of your quality. To measure their perceptions of your quality, you have to collect and share data from your surveys so all team members see their role in overall corporate quality. NPOs and their key indicators are the tools you use to show them.

Imagine a baseball team that didn't track its standing in the league. What would happen if no one tracked the team's overall win-loss record? Think of the powerful spurt of "extra effort" you've seen from athletes who knew a particular game was important to their league standings. You'd probably never see any extra efforts if the team's results were unknown all season.

Think of how heartbreaking it would be if the final standings, compiled after the season, showed that with only one more victory you would have made the playoffs. If you don't track key indicators and make them a topic of daily discussions around your business, you'll be like a baseball team that doesn't know its league standings.

Give your team members the extra energy boost that can come from seeing their "league standings" posted regularly. Your key indicators can infuse the same excitement level into your team members as when baseball fans talk about their favorite team.

TRACKING YOUR LEAGUE STANDINGS

The league standings for your company will be based on factors that directly support your mission statement. Those factors, your key indicators, are the statistics you use to measure your NPO results.

To help you set up your own key indicators, we'll list some of the priorities we use, which any company could establish as NPOs, and then follow them with key indicators that can be used to track them:

Improve Overall Product Quality

• Percent of favorable customer survey responses.

• Independent consumer lab quality measurements.

• Number of favorable product reviews published by independent publications.

• Total sales or market share growth.

Decrease Late Deliveries

• Late deliveries as a percent of total deliveries.

• Number of times a customer's business is hurt by your late deliveries.

• Percentage of early deliveries.

Increase Sales

• Total dollar sales.

• Percentage increase in sales over prior year.

• Percentage market share achieved.

• Your own sales increase compared to other companies in the same industry.

Improve Quality of Work Life

• Improvement in monthly employee survey.

- Decrease in employee turnover rate.
- Percentage of team members happy to be here.
- Number of complaints versus the prior year.

Improve Efficiency

- Profits as a percent of sales.
- Total expenses as a percent of sales.
- Average sales per employee.
- Average output per employee.
- Expense dollars per employee.

In each area you identify for your company, establish the set of ratings—exceptional, expected, and crisis—and include those numbers on the list of published NPOs. Once you adopt this system, you will undoubtedly discover your own innovative and unique key indicators to track your NPOs.

AN INNOVATIVE SOURCE OF FEEDBACK

One of our leading feedback systems—initiated by Tom Monaghan for Domino's Pizza, Inc., and also now used in another form by Distribution—is the *mystery customer*. Launched during the summer of 1975, the original plan was to have a mystery customer order at least one pizza per month from a store and report how long the delivery took, the driver's appearance and manner, whether the pizza was hot and tasty, the phone manner of the person taking the order, and an overall impression of the service.

The mystery customer's identity is closely guarded. No one at any of the stores knows which customer is the mystery customer. There are now two mystery customers per store who each buy one pizza per month, receiving a refund on their pizza order.

As the program developed, a challenge was set to maintain a 30-minute delivery service. By 1985, the systemwide average time was 24 minutes, with a significant number of stores averaging 18 minutes.

With the support they receive from the Distribution commissaries, a typical store can now bake a pizza in 10 or 12 minutes, leaving 18 to 20 minutes to safely deliver a pie less than 2 miles, which is the recommended delivery radius for all Domino's delivery stores. By 1985, across the board, Domino's was delivering in 30 minutes or less 91 percent of the time. Our current slogan sums it up best: "Our speed is in the stores, not on the streets."

Information collected from 15 years of surveying mystery customers has prompted many positive changes in Domino's operations. The data have been used to improve dough quality, other ingredients, and packaging, as well as other system refinements.

ADOPTING THE MYSTERY CUSTOMER SYSTEM

What works in one division of the company is often implemented in another. The mystery customer system also was installed within Distribution in the form of our Ideal Service Survey (ISS). Domino's Pizza stores, our customers, care about the price of the goods they receive, the quality, how quickly they are delivered, and if the Distribution commissary is friendly, cooperative, and supportive. Sounds like a typical pizza customer, doesn't it? That's why we copied the mystery customer concept ourselves, choosing them from among our pizza store customers.

No one at any commissary is aware which stores and store managers are serving as our mystery customers, so the feedback we get is unfiltered, revealing, and used to increase our level of service even further.

Your business can adopt the mystery customer system. Many companies use a program they believe to be similar when they have "company spies" pose as customers. That's not the same as a true mystery customer.

A company spy isn't in touch with all that a customer wants from you. What's the real purpose of most company spy programs? Typically, it's to catch people making mistakes, often resulting in reprimands or firings. Keep your mission statement in mind. As a mission statement-oriented company, you want to measure key indicators that track how you're upholding it.

Only an actual customer, adopted temporarily as a mystery customer, can provide the feedback that will prove most valuable to you. Besides tapping the unmatched insights of actual customers, the mystery program boosts your standing with them—you honor them by making them "insiders."

Let your customers know you've got such a program in place. And to keep the program fresh, pass it around. We limit our mystery customers' tenures to six months.

ENROLLING TEAM MEMBERS

How do you get your team members to support the NPOs you choose? We've got two powerful tools that make that happen. The first tool, to which you've already been introduced, is the summer survey, which helps identify our areas of national priority. All our team members are fully aware that we identify our NPOs from the results of summer surveys of customers, team members, suppliers, the parent company, and the community.

The second tool to ensure interest in our NPOs is our reward system. Our performance on NPOs drives our bonus system—we put our bonus dollars against the NPOs.

Under our bonus system, up to 20 percent of company profits are allocated, proportionately, to the items on our list of NPOs. Each NPO receives a weighted point value that is tied to a key indicator. The performance of the associated key indicators generates a number that is used to determine how much of the bonus is distributed (see calculations below on page 174).

At Distribution, each team member's total compensation is a product of both the team's overall performance and their individual contribution to it. A powerful aspect of this system is that the key indicators and the team member bonuses are calculated every four weeks. Our people don't lose sight of the big picture by trying to excel in one area for a year before seeing any rewards for their efforts. Every team member receives three checks a month from us, two regular payroll checks and a bonus check.

Try giving your staff an extra check, regardless of its size, every four weeks and see if people immediately take notice of company objectives and what it takes to keep these extra checks coming. *You've got to believe each of our team members has a strong, vested, continuing interest in racking up bonus checks.*

Essentially, every four weeks is like a new fiscal year for us. We "close up" shop, add up the profits, poll the customers and team members on how we've done on nonprofit objectives to determine the NPO points, and distribute the resulting bonuses. All team members can summarize their personal performance at the end of each month and easily calculate the amount of their bonus check. To do that, they need to know three things: the number of bonus shares they receive (a function of position and compensation level), the value of each share that month (determined by Distribution's profit level and NPO score), and their individual performance objective score, which is known following the end of the month (see Chapter 11).

After an exceptional month, we'll see communications on our computer system between commissaries all over the country talking to each other about what a great month the company had. We don't mind them dwelling on what they made—it's all system reinforcement. Team members will be talking about what they're going to do with their bonus checks even before they arrive, because the computer gives everyone instant data as to what they'll receive.

Team members respond directly to prompt bonus payments. They can watch the scores of a key indicator grow each month, whereas with an annual system, the excitement of the chase wouldn't show up in daily operations.

CALCULATING THE NPO BONUS

Let's look at how to figure the monthly bonuses for each team member. For now, the emphasis will be on the contribution of the NPOs to the bonuses. The next chapter will cover how each team member's individual performance further affects his or her bonus once the overall calculations are made from corporate NPOs.

Using our 1990 NPO chart as a reference point, you can see that each NPO receives its point value on the basis of our three-level rating system—exceptional, expected, and crisis.

If you add up the middle column—the expected performance level—you'll see that 100 points are available. In other words, if everyone simply does their job, we make 100 percent of the profit allocation available for bonuses.

If you total all the exceptional points on the chart, you'll see that the NPO score could reach as high as 125 points if we scored exceptional in every area. Therefore, the bonuses available to team members can reach 20 percent of profits. This serves as incentive for everyone to be innovative and to diligently pursue our overall mission.

If every area was in the crisis range, the total would be only 25 points, but we've limited the downside of the NPO score. If the NPO for any period results in fewer than 50 points, we award no bonuses. The lowest bonus we pay is based on 50 percent of the 20 percent profit

NPOs for Period 12, 1990

NPO—Period 12/90	Crisis	Expected	Exceptional	Result	Points
Net Operating Savings	3 Points 12% > 1989	12 Points 28% > 1989	15 Points 41% > 1989	$1,223,981 27% < 1989	0.0
Key indicator: Current period NOS compared to the same period last year.					
Cash flow	2 Points 9% > 1989	8 Points 29% > 1989	10 Points 48% > 1989	$1,704,938 23% < 1989	0.0
Key indicator: Current period NOS + DEPR compared to the same period last year.					
Package survey	3 Points 25% say no	12 Points 15% say no	15 Points 5% say no	0.60%	15.0
Key indicator: Package survey question: "Considering everything, are you satisfied with Distribution as a place to shop?"					
Dough quality	3 Points 25% say no	12 Points 15% say no	15 Points 5% say no	10.70%	13.3
Key indicator: Package survey question: "Where you satisfied with the last dough you received from your commissary?"					
Store closings	3 Points 3 closings	12 Points 2 closings	15 Points No closings	0 closings	15.0
Key indicator: Number of confirmed store closings this period.					
Present survey	3 Points 25% say no	12 Points 15% say no	15 Points 5% say no	9.5%	13.7
Key indicator: Present survey question: "Considering everything, is Distribution the best place for you to work?"					
JPR/IPO	3 Points 75% had a JPR	12 Points 80% had a JPR	15 Points 90% had a JPR	85.56%	13.7
Key indicator: An actual count of the percentage of team members who had a JPR in the last 6 weeks.					
Worker compensation	2 Points 9 injuries	8 Points 7 injuries	10 Points 5 injuries	2 injuries	10.0
Key indicator: Number of serious lost-time injuries (over 5 days in duration not counting day of injury) compared to last year's average					
Market share	3 Points 93.55%	12 Points 94.61%	15 Points Above 94.61%	94.85%	15.0
Key indicator: The percentage of stores serviced by DNC.				Total NPO points = 95.7	

pool—i.e., 10 percent of profits. Below that, we figure we've got too many crisis areas for anyone to receive bonuses.

If Distribution achieves a score higher than 100, then we give gifts to each contributing team member such as a tree sapling to plant or a car emergency kit. We choose gifts that make the team members' lives better but that they probably would not have bought for themselves.

As part of our national performance objectives for 1990, we monitored whether our customers, the individual pizza stores, were satisfied with Distribution as a place to shop and if they were satisfied with the last dough they received from their respective commissaries.

To be specific, with both questions to the stores, if 5 percent of the respondents said no—in other words, 95 percent responded yes—we would have considered that our performance was exceptional. If 15 percent of the respondents had said no, we would have considered that to be in our expected performance range. If 25 percent of the respondents said no, we would have been in the crisis range.

Using similar criteria for each area, we calculate the overall NPO point total. Along with each area, we've listed the key indicator we use to determine our performance in that NPO.

On the chart above, for Period 12 in 1990, you can see the exceptional, expected, and crisis numbers for each area, the actual score attained, and the resulting points allocated to each area. In this case, the total came to 95.7 NPO points.

This number is a percentage that is multiplied by the overall bonus pool available for the period. For Distribution, the pool always begins as 20 percent of our pretax net profit. If the overall NPO score is 100, then 100 percent of that profit allocation goes toward the bonus pool for team members. For the period in this chart above, the total dollars available were 95.7 percent of 20 percent, or 19.14 percent of our profits.

DISTRIBUTING THE BONUS POOL

Each team member position within Distribution has a number of bonus shares allocated to it. For example, all truck drivers are given 40 shares. Doughmakers are given 30 shares. Team leaders are awarded 100 shares or 300 shares, depending on their salary level; company vice presidents are allotted 1,000 shares each; and the company president is allocated 3,000 shares. The shares allocated to any team member only change with a promotion or transfer. This means the greater responsibility a person has in our company, the more his or her overall compensation is tied directly to performance. Top executives have the potential to earn more through bonus than through their salary, but they also put more at risk. I figure it personally costs me about $1,000 every time Distribution closes a store. A doughmaker, whose facility did not close the store (such a group would lose their entire bonus), stands to lose about $10.

Here's the four-step process on how our team members get their checks from the pool:

- At the end of each four-week period, our corporation completes the NPO point value calculations and determines the dollar value of the total bonus pool—up to 20 percent of pretax profits.

- The total dollar value of the pool is multiplied by the NPO score, either awarding the full allocation, or reducing it to as low as 50 percent. (No bonuses are paid below 50 percent.)

- The resulting dollar amount of the bonus pool is then divided by the total number of individual shares earned to produce a per share dollar amount.

- Each team member then receives a separate bonus check that equals his or her share allocation—ranging from 30 to 3,000—times the dollar value of each share.

Here's a typical calculation as an illustration. Let's say Distribution made a pretax profit of $2 million for the four-week period. The bonus pool allocation of 20 percent equals a dollar total of $400,000. If the NPO score for that period was 95.7 percent, then the actual amount of the pool to be distributed would be $382,800.

Suppose there are 100,000 team member shares within the company. Dividing $382,800 by 100,000 shares produces a value of $3.83 per share. A doughmaker, entitled to 30 shares each bonus period, would then get a check for $114.84 if he or she earned 100 or better on his or her IPOs (Chapter 11). A truck driver, earning the full amount entitled to 40 shares, would get a check for $153.20, and so on.

Like learning to drive a car, the system is not complex once you become familiar with it. However, things could get unwieldy with a large number of team members. For any business running its payroll and accounting off a computer system, the calculations can be easily programmed and become automatic and painless.

The point is to adopt a system that automatically rewards team members *directly for measured performance* based on the company's overall performance and their individual contribution to that performance. The next chapter will help you translate the concept of national performance indicators to each team member's daily work performance.

CHAPTER CHECKLIST

* Don't limit the performance measurements of your company to next quarter's bottom line.

* Create your list of "do or die" areas and include them in every year's set of NPOs.

* Help your team leaders create innovative ways to support the company's "do or die" areas in case of contingencies that you can reasonably predict may occur.

* Make a commitment to become a leader in some areas of your company's industry. Even if you fall short, you'll surely end up with outstanding performance.

* Encompass every vision in your mission statement in your company's performance objectives.

* Use the results of your surveys to determine your NPOs.

* Ensure that your NPOs are not pipe dreams of the executive team, but reflect widespread concerns of team members, suppliers, customers, and the community.

* Encourage all team members to address every issue that arises by relating it to your mission statement.

* Establish a set of key indicators as a scale for the NPOs you set, so you can track them as easily as most companies track profits.

* Initiate a mystery customer program to track product quality, customer satisfaction, and team member performance.

* Rotate the honor among your customers and emphasize the importance of maintaining total secrecy about their participation.

* Help every executive, team leader, and team member see how their performance affects the company's overall performance.

- Award your bonuses based solely on performance and never on seniority or salary.

- Distribute awards frequently to team members to maintain inertia.

- Pay bonuses in a check separate from normal payroll. The bonus dollars will work harder for you when team members see them as something other than normal pay.

- Create the excitement of the chase daily in your company, rather than aiming at a set of vague year-end goals.

- Designate a portion of your profits as belonging to your team members, by creating a bonus pool. Increase it above the normal level if performance is superior and decrease it or temporarily suspend it if performance suffers.

Chapter Eleven

Job Planning and Review

Despite the quantity of systems involved in gauging performance and establishing key indicators, we can't lose sight of the fact that human performance drives every aspect of our operation. Shipments aren't late or early by themselves. A good driving safety record is more than numbers on a page; it represents thousands of hours down the interstate by some of the most skilled, dedicated people who ever got behind a steering wheel.

The numbers we use, in all cases, are simply a useful means of monitoring human progress in a manner that enables everyone to see how his or her contribution fits into overall operations. In a sense, we use numbers at Distribution to *depersonalize* corporate operations, level of service, and growth.

We've created a team-oriented system that offers regular rewards for entrepreneurial-type thinking within our corporate setting. In this chapter, we'll look at Steps 6 and 7 of the Super Vision process. We'll cover our job planning and reviews (JP&Rs), individual performance objectives (IPOs), and performance-driven reward system that has produced superior communications, motivation, and success throughout the organization and has supported healthy growth for more than 10 years.

The current JP&R system at Distribution actually began in 1976 at

Domino's Pizza, Inc., with the help of Phil Alexander, president of Ann Arbor Consulting Associates, Inc. Phil had launched a business forum he called the Ann Arbor President's Seminar. It was a small group of six or seven presidents of small to medium-sized businesses (in 1976, Domino's Pizza was not a big business).

The JP&R arose out of a request of one of the other group members who had been using a performance appraisal system in his firm. He didn't like the one he had, so he asked Phil to come up with something better. The original job planning and review system began as a replacement for this company's performance appraisal system. Phil researched the field, came up with a couple of key innovations, and developed a workable approach to replace the inadequate performance appraisal system.

Phil had two mentors in his career. One of them, Dr. Rensis Likert, was founder of the Institute for Social Research at the University of Michigan and best known for his pioneering work in participative management. After Ren took early retirement in 1970, Phil worked for three years as part of Ren's newly formed consulting firm. By correlating extensive survey studies on management styles with hard data results, Ren could conclusively demonstrate that a participative, team-oriented management approach was 25 to 40 percent more productive than a "top down" autocratic system. One of the primary things Phil wanted to accomplish in changing the performance appraisal system was to build an organization in which teamwork would be the norm.

Phil's other mentor, Dr. Jack Gibb, was one of the founders of the National Training Laboratory in the late 1940s. Jack was a longtime president of the American Society for Humanistic Psychologists and particularly active in developing small group theory and dynamics. During a three-year intern program with Jack, Phil studied trust relationships in organizations, how they are created, and their impact on communication and performance.

SYNTHESIZING A NEW SYSTEM

Phil built the foundation of Distribution's present JP&R system out of the two basic concepts he had worked on with his mentors. One was basically committed to team-oriented management. The other was committed to the idea that trust underlies almost all effective organizational performance.

Most good managers would agree that communication is basic to accomplishing organizational goals and objectives. Without good communication, you can't make good decisions, you can't plan, you can't supervise, you can't really do anything of organizational importance. The foundation of good communication, of course, is trust. If you have trust, then you can build relationships that foster good communication.

The performance system Phil was working to replace typically generated a negative relationship between a "boss" and "subordinate." His theory, which grew out of the synthesis of the ideas from both his mentors, was that when you can build trust between the boss and the subordinates, you create a positive relationship on which a foundation for a team approach can be built.

We took this new performance management tool—for which Phil coined the term job performance and review (JP&R)—implemented it, found that it really did develop trust and positive relationships, and have continued to build on it. How does JP&R, as now implemented at Distribution, compare with the original version Phil introduced 15 years ago? When he was here for a recent review of Distribution's integrated system, we asked him.

Phil responded, "When I see what you are doing, I feel like I expect the Wright brothers probably would have felt if they saw a Concorde jet airliner. I can see the basic JP&R design is still there, the principles are the same, but it has been improved in all kinds of ways and adapted specifically to the Distribution mission statement to take it well beyond what I originally created.

"I think that sort of flexibility and growth potential is the mark of a good management tool. That's why JP&R in its present form at Distribution can be studied by any company and then be modified or improved further to adapt to nearly any type of business."

Phil's JP&R system continues to evolve and improve at Distribution to better serve every element of our mission statement. Here's where it stands today.

THE CONCORDE OF PERFORMANCE LEADERSHIP

Our current job planning and review system is based on the premise that each person merits the opportunity to regularly communicate his or her dreams, goals, and aspirations—as well as progress, frustrations, and plans—to the team leader. We tied the effective planning and review of the JPR with the power of our IPO reward system to create a comprehensive system. Individual performance objectives are set by the team member and team leader during the JPR session. When combined, you get effective planning, performance review, and automatic rewards—keystones of Super Vision.

Together, the JP&R/IPO leadership system forms the basis of the relationship between a team member and team leader. JP&R sessions are held every four to six weeks. In these typically hour-long sessions, team members discuss their roles, personal missions, performance, and future plans with their team leader. The team leader acts as a coach to guide team members, help plan, institute corrective actions, and offer reward and praise within the context of our mission statement. Although a JP&R typically takes from 40 to 90 minutes, it may last several hours if major corrective action, long-term plans, or long-range goal setting is required.

JP&R sessions are private, face-to-face meetings typically held away from the normal work setting to help put the team member at ease. Before the session, the member prepares a set of simple forms that becomes the basis for the session's agenda.

The team leader is responsible for helping the team member understand what constitutes expected and exceptional performance and for providing the resources, tools, and support necessary to achieve such performance. The team leader is particularly concerned with avoiding team member failure and, in general, with providing a work environment conducive to that team member's individual success.

The JP&R/IPO session renews the focus of the team member and offers him or her a greater sense of freedom to make decisions on a daily basis, while ensuring that those decisions support the overall company mission statement.

This may appear to be a significant investment of time on the part of the Super Visor, but it is a most effective use of time. Our consulting clients find that a few hours regularly, wisely invested in each employee results in months and years of improved performance and job satisfaction. Another significant benefit is the reduction in time being wasted by on-the-job arguing. Every team member knows he or she will soon have an open forum where their gripes will matter.

This simple, powerful mechanism helps maintain a flexible, well informed work force, provides team members with a sense of ownership over what they are doing, streamlines communication between team members and team leaders, and enables both to keep adjusting to the constantly changing marketplace.

The system also is an inherently effective response to the cultural diversity in the American workplace of the 1990s. We've discovered—as have many employers—that we increasingly have to be sensitive to the backgrounds, values, and needs of a multicultural work force.

Since the JP&R allows the team members to set their own goals, there is a natural allowance for the cultural diversity that each individual brings to us. Because the JP&R/IPO system constantly clarifies roles and priorities in terms each team member most clearly understands, he or she spends more of each day, more of each hour, more of each minute in a productive mode, focused on achieving the mission statement.

Our philosophy is that the stronger each individual's sense of perspective and self-worth, the more likely that person will respond appropriately to what happens around him or her. The better the team member understands the company's mission and his or her role in fulfilling it, the more likely the role will be filled effectively. Having personal mission statements framed in personal terms helps each team member visualize his or her part—and share—in the overall success of the company.

TAKE ME OUT TO THE BALL GAME—REPRISE

We all agree that if batting averages were not kept in Major League Baseball, a player might not know his contribution to the team's overall league standings. Tracking IPOs and reviewing them in the JP&R session give each team member a clear understanding of what he or she brings to the game.

Once team members learn to measure their own performance—as Major League ball players understand their own stats—they discover what resources they need to successfully accomplish the task or tasks at hand. For a professional ball player it might mean increased time in batting practice or extra coaching in an area where he can contribute to the team's overall standings.

At Distribution, the needed resources might include computer software, tools, training, brainstorming sessions, or a budget—among other things. Team leaders are charged—as are Major League coaches and trainers—with the responsibility of securing the needed resources and tools for their team members so that each can achieve his or her highest potential within the company. This commitment to supporting team members is specifically built into the JP&R session.

Often, team members simply need to have someone listen to them to help them break through frustrating barriers that arise in the course of doing their jobs. Once the team leader establishes a track record of providing support and fulfilling promises to his or her team members, the team leader begins building credibility. And credibility leads to trust, the foundation of communication.

BUILDING GOALS AND ACTION PLANS

The strategies determined during the JP&R/IPO session are action plans to be implemented in the following four to six weeks. These plans typically represent small portions of an overall goal. They're specifically described, include a list of any material or human resources required to accomplish the goals, and set a target date for their completion.

The key to success is that the action plan is developed primarily by the team member, not the team leader. This key factor safeguards against the action plan being merely a series of dictated tasks in disguise.

With the responsibility for charting their own course for the next four to six weeks and the resources and support to tackle the problems identified, team members are more likely to be innovative than if the goals and implementation strategies had been imposed by their team leaders. The JP&R/IPO system builds on the premise that team members most often have the greatest understanding of and are closest to the task at hand.

A particularly creative and energetic team member will regularly identify opportunities and request resources to pursue them through the JP&R sessions. Thus, any team member with any good idea quickly learns that he or she is an integral and important part of a system that acknowledges, supports, and celebrates his or her innovative ways of helping the company. In essence, they're inherently inspired to do their best.

Rather than conducting business as usual, or brushing innovative ideas aside with comments like, "This is the way we do it," the creative power in each team member is tapped.

Now, let's turn now to the nitty-gritty of our JP&R sessions and tell you how they are used to create the goals and action plans (IPOs), and how each affects the reward system for individual team members.

BASICS OF JP&R/IPO SESSIONS

All team members and team leaders receive a two-day course that teaches them how the JP&R/IPO system will affect their everyday activities. Because the system may confuse some team members and company newcomers, we've developed a complete training program that uses videocassettes, training materials, and workbooks. The course teaches the basics of the system and all its terminology.

You are already acquainted with most of the terms, such as NPOs, shares, share values, and bonus pool. This chapter has introduced JP&Rs and IPOs. The only remaining term is one we call *premium shares*, which you'll soon understand.

We teach team members how to prepare for and participate most effectively in each session. We begin by showing team members "what's in it for them" personally and professionally. Focusing on personal involvement significantly increases team members' awareness and enthusiasm for the overall program.

Here's what's in it for them:

- Health and on-the-job safety.

- Accomplishment of their responsibility.

- Support of their team and the overall mission statement of the company.

- Satisfaction of improved performance.

- Their bonus.

Once team members understand the significance of the session, they will be primed for a productive meeting with the team leader. The meeting will help them focus on how to best fulfill work responsibilities and understand how they will be rewarded.

Team leaders are given extensive training in listening, coaching, and effective use of the process thanks to Linda Schow, our 1987 olympic team leader champ, who fought to institute this training after she recognized our particular needs in this area.

Each JP&R session has three basic sections: responsibilities and needs, achievements and needs for improvement, and goals and action plans.

RESPONSIBILITIES AND NEEDS

The JP&R session has to be viewed as an opening for team members to get support from their team leader to help them accomplish their IPOs. It's not a gripe session for team members to get in their licks against their leader, nor is it a scolding session for leaders to rail against poor performance.

Both people are to assume the other wants to do the best job possible. Both are charged with helping the other fulfill his or her responsibility.

The responsibility first falls to the team member to prepare for the session. We've developed a checklist of responsibilities so a team member can know how best to prepare:

- Make an appointment with your team leader for the session.
- Schedule a time to fill out your forms in advance.
- Collect your thoughts. Don't wait until the last minute to identify what to say. Keep a notebook of things you think of between review sessions that includes:
  - Questions, concerns, unknown direction.
  - Unkept promises.
  - Problem areas.
  - Needs.
  - Accomplishments.
  - New goals.

- Review your role.
  - Performance key indicators (KI).
  - Make sure KIs are possible.
  - KIs that need improvement.
  - Tools you need.
  - Identify new KIs.
  - Achievement KIs.

- Take responsibility for your role in the JP&R process.

- Be open and honest.

- Practice the Golden Rule.

The first part of the process directly addresses the team member's responsibilities toward the company's mission and the team's performance. The team member writes a personal mission statement that prompts the team member to think of how he or she could best participate in the achievement of the company's goals.

Team members who know their role in an organization and who know how well they are performing to meet company and personal objectives are a great defense against the gradual erosion of quality. Motivation systems are more effective in the long-term when they employ carrots rather than sticks.

The session opens the door for team members to communicate with their leaders about any help the team needs to advance the company's mission statement as well as any upsets that may be lingering from the leader's unkept promises. Thus, motivation is always presented in a positive manner.

After the JP&R session has been initiated with this open communication to focus the entire process on the mission statement, the team leader moves on to the next section. In this stage of the session, both participants review the team member's IPOs and other achievements or struggles.

ACHIEVEMENTS/NEEDS FOR IMPROVEMENT

The JP&R/IPO session is the tool the leader uses to acknowledge each team member for superior performance in all areas of his or her job. Not only does it note the team member's IPO scores, but it also provides an opening for both to discuss areas outside the scope of normal IPOs.

One of the most important facets of this session is the opportunity it provides for the team member to identify help he or she needs in specific areas and for the team leader to commit to providing that help.

If any of the IPOs are in crisis, the team member and team leader enter a serious problem-solving mode. The team leader takes on the task of putting out the fire immediately—before the individual team member's crisis IPO score can affect the overall performance of the team. The team leader will do nearly anything necessary to provide the needed tools, knowledge, direction, or training, or to find someone else who will help the team member quickly clear the crisis hurdle and return to expected performance.

Once both participants in the review understand their role in the team member's support of the mission statement, they're ready to move on to the final stage of the session. As the meeting draws to a close, the team member will commit to his or her IPOs and agree to the key indicators that will measure them. The team leader will commit to helping the team member in any way possible to accomplish all appropriate IPO and non-IPO goals. Here's the final form used in a JP&R review.

GOALS AND ACTION PLANS

This final part of the JP&R creates the extra energy we need to prosper in today's challenging world. When completed, our team members will know their unique role in supporting our mission statement, what specific tasks they can accomplish to uphold it, how they can readily track their progress, and how they'll be rewarded for their hand in the company's success.

When the JP&R session ends, the team member will have developed and committed to between six and eight IPOs for the following review period. Each IPO is assigned a point value based on the familiar three-level system of exceptional, expected, and crisis performance.

A couple of typical IPOs at Distribution are for our delivery and service team members to track their gas mileage and late deliveries. Whatever IPOs are chosen, they need to be easily measurable with key indicators that translate into objective data. Choose key indicators that measure the most important aspects of the job and set challenging expectations that will both move the company toward its goals and be achievable by a skilled team member.

Once team members' IPOs are set, they and their leader will agree between them what the key indicators and target performance numbers will be for each. As with the NPOs, each IPO needs to track *results* and not *effort*, while encouraging long-term problem solving over quick fixes. Striking such a balance always relates the issue at hand to the mission statement.

KEEPING TEAM MEMBERS FULLY INFORMED

No one likes to be set up for failure. Unfortunately, many managers unconsciously do precisely that to their team. Priorities and focus evolve rapidly in our changing world, but most companies do not have a system to rapidly communicate those changes to their team members and to implement new goals and procedures necessary to stay ahead.

How often do new team members begin their jobs with a whirlwind orientation that gives them little more than the location of the restrooms and the coffeepots? Our team members are prepared for their jobs with specific knowledge of what to do, the resources to get it done, and a commitment from their leaders to help them.

JP&R sessions for new team members create an excellent training tool. Since performance bonuses are not paid until a team member has been with us for six months, they have a transition period to fully understand how their performance will be rated *before* there is money on the line.

One of the most important aspects of the last part of a JP&R session is that the team member has input into the creation of his or her goals. This eliminates on-the-job surprises and hurt feelings and enables team members to see the objective results of the performance to which they committed themselves. In fact, the team member will check his or her own performance data (IPO scores) before the review session.

Similar to a baseball player meeting the team's manager when both know the player's stats, the personal elements that can produce flared tempers are avoided. Team members with poor scores will clearly see them for themselves and the team leader will not be viewed as the bearer of bad news.

The only significant potential in our JP&R system for hurt feelings is when team leaders "change the rules" between sessions without communicating the new conditions or requirements to the team member. Team leaders must be trained to make such changes only when absolutely necessary and to do so with the input and knowledge of all team members affected by the new set of requirements.

TRANSLATING IPOs INTO INCENTIVE AWARDS

No bonus system can provide a good return on investment unless it's tied to performance. We discussed that in the last chapter, showing you how we use our NPOs to calculate a share dollar value for each team member's bonus.

However, team members do not automatically receive the full bonus produced by multiplying the number of shares they're allocated times the share value. That number reflects only their potential bonus earnings. Factors other than overall company performance affect each team member's actual bonus.

First, new team members have to be with us for six review periods before being eligible to receive bonuses. Participation starts at the beginning of the seventh period, and the first bonus is paid during their eighth.

The next factor we consider in incentive calculations is the performance of each individual team. One sure way to sabotage a good bonus system is to distribute the rewards evenly among all eligible team members, regardless of how their individual teams contributed to the overall company performance. In a company as large as ours, it's possible to have the company operating in the exceptional range while one unit operates in the crisis range.

The vehicle for recognizing and balancing differing team performance is something we call *share premiums*. That's an adjusted share value assigned to each member of a team if their facility had overall exceptional performance. With this share premium, an outstanding unit in the company will be appropriately recognized and rewarded.

Any units in crisis fail to share in the overall reward the others produced. An allowance for share premiums is essential to the long-term success of the reward system because one unit in crisis drags down the overall NPO scores, affecting everyone else's bonus.

Share premiums are added to the share value before any other calculations are made. It's a dollar amount above and beyond the normal bonus. Based on each team's performance—the level of efficiency of the commissary or operating unit—the share premium can be anywhere from $0.50 to $5.00 per share. As mentioned in the last chapter, shares are based on each team member's level of responsibility and potential to affect NPOs.

After share premiums are calculated, they're deducted from the overall bonus pool and what's left gets distributed to all eligible team members throughout Distribution. So, if one facility stands out from the rest, it gets first crack at the bonus pool.

MAKING IT PERSONAL

IPOs are used for individual team members as NPOs are for corporate key indicators; that is, if a team member's IPO score is 100, that team member gets 100 percent of his or her share value, otherwise it's reduced. As with NPOs, we've set a floor on this reduction. If a team member's IPO score drops below 50, no bonus is paid. At that point, the team leader will become highly involved in clearing up that person's crisis.

However, if a team member's IPO score is in the range of 101 to 125, no additional share value is paid; the dollars simply are not there. In that case, it's the team leader's responsibility to quickly and appropriately celebrate that performance. This reinforces the success for the team member and helps promote future exceptional performance.

Celebrating exceptional IPOs can take many forms: the team member can expect an extra pat on the back from his or her team leader, or some nonmonetary premium, such as tickets to a favorite sports event, or extra vacation time. Another terrific response is to mention it in the company newsletter.

Whatever the reward, the team leaders try to make it something the team member will truly hold dear, while remaining within common-sense budget restraints of the company.

The bottom line is that a company cannot *make* its people happy. It can, however, do many things to remove frustrations that block happiness, such as failure to reward exceptional performance.

People will be more effective if they are happy doing their jobs. One of the ways a company can contribute to the happiness of its team members is to grant freedom based on demonstrated performance; that is, if a team member handles a job well, give him or her greater latitude on the next project. This freedom, in turn, breeds continued satisfaction on the job and effectiveness is increased.

An effective JP&R/IPO system that is tied to a reward system is a fabulous tool for granting the freedom your team deserves and for tapping the team's energy. You'll have an effective system to allow freedom because performance is tracked regularly, and you'll be able to identify those people who take advantage of the creative atmosphere it breeds. All your team members will have tremendous incentive to perform well, knowing they'll be supported in their efforts and rewarded for their performance.

Team members who know they will get a bonus if their performance meets or exceeds goals are most likely to overcome performance problems and excel. In fact, motivation to improve sometimes comes from peers whose own bonuses depend in part on overall team performance. Again and again, we find that a performance-driven, integrated system such as our JP&R/IPO process creates a cooperative atmosphere of innovation between all team members and their leaders as all strive to serve the company's mission statement.

CHAPTER CHECKLIST

- Create an integrated system of performance-driven rewards that will produce superior communications, motivation, and success throughout your organization.

- Focus on a participative, team-oriented management approach in which teamwork becomes the norm.

- Use open communications within your company to build trust between team leaders and team members.

- Base your communication on the premise that each person merits the opportunity to regularly communicate his or her dreams, goals, and aspirations, as well as progress, frustrations, and plans to the team leader.

- Have team leaders and team members work together in support of the job performance and review system to establish individual performance objectives.

- Use such sessions to renew the focus of team members and offer them a greater sense of freedom to make decisions on a daily basis, while ensuring that those decisions support the overall company mission statement.

- Set specific, measurable key indicators for each IPO in a rating period. Tie the key indicators to results and never to effort.

- Let team members establish their own goals, phrased in their own words, so as to acknowledge the multicultural diversity that is now a permanent part of every corporation's work force.

- Arrange for face-to-face sessions away from the normal work setting to help put the team member at ease.

- Establish a file in your company's computer system so each team member can easily track his or her progress toward goals and bonuses.

- Train team leaders and team members to ensure that the goals they set represent small portions of the company's overall goal.

- Orient your team member training to answer the question, "What's in it for me?"

- Train team leaders to make changes between JP&R sessions only when absolutely necessary and then to do so with the input and knowledge of all team members affected by the new set of rules.

- Create a vehicle for recognizing and balancing differing team performance, such as share premiums.

- Empower your team leaders to celebrate exceptional IPOs among team members with whatever reward they believe the team member will truly hold dear, while remaining within commonsense budget restraints of the company.

- Above all, tell your team members exactly what needs to be done, give them the tools to accomplish the mission, track their progress, and then get out of their way, letting their natural abilities take over.

Chapter Twelve
Blueprints

Suppose you've gotten your mission statement to be focused suffi-
ciently on all you impact and general enough to guide day-to-day decision making. There still could be some instances when more clarity
regarding a specific goal or task is needed. Producing and circulating
your mission statement, however well-crafted, will not result in understanding all the ramifications of every subject, each day, over many
years.

In this chapter, we'll discuss a tool that keeps Super Vision working
when particular situations call for an added measure of guidance or the
team members assigned lack a balanced perspective of the situation.

Some team leaders and team members, even top executives, may
lack the direction they need in specific cases, and their next JP&R
session is weeks away. This is a problem that periodically occurs to
everyone. Some team members may see the mission statement as so
top-level oriented that it doesn't apply to the issues they're facing. Or I
may need to issue a special quick-turnaround assignment.

To bridge the gap between the mission statement and the guidance
someone may need to face a particular problem or to handle late-
breaking developments, we created the blueprint, which is simply a
handwritten tool, usually a page or less. Blueprints are a direct by-
product of my leadership style, but other leaders like David Materne,

head of our equipment division, have since adopted them for use with their team members, with excellent results.

A blueprint is easy to produce, and both team leaders and members like using them. Often, blueprints provide an individual with the big picture, including influences on the company or future possibilities, and the available options the team leader envisions as to how the team member might proceed.

Like Design Engineers. One way to understand how blueprints work at Distribution is to think of company leaders as design engineers. They design the next generation of technology, work with draftsmen on blueprints that accurately detail how to build the new design, then move on to further the technology.

Design engineers *don't* follow the blueprints through the factory and watch over the shoulders of team members on the assembly line to catch mistakes. The engineers need to be familiar with the assembly-line procedures and be able to screw in a bolt, or make dough, because they can be more effective designers if they understand how the product will be assembled. But it's not their job to hover over people.

You've already been exposed to one blueprint. In Chapter 9, I described how we envision what we want from the next year's summer survey. The single page pro forma planning sheet (see page 150) is actually a blueprint.

We developed our original blueprint to deal with the overwhelming amount of calls from company executives who wanted to visit us in Ann Arbor and learn our systems. The blueprint established the Domino's Pizza Innovation Network. Headed by Peter Niedbala, the network helps companies adopt our systems through one-on-one assistance. On a single page, we were able to define this profit center, which has grown steadily over three years.

FROM HERE TO TOMORROW

Often a blueprint explains how the world used to be, how the world is now, and what we are trying to accomplish for tomorrow—through numbers, prose, a series of pictures, a flowchart, or a combination of the above. The examples on the next pages, both on aspects of setting priorities and goals, represent an outline style and diagram style of blueprint.

Any team leader can create a blueprint to help accomplish some

---

INTRODUCTION: Once a year our company must take time to reflect—where do we stand compared to accomplishing the Mission Possible? We must then set forth goals for the upcoming year according to our self-analysis. The group selected to do this must have a well-developed view of the long-term destination of our company. The following serves as information to that group as to the planning systems our company uses to set goals for the next year.

PREPARATION TO PARTICIPATE IN DISTRIBUTION'S 1991 GOALS:

Step 1:   Absorbing Potential Improvement Points

By mid-year, our company is usually on its way to meeting the goals that have been set forth the prior year. Times change and so do the needs of all the people mentioned in our mission statement.

- To set next year's goals, you should begin to investigate the needs of these people by keeping your ears opened and asking questions regarding their needs for the upcoming year.
- Make notes if you have to and store them in the file "Next Year's Goal Setting." We will start setting goals in September/October of each year.

Step 2:   Accumulation of Ideas

- Just before the October goal-planning session, take a day and grab the following materials: Mission Possible, P&Ls, NPOs, key indicators, summer surveys, ideal service surveys, notes from your meetings with customers, and visits of commissaries and stores.

- Get selfish and get greedy! Try to envision an upcoming year in which there would be no surprises, no anxieties, no frustrations, and no crises to disrupt your steady routine and happy lifestyle.

- Believe your dreams will come true by merely putting down your desires in writing.

- Make a list—not of problems but of *desired results, achievements, or resolutions.* DO NOT worry about any action plans or how it will get done. That comes later in the process.

Step 3:   Go for the Big Win

It's safe to assume that everyone participating in the goal setting really wants to run a perfect company and resolve all our problems. Realize that that is what a "manager" does. As "leaders" of this company, we need to focus on THE MOST IMPORTANT THINGS that will bring success. It may perhaps be in the best interest of our company just to resolve ONE MAIN ISSUE in a calendar year. Chances are there will be 5 to 10 issues that likely will bring the most significant positive results.

- Divide your list into *"Top Priorities"* and *"Secondary Targets."*

---

specific end. Frequently they're used to help a team member understand a situation as the team leader understands it. The key, however is to provide a thorough blueprint session that doesn't end until everything is clear.

With the situations I face as president, my blueprints may include government action, consumer preference, competitor moves, or size of the current harvest. I dispense blueprints as often as 10 times a day or periodically throughout the month—whenever I see or sense a change in the environment or following new input from key staff.

My blueprints are often nothing more than roughly hand-drawn charts and diagrams, like the sample provided on page 196. It may look like chicken scrawl to you, but once a team member understands it, it's an excellent one-page management system. Whatever form it takes, the person who grasps the concepts has something to refer to as he or she initiates action.

INTENTIONAL LEEWAY

As you know, dough is an important item in our business. Dough has to be a certain quality, able to be easily shipped, and not require constant capitalization and retooling. My blueprint on dough, a single page, is circulated to the people in charge of making dough. How they will accomplish these ends are left intentionally unspecific.

Team members assigned to the task will figure out the "how," perhaps in a work-back-from-the-goal process. This enables them to maintain an entrepreneurial focus, while achieving what I'm seeking. They pursue the goal rather than a given process.

Another term we use in association with blueprints is *tights*. Like the mission statement, blueprints contain boundaries. Tights are guiding principles. Some are in force on all blueprints, that is, the solution to a situation outlined in a blueprint has to always be ethical and legal.

Other tights are case specific. Perhaps the solution is to keep the cost below a certain amount or to limit a time frame. Other than drawing the blueprint and determining the tights, the task is left as open as possible.

The customer might want a lower price, while the parent wants greater revenues. These dynamics would be included within an individual blueprint. The team member, given such a blueprint, might then surmise that the solution is to become more efficient—cut operating expenses to be able to lower prices.

This illustrates how we balance our mission. Cost savings come out

Original Blueprint for Chart on Page 144

(*Blueprints often start in rough forms. This blueprint, however, was clear to everyone present when it was drawn!*)

of total operating expenses, so we could lower prices (one win), keep paying bonuses (two wins), and return the same level of profit to the parent company (three wins).

APPLYING KEY INDICATORS

Key indicators are a part of blueprints. They are introduced by standard phrases such as: "an exceptional job is indicated by . . . ," "expected performance is indicated by . . . ," and "a crisis is indicated by . . . ." Thus, team members know in advance how their performance will be rated, as they do with all other tasks and responsibilities they face.

If an exceptional performance in the case of dough means that 88 percent of store managers are satisfied with dough shipped from the commissaries, that is the figure team members ultimately work to achieve.

Performance Earns Freedom.   Suppose an exceptional performer has an idea to double the effective life of a green pepper. Given that she has consistently met performance objectives, she can then turn to her team leader and say, "I see a need to initiate A and B." When team members are given blueprints and they meet or exceed expectations, they automatically are given more leeway and personal autonomy to meet future tasks. Because team members have success in meeting other objectives, our confidence in their future performance increases and fewer or less restrictive "tights" are tied to the project.

We describe the process of granting freedom after exceptional performance using something I call the *Pajaro principle*. Simply stated: performance earns freedom; freedom used to further performance earns reward. For the SuperVisor, trusting team members to achieve without close scrutiny is a windfall; it frees the SuperVisor for his or her proper leadership roles. The SuperVisor trusts the natural instinct of a person to improve and relies on the proven ethics of the team member. A supervisor, however, could never be comfortable giving up control of a team member's actions. A supervisor looks for times that natural instincts fail and creates audit trails to control and prevent possible dishonesty.

A DYNAMIC ATMOSPHERE

Blueprints also can be issued at the department or group level, and departments or groups that have performed exceptionally are also given leeway to pursue new projects they have identified. Hence, innovations and new areas of exploration are constantly being launched at Distribution, with the approval and blessing of the appropriate team leader.

Projects could be as simple as reorganizing a report form or as complex as redesigning key equipment in the commissaries. Or they could be improvements in shipping, packaging, delivery, or communications procedures—there are no limits on innovation.

CHAPTER CHECKLIST

- Use blueprints to bridge the gap between the mission statement and the guidance someone may need to face a particular problem or to handle late-breaking developments.

- On one page, sketch for your staff the big picture of an issue, including influences on the company or future possibilities, and the available options.

- Don't hover over the person assigned to handle the blueprint.

- Offer guiding principles or set some boundaries if you have to, but leave accomplishment of the task to the member. The "how" is his or her responsibility.

- Include key indicators as part of the blueprint, giving team members advance notice as to how their performance will be rated.

- When team members meet or exceed expectations established for a blueprint, give them more leeway and personal autonomy the next time.

- Offer the necessary guidance and resources to exceptional performers as they initiate the new task they've identified.

- Employ blueprints at the department or group level also, and give leeway to departments or groups that perform exceptionally.

PART

IV

Tools for Reinforcing
Super Vision

All the tools to measure and enhance performance work notably well. Our commitment to sharing information, supporting team members, avoiding duplication of effort, and seeking the input and support of everyone in the organization, however, extends much further.

As such, we employ tools for reinforcing Super Vision that provide company-wide team member communication and support systems. Whether it's the 007 Reports, monthly State of the Union Reports, the high-spirited Distribution olympics, the ever-flourishing Team Member Workbench, the Satellite Network, or other communication vehicles, we cover every angle in pursuit of our mission.

Since we began using these reinforcement tools, home office administrative costs as a percentage of sales have declined from a 10-year average of 2.8 percent to 1.5 percent, occurring largely during the past 18 months.

Reinforcement tools need not be expensive. Every company has options for upping its employee communication and support systems. As each of the next four chapters unfold, you'll see that in all cases there are nonexpensive corollaries to our tools.

Chapter Thirteen

Reporting Live, 007 and the State of the Union

Consider what is happening in many companies today; does any of the following sound familiar? There is a growing rift between the corporate administrative offices and the regional and field offices. Regional and field staff often think the people in the home office don't understand them, are drifting apart from them, or have a different concept of what the company is all about.

These perceptions from the team members in the field are often reinforced when the company suffers a business downturn. Morale in the lower corporate echelons can be irreparably damaged when they're forced to swallow cuts in pay and benefits, at the same time that the managers who were responsible for the difficulties pull the rip cords on their golden parachutes.

Many companies also hire office managers from outside the company, people who have not come up through the ranks or do not have an operations focus. Understandably, these people end up running offices rather than managing the company's operations. To prevent this rift, our team members are operations-oriented, and management slots are filled from within.

Mike Soignet, the vice president of our commissary system, for example, began as a tray washer, moving to truck driving, team leader, commissary leader, regional manager, and then to vice president.

Such internal promotion, coupled with regional managers who have close personal relationships with their team members and commissary leaders, is how we "keep a large company small."

As companies grow, they tend to decentralize, spawning regional offices with regional managers who begin building their own regimes. However, the people who make the best regional managers rarely have top office-management skills. At Distribution, for example, we have at least 15 to 20 executives who could easily manage a region, but few that could manage a region *and an office*. We decided to split the functions so we'll no longer have anybody in the regions running offices.

DISBAND AND FLOURISH

At one time, we had three regional offices—in Ann Arbor, Atlanta, and California. The regional offices were costing us $1 million a year to run. Each regional office was staffed with an average of 11 people. However, we found that instead of helping the commissaries operate efficiently, regional managers ended up supervising the people in their offices, managing paper flow, and handling administrative tasks, rather than providing the critical assistance and monitoring we needed to run our commissaries.

Thus, we made the crucial decision to disband our regional offices and instead charged regional managers with the responsibility of visiting and assisting field operations.

Instead of "managerial types," we opted for hands-on people, equipped with worldwide beepers, who are expected to travel from commissary to commissary rather than stay in a regional office. We want each manager to be totally in tune with between four and six commissaries.

On a daily basis, the regional managers have to report back to headquarters, "Here is what I learned, here is what I recommend, here is what I need." This reporting process became known as the *007 Report*. It lets us know exactly what is happening in the field, what the needs were, and how to best respond. As a bonus, the reporting requirements keep the regional managers alert and on their toes.

Depending on where the regional manager lived, he or she would visit some commissaries by car and frequently stay over night at the home of the commissary manager. In other instances, the regional manager had to fly to commissaries. In all cases, we were looking for the regional manager to form strong professional relationships with the commissary managers and to be somewhere on-site everyday.

In disbanding the regional offices, we also reallocated the work and people so that everyone continued to be employed with the company, either at the home office or within one of the commissaries. We sought to give all team members opportunities and challenges equal to or greater than what they had faced in the regional offices.

Regional managers retained their titles and salaries but were given the responsibility of visiting every commissary once a month. Their agenda included determining if field staff and customers were happy, sampling the product, holding meetings to discuss problem areas, and providing any information from headquarters in Ann Arbor that would help operations.

I Am, Therefore I Resist. Understandably, both regional managers and the home office people to whom they reported initially resisted this change. After all, regional managers are supposed to have offices, right? Also, home office people were not happy about having their sense of protocol disturbed and were not enthusiastic about the response network they would be providing (more below.)

Once again, as it has been in so many of our interconnected operations, our mission statement was the glue that held the whole system together. Both sides began to view their roles as vehicles to support Distribution's overall vision and started offering suggestions for system refinements that supported the mission statement.

After hundreds, if not thousands, of hours of observation, we finally got a feel for how the system actually worked, and we were able to compile a roster of regional managers' duties and responsibilities. The resistance gradually faded, and a solid, effective network of intracompany communications took shape. Now our regional managers have all the advantages of a regional office without the disadvantages of cost and administration.

As time passed, some regional managers devised a checklist to fill out monthly at each commissary. The checklist rates such categories as sanitation, cleanliness, and receiving. As with other key indicators, each area on the checklist has a crisis zone, an expected or sleep zone, and an exceptional zone.

We asked the regional managers to share this evaluation with the commissary team members at team huddles so that together they could agree on its accuracy before it was sent back to Ann Arbor. This diminished the problem of a regional manager blasting a commissary manager on paper, precipitating the need for the home office executive staff to resolve the matter.

In all, the conversion to this form of field support, a bold innovation for us at the time, has worked well and today it is the fulcrum for our operations-focused company.

FEWER TASKS, NOT FEWER PEOPLE

Our operations focus initially came about when we realized we were paying too much for administrative activities, compared to operational. Of course, this didn't make sense because operations (service) is what we're all about.

What we sought to do at Ann Arbor, in the words of Jerry Graf, one of our region managers, was "to remove tasks, not people." To do that, we needed to hear from our commissary managers what they were not getting but wished they had, and what they were getting but didn't want. More than that, we needed to know how we were getting in their way, and where they wanted us to back off.

I had to acknowledge that even some of my requests of the commissaries hampered their operations.

We decided our home office would be structured based on what the commissaries needed to have from us, and not necessarily vice versa. So we inventoried what we were doing in the home office, what regional managers were doing, and what the commissaries were doing.

Nicety but Not Necessity. We found that each of the three areas undertook many types of activities that were nice but didn't contribute to overall operational efficiency and had little positive effect on the organization as a whole.

The more we looked at operations, the more we realized how heavy our administrative burden was. Of 11 people reporting to me, for example, 4 were in operations and 7 were administrative. Administration does not run the company; operations does. Administration exists only to serve operations, not to command them. Hereafter, we needed to have the people reporting to me all be operational.

The funny thing about administrative systems is the more creative and inquiring your mind, the more inclined you are to introduce all kinds of measures and controls that are wonderful, but on scrutiny don't forward the progress of the company. In our commitment to being a totally operations-driven company, we decided home office administrative staff posts would report to operations people.

FALLING INTO LINE

Once we made the great leap to an operations focus, many system components fell into line. With operations as our chief focus, how could we support our operational people in the way they wanted to be supported?

We decided that if Mike Gordon, one of our commissary managers, or any other commissary manager had a question, concern, or need on Thursday afternoon, we would respond in Ann Arbor by Friday noon either the solution, or a firm date and time as to when the solution would be forthcoming.

To be that responsive to Mike and each of our other commissary managers, we decided to diminish the workload of everyone at headquarters, eliminate redundancies, and most importantly, have everyone's schedule clear every morning through noon. With this policy in place, wonderful results quickly followed.

Now, any time a commissary manager calls, his or her request is logged into our system, routed to the appropriate person by early the next morning, and answered by that noon. No one at headquarters should engage in a meeting during the morning until requests are handled, so that everyone can remain totally responsible to incoming requests.

Concurrently, to reduce the number of unnecessary requests, (i.e., the information already exists in some media), we developed a computer network called Team Member Workbench (see Chapter 15). The network can store and make readily available on-line to anyone in the company our corporate history, mission, and policies as well as a library of questions, problems, and concerns phoned in by commissary managers and their solutions.

With these measures in place, we greatly reduced the amount of paper that had been inundating our home office staff. Per staff person, we are getting fewer requests, and the requests that do come in are often single-focused, clear, and to the point.

ON EVERY QUESTION, A TEAM

Each staff person handling requests from the field relies on a team; no one ever shoulders an inordinate burden. This plan has allowed our home office people to get more involved with more aspects of operations.

Understandably, this makes each of our team members in the home office more valuable; as each week passes, he or she understands the company with a wider and wider perspective. In addition, each team member at headquarters is free to sit in on any number of groups responsible for different operations. In short, team members can choose their areas of interest.

Jeff Smith, for example, at one time worked simultaneously on WDPD, an innovative internal communications tool (see Chapter 16), transportation, and other work-related issues. In a more formally structured company, there is no way he could work in these three groups. He would be told where to work or, if fortunate, given the chance to make a single selection.

REDUCING PING-PONG PROBLEM SOLVING

With the 007 call-in system in place, as we now refer to it, we are able to short-circuit many requests for assistance from the field. The actual protocol is for the field or commissary leader to request assistance from the regional manager. The regional manager will first assess the situation to determine whether his or her input is needed. If not, the manager will turn it back to the field or commissary leader.

If the regional manager believes the problem needs to be turned over to the home office, he or she makes it part of the daily report, with the understanding that a reply will be received by noon the next day. Requests coming in from the field are screened to make sure they are not make-work requests. Thereafter, the home office staff person by noon the next day either solves the problem or states a day and time when it will be solved.

This system reduces resentment people in the field may feel toward home office staff. Being given a day and time by which a problem will be resolved helps the manager more easily maintain a strong human connection with the home office representative.

As the information entered into the Workbench grows, the number of calls from the field subsides. For example, cheese prices fluctuate. Commissary leaders need to know whether or not to stockpile cheese. Instead of calling the regional manager or the home office, they can consult Workbench to see what others have done in a similar situation.

THE 007 SYSTEM AND THE REGIONAL MANAGER

Let's look at the call-in system from the regional manager's perspective. David Whitacre is one of our regional managers and has responsibility for four commissaries. He stays in touch with those commissaries and visits them as often as possible. Every evening he calls in to corporate headquarters through a voice mail system on Team Member Workbench.

David's report contains two elements—information and needs—and will be stored on file and available for anyone to review. He reports his needs in precise language so we can route his concerns immediately to the right party.

For example, he might say, "I need to talk to the transportation group. I want them to call up the Florida commissary because one of the commissary's truck leases is expiring and the commissary is not sure what decision to make." David knew somebody would follow up on his need statement and get back in touch with the Florida commissary by noon either with the solution or the date and time the solution would be forthcoming.

This system frees us to get in touch with another commissary the next day and focus on their concerns and needs, without having to make a lot of follow-up calls to determine if the commissary that had the question is being served. We now know they are being served because of the basic system design and the fact that everybody in the company supports it.

When the headquarters transportation group comes into work that morning, David's request is in their in box. It is immaterial whether Gary Kelly handles it or Dianne Thuen or any of the other members of the group. The important thing is that one person will take responsibility for the assignment. In all cases, the headquarters staff goes right back to the commissary, and not to the regional manager.

A NEW LEVEL OF TRUST AND FREEDOM

Over the years, the commissary people have come to trust and rely on the home office staff, realizing the home office staff has their needs and concerns at heart.

Kathi Seglund, part of our communication team, presides over this system. Whenever important issues surface, she gives me an immediate report. Meanwhile, she looks at the pattern of requests and needs coming in from the field. If she notices the commissaries are experiencing some common difficulty, she also reports this to me.

We look at the picture systematically and decide if there is another way we can handle this issue, thereby further reducing the number of requests coming in from the field.

Suppose some complaints are coming in about the commissary in Maryland. Under the old system, Kevin Williams, head of store operations, would hear about it 10 to 14 days later and understandably be upset. Following a flurry of phone calls back and forth, he might get to the root of the problem.

Under the 007 system, the problem is reported at once, and someone is on it by the next day. We check the file to see if this problem is a repeat, and if so, we examine the earlier solution. If not, we look for a novel solution for this commissary. Meanwhile, if Kevin Williams wanted to find out more about this situation, rather than having to flag me down, he could simply ask for a printout of the initial request and all other communication that has ensued. On reviewing this information, Kevin might conclude: "They don't need me." And that would be fine. He has plenty of other things to handle.

STATE OF THE UNION REPORTS

At the end of every period (remember, we have 13 in the year, lasting for four weeks each), we ask the regional managers for a state of the union report, a standardized briefing on each of their commissaries. The reports cover the vital areas: total operating expenses, dough, zero payables, team member happiness, no store closings, golden rule. We also report on current issues. The reports highlight only what is exceptional and what is crisis. There is no need to report on sleep zone performance.

A second section of the report reviews the status of particular programs. If a program is not proceeding according to plan, the state of the union report would alert us to this, and the regional manager would continue to update us in subsequent reports.

Meanwhile, at the home office, we have a report every four weeks on each of the 32 commissaries. These enable us to spot trends and compare and contrast commissary operations. The data are stored in the Workbench system and available for anybody in the company to review anytime. No one need call the commissary, ask for requests, or go through any clearances. It is all there with a touch of a button. There's no need even to print on paper.

STATE OF THE UNIONS FOR SUPPORT GROUPS

Every support group also files a regular state of the union in the form of a job planning and review sheet. As with a team leader and team member, the group meets once during a period, decides what its overall mission is, what project each is working on individually, and what was achieved individually and as a group.

The team leader incorporates information on individual projects and achievements in the state of the union report for the group. Rather than preparing an elaborate state of the union report each period, the team leader only needs to focus on what changed and what is new.

For example, if South Florida team member Peggy Powers' role has expanded and she had two new achievements that no one else knows about, the team leader puts a red star by these when reviewing her JP&R. When the team leader combines the JP&Rs to bring to the group's next monthly state of the union meeting, he or she has only to look for the red stars indicating changes. As such, the state of the union report is simply an evolving document, reflecting the changes since the last report.

All state of the union reports from the groups are submitted to the communication team, as are the reports from the regional managers. Again, communication team members highlight anything they think the executives or I need to know. As a result of this process, overall paperwork on everyone's behalf is drastically reduced.

Accelerated Experience. If an individual is in three different groups, every four weeks he or she may sit down with three different team leaders in preparing these reports. Hence, the team member benefits by getting guidance from more than one person.

If you think that isn't a tremendous aspect of the system, consider what it is like to work in a corporation with hardened, formal lines of communication, and the boss turns out to be a royal jerk. You end up with employees who are frustrated, less than loyal, and prone to turn over more quickly. Under our system, if you are looking to improve yourself or are struggling in some area, you always have the opportunity to work with a team leader who is strong in the areas where you want to be strong.

ROAD TRIP

Suppose a particular commissary is having trouble in one area, let's say pizza sauce. We assemble a group from headquarters to visit the commissary and scrutinize the problem. We arm such travelers with camcorders and tape recorders to document their findings.

At headquarters, we assemble a group to examine the situation, review the film, and listen to the tapes. This group takes a wide-angle view of the commissary's operations, focusing on much more than the immediate problem. They also look at what is going right, who is doing a good job, and other potential challenges that may be forthcoming.

Under this system, home office, more than ever, is visibly in tune with what is going on in the commissaries—not that home office steps on the toes of the regional managers. Rather, home office is an additional resource for the commissaries.

As home office groups are assembled to focus on particular commissary issues, and as solutions are developed, we also make sure all other commissaries are kept informed. Too often in the past, a unique or brilliant innovation in one commissary remained there or spread to a few other commissaries. Not anymore.

INITIATING ACTION AT HEADQUARTERS

A group manager of transportation, for example, may identify an issue at headquarters as the result of handling requests from the field or examining a regional manager's state of the union reports. Similarly, regional managers may suggest areas where they would like to have formal presentations or more information.

Mike Soignet devised a three-person committee that addresses these concerns. As you might imagine, with creative, concerned people, a list of agenda items could go on for pages and pages. Mike draws on his experience and the counsel of the rest of the Distribution executive team to prioritize their concerns.

TRACKING OUR PROGRESS

We now track the ability of the home office staff to respond to questions from the field. It becomes part of each home office staff person's individual performance objectives. Everyone knows that answering the field calls effectively is a priority and an important component of an individual's bonus.

We also recently instituted another effective monitoring technique. In essence, the "customers" of the home office staff are the people in field operations. By providing a survey form to the field staff to rate the effectiveness of the home office staff in responding to needs, the entire organization is strengthened: The home office staff members get regular, valuable feedback regarding their performance. The field staff members get to play a major role in the type of services they receive and also have a regular and appropriate outlet for their concerns.

The problem of more paperwork or more forms doesn't come up— the field staff looks forward to the opportunity to compliment or blast the home office staff, whichever the case may be.

Each period, we present a "North Star Award" ("north" as in Ann Arbor, Michigan) to the home office staff person voted most helpful by the field office staff. It's a most distinguished honor and one that's not easy to win twice. Team member Carol Frey has won the award four times, which means she is providing an extraordinary level of responsiveness to the field staff. We've explored having the field staff vote on whether or not the home office people receive raises. It's a way to ensure the home office staff members perform up to the expectations of their team leaders *and* the expectations of their customers—the field staff.

CHAPTER CHECKLIST

- Promote from within, especially when it comes to operations.
- Disband all administrative functions that are nice but unnecessary.
- If it's what drives your business, have your field people report in every day.
- Expect resistance whenever you introduce change, and expect to succeed.
- When in doubt, go back and read the mission statement.
- As soon as you can, define the new positions you create, and keep refining roles and responsibilities with the help of your team members.
- Look for ways to give your people less to do, while concentrating on a few important areas.
- Make operations the fulcrum of your activities—administration serves it, not vice versa.

- Constantly look for ways to resolve issues without generating more paper.

- Avoid Ping-Pong problem solving by requesting that all staff give specific dates and times as to when questions will be resolved.

- Have your team members cast an annual ballot to vote on the most helpful fellow worker. Present an award, similar to our "North Star Award," to honor the winner.

Chapter Fourteen
An Olympic Idea

The noted author and psychologist William James once wrote, "I now perceive one immense omission in my *Psychology*—the deepest principle of human nature is the craving to be appreciated." Who are the unsung champions in your organization, division, or department? And how are you going to show your appreciation for their efforts?

When one of your key indicators reveals team member morale is low and people in the commissaries don't believe they're being adequately recognized, you look for a way to balance the situation by making a big, key statement that you do recognize their contributions and hard work. At one time, team member surveys revealed many of them thought they were never recognized for outstanding efforts. We had missed a basic need of one segment of our public, and I was frustrated because it was true: We weren't giving proper recognition to our team members. Instead, we kept honoring a central pool of executives for work their team members had accomplished.

People will not long sustain enthusiasm if the reward for hard work is indifference. Our performance numbers (Step 6) clearly showed that we needed some type of innovative program, a powerful reward system that would greatly increase the incentive of team members to improve performance.

Each year, we now sponsor a Domino's Pizza Distribution olympics. Finding and rewarding outstanding performers is crucial to success—in our company, and in yours. Let's turn to a winter afternoon in January 1985 to see how our olympics evolved and why it's become such a highly anticipated event companywide.

Valeria Russell, our director of commissary product development, gave me a gold medal idea for our annual awards banquet in June, which she was coordinating. She told me that while she was visiting one of our commissaries, a regional manager, Keith Brown, saw team members making dough by hand.

Keith challenged them to make the dough more efficiently. Everyone engaged with surprising fervor in this impromptu mini-competition. As result of this experience, the production team respected Keith more because they could see he was proficient at doughmaking. And Keith gained new respect for the doughmakers because he had a more accurate view of their obstacles.

The Los Angeles Summer Olympics had concluded only months before. Coincidentally, Distribution had already chosen greater Los Angeles as the site of its awards banquet—the Queen Mary docked in Long Beach, to be precise. Valeria originated the idea of having the executives compete with team members in a mock "olympics." Later, we changed the concept to competitions between team members in their job categories.

I had been struggling to find a way for the executive team to honor outstanding team members. I had known for a while that many people in the field had doubts about whether Distribution represented the best place they could be working. Valeria's idea of staging an olympics for our company intrigued me. I had long dreamed of becoming an athlete, earning a six-figure income, seeing my name in the newspapers, and having people approach me for an autograph. Obviously, my career took a different route.

As president of the division, however, I was making a good income, and my name was appearing in magazines and books. Occasionally, people throughout the company and from other companies asked me for my autograph. I was getting the credit, however, for the efforts of many people who worked hard to keep the company flourishing. My dream remained. It emerged in a new context with the opportunity for other people to participate. These were unsung heros with little chance of being in the limelight.

Simultaneously, my leadership style was ready for a healthy change. I'd been a good problem solver and could turn around a tough situation. I could rally the troops and kick some derrieres when needed. My weakness as a leader had been the inability to offer appropriate, positive feedback when merited.

The olympics could be a good vehicle for recognizing and rewarding jobs well done. As I further explored the idea, it became clear this was the type of big, positive statement our team members deserved and I had longed to make.

THE UNRECOGNIZED CHAMPIONS AMONG US

We decided to hold the awards banquet at the olympics. From this decision, a skyful of opportunities opened up. Who was the most skilled truck driver in the company? Who was the best doughmaker? Here was the chance to identify and reward these individuals and share their knowledge and techniques with others throughout the company.

For the past year, our truckers had maintained a record of 99.97 percent on time delivery—*only three in 10,000 deliveries were late.* In their book, *In Search of Excellence,* Peters and Waterman lionized Frito Lay^{TM} for an on-time percentage that didn't come close to ours. Besides a superlative on-time record, our truck drivers earned the U.S. Department of Transportation's highest possible safety rating. It followed that if we had outstanding truck drivers, our best truck driver was certainly among the best truck drivers in the nation.

If our best driver was among the best in the United States, why didn't I know who he or she was? What kind of company would let that kind of talent go unrecognized year after year? Hereafter, it certainly would not be us. What does the leading home-run hitter in baseball get? A $3.5 million salary, standing ovations, press coverage, adulation, commercial endorsements, you name it.

What does the best truck driver get? Nothing extraordinary. My vision was to have team members compete against each other and be judged on their performance and to give the winners a cash prize, rewards, applause, coverage in their local newspaper and in our company publications. For their stay with our company, we would give them the recognition and respect of a champion.

My executive staff was not enthusiastic about the idea of sponsoring our own olympics. Leading up to the big event, I feared the whole venture would be a costly flop. Nevertheless, we continued with our efforts to stage the first Distribution olympics.

We created starting blocks and sprint lanes on the floor of the Queen Mary. We installed rubber mats, washtubs, and all the other components of a real life commissary. Contestants would compete in a setting similar to what they faced daily on the job. In all, we would honor champions in 15 job classifications.

A MEMORABLE FIRST

The ceremonies began with the lighting of a torch, the blaring of trumpets, and an opening procession that sent chills up my spine. Tom Monaghan was flanked by Steve Fraser, the 1984 Olympic gold medal winner in Greco-Roman wrestling.

Teams carrying identifying banners followed. As competitors stepped into the transformed arena, astonishingly, the crowd offered a spontaneous standing ovation that did not subside for 20 *minutes*. No one would sit down. The pomp and circumstance was unprecedented.

Tray washing and scraping was one of the early events and proved to be memorable. Tray washing is a miserable job. Team members physically scrape hard-crusted dough from large trays and, using steaming hot water, exert considerable effort to get the trays clean. During the competition, the contestants got soaked from head to toe.

Contestants lined up at starting blocks and when the starter pistol was fired, raced toward sinks filled with stacks of trays with crusted dough. In a controlled frenzy, competitors battled for the right to be called the fastest dough scraper and tray washer in the company. For some, it was their first opportunity to gain recognition for being the champion at something.

In the stands, normally reserved executives, team leaders, and team members chanted, "Go, go, go" in support of their favorites. All attention was firmly fixed on the "playing field." We had no idea that this kind of spirit and enthusiasm would be released. From the opening procession, the olympics easily outstripped expectation. Whether you were competing, or simply rooting, this was a life event not to be missed.

HEARTFELT EMOTION

I sat in the stands feeling ecstatic. In minutes, the olympics had taken on a life of its own and had exceeded my vision. The camaraderie among the competitors was heartwarming. Participants would say to each other, "Good job! You beat me, but I'll be back next year!" Individuals who had never met hugged and parted with a rare bond.

Each event's first-place winner received $4,000, a gold medal, and a jacket. Second- and third-place winners received silver and bronze medals, respectively.

We hadn't planned it, but before the first check was dispensed, Gary Josefczyk, who managed our equipment division, requested that the top winners take the microphone and say a few words. What followed were some of the most heartfelt, unrehearsed expressions of human emotion I have ever had the privilege to hear. One winner said, "I want to thank the Lord. I want to thank my family. This is the greatest company in the world to work for."

Team member Chris Allen, a double winner, earned prize money of $8,000. On top of his salary of $14,000, it was like getting a 57 percent bonus! Chris got up and said, "If you want to win this, you've got to do what I did. For days and days before this, I timed myself every day." With that kind of dedication, it's no wonder our productivity improvements have skyrocketed.

As I watched the events, tears filled my eyes. I realized I was no longer in control of all aspects of the company—for the good of everyone—and from this day on we were going to be more successful than we had imagined. I had helped to formulate an idea, but other people took it and ran with it. They made it *live* as no executive staff committee could. This was one of the greatest displays of Super Vision in our history: our team made it happen and my role as SuperVisor was to come out to celebrate exceptional performance.

SPOTLIGHTS AND DRUM ROLLS

At the awards ceremony that night, Valeria Russell had arranged for actors to dress up as Marine honor guards. With crossed swords, they formed the entrance way under which the champions entered the arena. Each champion wore a banner across his or her chest indicating the type of competition, such as vegetable processing, they had won. Most were accompanied by a spouse.

As each champion emerged from under the crossed swords into the single spotlight in the darkened arena, the announcer would say, "and now your 1985 Domino's Pizza Distribution national champion . . . , in fork lifting, from the Equipment and Supply Division, . . . Tim Barr and his partner, Judy Soth." And Tim and Judy became the center of attention to throngs of cheering people—some weeping—who rose to offer a standing ovation. As each winner made his or her way into the arena, the uproar continued. Many champions also got teary-eyed. For many, it was an indelible moment.

SUDDENLY, A TRADITION

In 1986, Steve Fraser, the gold medalist in the 1984 Olympics, joined our company. Steve and Valeria both became heavily involved in helping plan and organize the competitions that year. They restructured events, fine-tuned award criteria, and placed greater emphasis on teamwork and rewards. They coordinated the introduction of warehousing, production, and office skills to the olympic competitions.

That year, we introduced a written test as part of the competitions, which checked everyone's company knowledge and specific job skills. Chris Seufert, a bronze medalist in the women's three-meter springboard diving event at the 1984 Olympics in Los Angeles, joined us as an administrative assistant.

The olympics and annual awards banquet took place at the Fairlane Manor in Dearborn. As each event concluded, the first-, second-, and third-place winners got up on the winners' stands and received a gold, silver, or bronze medal, a ring, and a jacket. Once again, the gold medal winner also received a check for $4,000. Yvonne Silvey, a receptionist from our Georgia Commissary, won the gold in Office Services; she repeated in 1987 to become our first two-year champ!

At the banquet, I met the father of one gold medalist, Jeff Parker. Jeff's father had taken off work for the afternoon to come see his son compete. He told me that all Jeff talks about is his job at Distribution and how much he loves it and he thanked me for running the company that gave his son so much pride. Chills ran down my spine. Tributes like that are among the most priceless bonuses I can ever get.

For the awards banquet, we invited Tom Peters, who lavishly praised Distribution for innovative methods of doing business and for investing in its people.

Later that summer, individually, the first-place winners were flown to headquarters in Ann Arbor. In the evening, we took them by limousine to a Detroit Tigers baseball game and escorted them to the owner's box. Before the game, we escorted them to the playing field and took a photograph of them. They received VIP treatment for the duration of the game and for their stay in Ann Arbor.

Next, we flew the champions to the company lodge on Drummond Island at the top of Michigan. There, they met with me and my executive staff and helped us do high-level problem solving. To win the olympics in our company means more than rewards, prizes, and honors; it gives you the opportunity to talk to the president and state what you think we ought to do. In fact, one of the questions we ask our champions when we invite them to the lodge is: "What would you do in the next 12 months to improve overall operations if you were president of the company?"

A few months later, I attended one of Tom Peters' "Skunk Camps." The session was uncharacteristically dragging, energy was low, and ideas were not flowing. One of the leaders of the Skunk Camp, Reuben Harris, asked me to play a copy of the olympic videotape I had brought. We played the tape and immediately the spirit and enthusiasm in the tape charged up the room.

FROM PROBLEMS TO OPPORTUNITIES

From the start, we invited our customers, the Domino's franchises, to serve as judges at the olympics. Who better to judge doughmaking, vegetable processing, and so forth, than the customer? Our customers love to serve as judges of our performance. So will yours.

Besides the instance when Ron Conkey, the franchisee judge mentioned earlier, helped us recognize the need for a national dough certification process, we've had terrific luck identifying areas where we can become better by having our customers critique our best.

We've launched several programs as a result of what we had learned through our local and national competitions. Hence, the competitions doubled as an element of R&D. Where else could you get such immediate, visible, high-level input as to how your most skilled performers did their jobs and could do them better? In one competition, the national champion for vegetable processing, Kathy Christiansen, didn't slice her vegetables according to our specifications. Nevertheless, her method was so superior to ours that we changed our specifications for vegetable slicing, worldwide.

MORE REFINEMENTS

We held our 1987 olympics in Ann Arbor, Michigan, at Domino's new world headquarters. As planned, we added several awards and incentives in doughmaking. The gold medalist that year in the dough production competition earned a one-time-only prize of $6,000 in

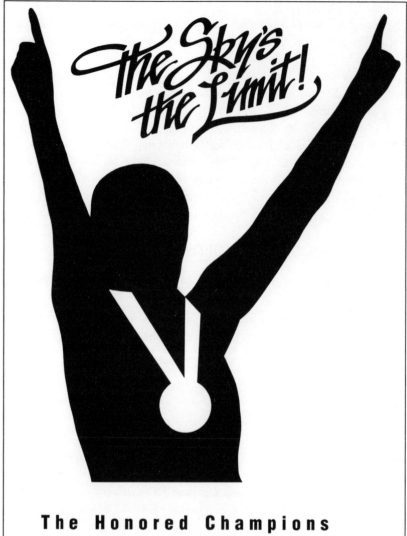

The Honored Champions
International Distribution Olympics

The Honored Champions   DOUGH PRODUCTION

Evaluates knowledge of dough production including procedures, placement, weights, bake evaluations, and teamwork.

Ed Kester and Jeff Schuman   Gordon Region: DNC Cross/MN

In his first year with Distribution, Ed is a sanitation supervisor on the Cross team. Hoping to be a team leader in 5 years, he says, "It is enjoyable to work with good people and with a very good company."

Also new to Distribution, Jeff is a Customer Service Representative/Trainee Commissary Field Representative. About the company he says, "It is the best in the world."

Tina Osborne and John Reese   Soignet Region: DNC Stansell/TN

Tina's goal is to make the best dough possible—touchdown dough! Success secret? The dough certification program and teamwork. About Distribution, she says, "I like the family atmosphere and the company pride."
John enjoys Distribution because "it allows a team member a voice in what happens, it creates a challenge through the Olympic process, and the people are great." A returning champ, John won the "gold" in 1986 and 1987.

Jimmy Frost and Ray Hutley   Team West: DNC Bresnahan/WA

Originally attracted to his job on the production team by a friend, Jimmy still finds it "a lot of fun." His success secrets: "Hard work and trying to learn everything possible about Distribution."

Ray first heard "many good things about Domino's Pizza" from a friend. Ray loves his job and hopes to become a commissary leader in 5 years. He is "happy to be part of a unique company."

Alan Collard and Mohammad Mohammad   Master Dough Center: Moran/MI

Alan was attracted to "Domino's Farms by its good reputation for treating people well." He feels Distribution offers great opportunities and says, "the rewards can be endless." His goal is to be in a leadership role in 5 years.
Mohammad, with Distribution for 6 years, enjoys working with his team and wants to be "the best I can be on my job." His goal is to be a leader and teach fellow team members how to do the job by following the company mission.

Charles Bargas and George Slaikeu, Jr.   International: DPD Vallero/HI and DPD Young/AK

Charles is production team leader and has been with Distribution for 6 years. Crediting his success to hard work, Charles says, "It's a great job. I look forward to going to work, and I like the company."

George thinks Distribution is the greatest company in the world. Hoping to be a commissary leader in 5 years, he says his current success is due to " dedication, watching, listening, and learning."

The Honored Champions   **TEAM LEADER**

Evaluates knowledge of company goals, policies, procedures, and philosophies. Also evaluated is the ability to address team member concerns about a store closing.

Marc Prud'homme
Gordon Region: DNC Cross/MN

Marc is also competing in the Controller event.

Mark Cahill
Soignet Region: DNC Peebles/LA

As production team leader, Mark says his secrets to success are "having an inner drive and providing leadership to my group." He feels Distribution is a company that allows him personal growth. "Good People + Fun = A Good Job!", says Mark.

Linda Schow
Team West: DNC Hendrix/CO

Linda has been with the Hendrix team since 1981 and is currently a team leader in production. After spearheading the campaign to develop the JP&R/IPO manual, she also did some of the writing of it and is now a master trainer. Her secret to success? "Persistence!" Linda is the reigning champion.

Tim Barr
Materne Division (E&S)

Currently sales manager of the Emporium, Tim has been with Distribution for 4 years. He was originally attracted to the company by its philosophy that people are its #1 resource. About success Tim says, "Don't promise more than you can do and do what you promise to do." Tim won the "gold" in 1985 in the Forklift event.

Evaluates knowledge of procedures, cleanliness of the trays, and the quantity of trays washed within a specified time that are acceptable for dough production use.

Cynthia Braxton
Gordon Region: DNC Kirchner/Maryland

Now completing her first year with Distribution, Cynthia believes it to be "the best company to work for and to grow with." She says that her secret to success is to work hard and to show the company how valuable she can be.

Pamela Richardson
Gordon Region: DNC Kirchner/Maryland

Pamela was attracted to Distribution by its reputation, the benefits package, and the fact that everyone works together. She says, "I find Distribution very exciting. It keeps me motivated. I love it — the people are fun and caring."

Gordon Region Finalist to be selected in a run-off prior to Events Day.

Art Cabrera
Soignet Region: DNC Lucas/FL

Art was attracted to Distribution because he heard about the family atmosphere. A gold medal champ for the Soignet Region in 1987, he attributes his success to hard work and always trying to learn more about the workings of the company. His goal is to be one of the best team members in the company.

Juan Macias
Team West: DNC Bahnemann/WTX

Currently production team leader at DNC Bahnemann/WTX, Juan started out 4 years ago in Delivery and Service. He says that he loves working at Distribution, and he exhibits it with hard work and care, with which he attributes his success.

cash, the gold medal, plus a watch, jacket, and ring, for total winnings of $7,500.

At the company lodge that summer, one of our champions, a young woman named Bev LaVasseur, was so jittery she could hardly talk to me. I sat down next to her in the lunchroom in the lodge. "Bev," I asked, "what do you think of the lodge here?"

"Mr. Vlcek," she said, "I can hardly speak—I'm so nervous sitting next to the president." So I said, "But Bev, you're an olympic champion. You can talk to me any time and please call me 'Don,' my dad's not here."

I thought she was going to run out of the lunchroom, but somehow she held together. Now, whenever I see her, she runs up to me and gives me a hug and a kiss. We talk over old times and more importantly, what we're facing today.

Some years, particularly if our people are working too fast and quality is beginning to suffer, we deemphasize speed and overaccent quality in the Olympics. In 1987, when dough was a big issue and complaints were on the rise, we gave it more attention. We made dough part of everyone's test, including the controllers who had to determine if the right mix of ingredients was being ordered. We even asked controllers, "What did you do during last year to improve dough?"

We also created a "master dough maker" award, which included stringent criteria. Qualifying required working 10,000 hours (roughly five work years) as doughmaker. A potential master dough maker also had to maintain a high customer-satisfaction rating, demonstrate success at their craft, and obtain the recommendation of a regional manager, among other measures.

Master dough maker award winners retroactively received a bonus of $1 for each of their 10,000 hours—$10,000. We announce one or two new masters each year at the olympics, a high point in the careers of individuals like Randy Miller of our Southern California Commissary.

DOESN'T HAVE TO BE COSTLY OR DRAINING

In case you think staging your own internal competitions will be too costly or too much to arrange, consider this: there are many ways to quickly and easily identify and reward your company's champions. You can hold modest competitions on a local basis. Simply schedule them and make sure in advance that you'll have some eager contestants in each category. As to the categories, you name them.

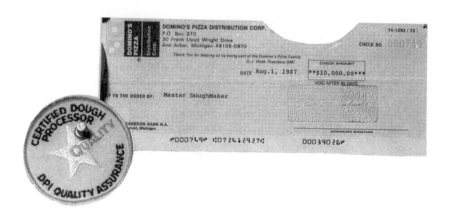

What are the crucial skills in your business? Addressing envelopes, unloading office supplies, slicing pickles, handling customer complaints, wiring circuit boards? A simple competition can be devised for nearly every skill vital to your operations.

After a third-shift line SuperVisor at Navistar International heard one of our executives describe our olympics, she decided to launch some competitions on her own. She established third-shift contests on an engine assembly line that were both challenging and fun.

One category was for "burnishing engine blocks per hour." The individual able to complete a given set of tasks most efficiently was the winner. The entire third-shift crew enjoyed the competition, and morale shot up—all for the grand prize of a chocolate bar.

Another company initiated a "two stall-time" competition to determine who could clean two bathroom stalls the fastest. This competition, for an otherwise thankless task, ignited a healthy motivation and drive on the part of employees. The winners simply received an extra break period.

After competitions, awards can be presented at monthly meetings, annual retreats, the company picnic, Christmas, founder's day. Within any company, there are many opportunities throughout the year to recognize top performers.

You could announce the winners in your newsletter or use any other effective communications vehicle, and you don't have to spend a fortune. In fact, you don't have to have much money, merely the resolve to recognize and reward your champions.

The First National Bank of Chicago devised its own "service olympics" in 1988 after seeing a tape about our program and hearing about it from the Tom Peters Group. To standardize the level of service from its 50 branch locations, the bank set up a contest where each receptionist at each location, randomly and unannounced, received three separate telephone questions:

"How do I get a debit card?"

"Why is there a fee when I use your ATM machine?"

"I have an IRA to roll over from another bank, what do I do?"

The branches know that within a six-week period, these kinds of questions will be posed over the phone by company employees who serve as judges. Participants are judged on such factors as their tone of voice, friendliness, accuracy of the answers they provide, or, in the case of the IRA question, if they promptly transfer the caller to the correct department on the first try. They are also rated as to whether the caller had a pleasant experience; that is, did the receptionist say "thank you" and offer more information?

First National offers awards at the branch, team, and individual level. Each manager is informed of where his or her group stands relative to the rest of the branches. At the end of the six-week period, those obtaining low scores get the opportunity to improve through the use of company resources.

Linda Cooper, the vice president and manager of consumer affairs, says the competition has been terrific, resulting in a high level of customer service. Moreover, the company spends little to maintain the program—the first-place individual winner receives a deluxe weekend for two at a Marriott, about a $600 value. Second place is dinner, a $150 value, and third place is brunch.

The winning branch gets $500; second place, $250; and third, $125. Usually the branch manager uses the money to throw a party for the staff.

THE MAJORITY OF OUR TEAM MEMBERS COMPETE

By the time we held our 1988 competitions, we were hosting many repeat regional and national winners. Competing and making the finals had become a companywide goal. Even the international regions geared up to compete.

At the local level, each commissary was free to choose its own representatives to the nationals. Local-level participants might be selected because of their spirit, job performance and review, performance in local competition, or through recommendation of area team leaders who spotted talent.

Of 1,600 total employees, up to 1,000 annually were engaging in at least one competition.

We held competitions in all aspects of operations, not only those involving manipulation of products and utensils. Our accountants competed by reviewing income statements and invoices to spot errors. Their task was to find quickly what was out of line and then respond to a panel of judges who would ask, "What steps should you take to resolve this?" The overall score encompassed both speed and quality.

Team leaders competed by demonstrating leadership and coaching skills, conducting a job planning and review session, or helping set individual performance objectives. A team member would role-play as someone who had turned in a "crisis" performance.

Through this event, we discovered that most team leaders were not completing job planning and review forms properly, so we immediately streamlined and simplified them. We also started a mandatory job planning and review certification program for all leaders compa-

Tentative Agenda
(Subject to change, please check in at Welcome Desk for latest agenda)

Attire: Written Tests/Events/Oral Presentations/Opening Ceremonies:
Uniform/Business for competitors; casual for non-competitors
Awards Day: Business
All other times: Casual

Friday, May 18

5:00 pm	Competitors Meeting	Marriott Hotel
6:00 pm	Judges Meeting	Marriott Hotel
7:00 pm	Dinner	Marriott Hotel
8:30 pm	Opening Ceremonies	Marriott Hotel

Saturday, May 19

6:00 am	Breakfast	Marriott Hotel
8:00 am	Written Tests	EBA Club/Fitness Center, Domino's Farms
9:30 am	Events Begin	Domino's Farms
12 noon	Lunch	Domino's Farms
6:00 pm	Dinner	Marriott Hotel
8:00 pm	Oral Presentations	Marriott Hotel

Sunday, May 20

7:00 am	Breakfast	Marriott Hotel
9:00 am	Events	Marriott Hotel
6:30 pm	Dinner	Marriott Hotel
8:00 pm	Auction/Fun Night	Marriott Hotel

Monday, May 21

6:30 am	Breakfast	Marriott Hotel
9:00 am	Awards Ceremony	Laurel Manor, 39000 Schoolcraft, Livonia, MI
3:30 pm	Closing Ceremonies	Laurel Manor, 39000 Schoolcraft, Livonia, MI

To make your air travel arrangements and your hotel arrangements, call your Region Coordinator.

Region	Region Coordinator
Burgerhoudt	Madeline Shear
Graf	Mike Brown
Lenzi	Tim Barr
Macksood	Shawn McKay
Materne Division	Dianne Anderson
McPherson	Roxanne Hall
Range	Judy Freeland
Whitacre	Peggy Powers
All Others	Carol Weaver

nywide headed by that year's team leader event champion, Linda Schow.

LET THE WORD GO FORTH

One of the many payoffs of the olympics is that the message we want to impart spreads rapidly through the entire company. Take receiving, a key area for us. Those with responsibility for receiving have to check the accuracy of invoices, the quality of goods, or temperature standards. If any of the above are awry, you can have major problems. Naturally, we devised a receiving competition.

Our people would never smoke in a commissary or at a loading dock. However, drivers from our suppliers often smoked. On the Queen Mary, we had rolled in a truck, a pallet jack, packages, and invoices. The truck driver/supplier was a cigarette-smoking role player who acted the part for each contestant.

Among many other responsibilities, our receivers were to point out that smoking was *verboten*. Yet, no one in the competition noticed it. Curiously, when viewing the next competitor, each previous competitor easily spotted that the supplier's cigarette was out of place. The judges made it a big deal when they reviewed scores with the contestants, who learned an enduring lesson.

Our Olympic Categories

Accounting
Controller
Customer service representative
Delivery & service
Dough production

Driving
Loading
Maintenance
Office services
Partners competition

Purchasing/inventory control
Receiving
Tray washing
Team leader
Vegetable processing

In the weeks and months that followed, the problem of cigarettes in the commissaries virtually disappeared. We have never had a problem with tobacco in the commissaries again. What happens at the olympics is big news throughout the organization. Our people care about doing the job right. When it comes to being more effective, any tidbit of information that they can pass to someone else gets passed quickly.

THE POWER OF BROADCASTING

To give our champions the same recognition as sports superstars, we broadcast our awards ceremony live via our satellite network (page 257). Imagine the excitement "back home" as people see their fellow team members awarded the gold medal on a live broadcast from a thousand miles away! Or, in the case of our commissary in Germany, half way around the world! Parents of competitors have even driven to our Florida Commissary to watch the ceremony.

All national competitions are also both recorded on video tape and described in writing. These items become part of the company's archives for team members to review. What we learned in the 1991 Olympics is already impacting more hundreds of team members across the United States and in 23 countries. Each function is examined, dissected, trisected, and improved on a continuing basis. No single aspect of operations is left untouched—if there is a better way to do something this system will uncover it. Similarly, every job and every task is viewed as critical to the overall success of the company.

THE CHALLENGES OF GROWTH

As with many companies that experience strong growth, we faced a period when we had employee educational and training problems. That was the year we gave participants a written test on what we believed was most important for them to know. Amazingly, all contestants scored well.

Afterward, I learned that the head of our olympic committee, Carol Weaver, had circulated the questions *and answers* before the competition. I hit the roof: "What the hell are you doing? How are we going to determine the champ when you pass out the questions and answers beforehand?"

Carol asked me if the purpose of the olympics was to find a few outstanding performers or to educate team members and, by doing so, have everyone perform better? I backed off immediately: "Excuse me—good move."

Now, each January we determine and then ANNOUNCE priorities. Alert team members recognize that these priorities heavily influence what will be emphasized at the summer olympics. Those who understand that company priorities are directly linked to the rewards system buckle down and work on those priorities.

FINDING THE HOT BUTTON

One year we had a 40-year-old fellow from North Carolina, Wade Burt, who won the silver medal in the receiving competition. His brother, Charles Burt, won the gold medal in truck driving. Amazingly, Wade could not read. He openly expressed that the only reason he didn't win the gold was because he couldn't read. After the competition, he enrolled in a reading course.

His experience in the olympics propelled him to learn a life skill that he had put off for so long.

We announced that next year's receiving competition would include a written test. The students in Wade's reading class obtained the questions and answers. The teacher and everyone else worked with him, endlessly, so he could become more competitive and vie for the gold medal.

Why don't stories like this happen in American business? Too often, they don't because those in positions of power don't stretch themselves to find solutions to help people get beyond self-imposed barriers. As executives, leaders, and managers, we are charged with responsibility for finding the hot button that turns on our employees and interests them at their level of excitement.

WORTH THE PRICE TAG?

Among our champions who reached the finals since 1985, there has been an 80 percent retention rate and a 60 percent promotion rate. Is the time and effort worth it? On video, reflecting on the first olympics and those following it, Tom Monaghan said it has been the most effective leadership tool he has encountered in his entire career, and Tom never makes such statements lightly.

Our olympics has become a continuing forum for team members to demonstrate that they know a better way to perform their jobs, or to demonstrate their belief they're the best at what they do. Not enough companies offer high-level recognition to their champions. Some organizations actually employ the best performers in their particular fields. Unfortunately, the higher-ups have no clue as to who these individuals are and understandably will learn little from them, if anything.

So, who are the unsung champions in your organization, division, or department; and how are you going to show your appreciation for their efforts?

CHAPTER CHECKLIST

- If morale is low in your company, consider that it may be a result of not offering adequate recognition to the job your team members are doing.

- Constantly seek ways to identify the unsung champions in your organization, division, or department; then find innovative measures to show your appreciation for their efforts.

- Consider hereafter that finding and rewarding outstanding performers is crucial to success in your company.

- For whatever competitions you devise, actively recruit your customers or suppliers to serve as judges.

- Throughout the year, induce branch offices, departments, or divisions to engage in friendly competitions.

- Learn all you can from your champions. Videotape them and/or interview them to glean the essence of why they are more effective or productive than others.

- Share these insights with others throughout your company. Set up an archives or resource center where anyone can review or take materials on loan.

- Be prepared to change company procedures as your champions demonstrate better techniques to accomplish tasks.

- Use the employee competitions to help meet the new challenges you face in your business. For example, if your shipments are not being packed securely enough and

customers are complaining, initiate a competition in secure
packaging.

• Use monthly meetings, annual retreats, the company picnic,
Christmas, founder's day, or any special occasion to make
awards. Or simply create an awards day.

• Set up a reward system that honors the champions several
ways—through prizes, an awards ceremony, mention in your
newsletter, via a special plaque in the reception area or a
memo on the bulletin board. Do whatever you can afford and
you feel comfortable doing.

• For long-term achievement, analogous to our "master dough
maker" award, look for areas in which you can award a
certificate, a badge, or some sort of special designation.
Money need not be involved, but it helps.

• Continue to add new events as your business changes. If you
install a new technology, make mastery of that one of the
competitions.

• Don't be afraid to involve executive-level staff in
competition—they can benefit from the challenge and the
whole company will get a kick out of it as well.

• Consider circulating "answers" in advance of competitions.
Remember—the goal is recognizing achievement and
improving performance, not simply handing out rewards.

• Continue to probe for the hot button that turns on your
employees and interests them at their level of excitement.

Chapter Fifteen

Team Member
Workbench

Our team members, from olympic champions to new hires, have a right to know all information and activities that affect them and their company. It is a simple but a powerful concept: trust your people to the maximum, give them the opportunity to air their views, and never have it any other way.

Another reinforcement tool of olympian proportions is what we call Team Member Workbench. I've tantalized you with the concept in several chapters. In a sentence, Workbench is an innovative, multimedia computer system designed to encourage our team members to communicate their ideas and to share solutions quickly and easily.

Looking back it seems almost like the age of dinosaurs, but about five years ago we didn't have a single personal computer at corporate headquarters, let alone the commissaries. Nevertheless, our commitment to efficiently sharing the results of the summer survey, our national performance objectives, and individual commissary performance led us to a bold experiment.

For two months, at our Minnesota and northern California commissaries, we tested an information and communications system that would put screenfuls of information about Distribution at the fingertips of everyone in the organization. As with all innovations, there were detractors. Some of our own people called the Workbench the "bleeding edge" of technology.

233

AN ELECTRONIC MISSION

Our objectives were straightforward: to communicate business information faster in both directions (from home office to the field and back), hasten the decision-making process, and improve education and training. We wanted to put into the hands of our team members all business data traditionally held by top executives and managers.

In short, our goal was to provide an electronically democratic workplace by turning the traditional communicating process upside down. Instead of information flowing up to a few executives at the top of the management pyramid and decisions flowing down, our goal for Workbench was to create an open channel to allow information and ideas to flow to and from any point in the company.

Once the system was successfully tested at the two commissaries, our intracompany task force began implementing the system on a nationwide basis. The accompanying chart briefly summarizes the technical details of the information flow. I will briefly describe how the system works, followed by user applications templates.

From our headquarters, we worked closely with Apple Computer and General Electric Information Services in developing this system. It is now fully implemented and on line at all 32 of our commissaries. Each commissary is equipped with one megabyte of main memory, special application software, and necessary interfaces—a hard disk, modem, and mouse.

**Domino's Distribution
Centers - Worldwide.**

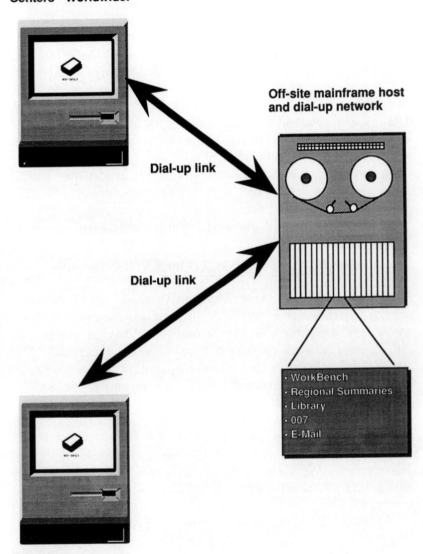

**Off-site mainframe host
and dial-up network**

Dial-up link

Dial-up link

- WorkBench
- Regional Summaries
- Library
- 007
- E-Mail

**Domino's
Headquarters**

Each operating unit can operate as a stand-alone system or can communicate via electronic mail with our home office. Any user at the commissary can both input and access local information. The system relies primarily on a point and click operation as much as possible. Most of our team members can master the basics in 15 to 20 minutes. In 60 minutes or less, one can almost be called an experienced user.

Our commissaries and distribution headquarters in Ann Arbor are all linked via a wide-area computer network. All Workbench-related data, regional summaries, libraries, 007 reports, and so on are logged in and stored, for easy retrieval. There are no special access codes or passwords only for executives.

Individual user sites, including several within headquarters and all commissaries, are equipped with personal computers and laser printers. At headquarters, we are linked through a local-area network and rely on a commercial computer bulletin board for daily interface.

AN IMMEDIATE BOOST TO OPERATIONS

As alluded to previously, Team Member Workbench greatly facilitates our 007 reporting system. While our five regional managers, each responsible for a portion of the U.S. commissaries, have no offices, they still have to phone in their reports from the field each evening. At 6 A.M. the following day, all regional managers' reports are collected from their voice mail boxes and logged into our computer system.

An operations manager routes the reports and requests to the appropriate support departments. All requests from the regional managers, and follow-up responses, are easily retrievable by any other regional manager, commissary manager, or team member. From any location, one can use the Workbench library to find out if a current problem has already been solved. This eliminates huge amounts of time spent reinventing the wheel.

The list of other applications and resources that Workbench offers is lengthy. Here are some of our most interesting ones:

- On-screen road map to guide you through the information needed.

- Company basics, general information about benefits, policy, and history.

- Company goals and priorities.

- Key performance indicators on visual and commissary performance.

- A library of video and audio and text that is used to create, illustrate, and animate training manuals and other communications.

- A computerized version of our annual report that uses animation and sound.

- Financial performance data about all company units updated, in many cases, on a daily basis.

- An electronic company newspaper with general and company news, job opportunities, and classified ads.

- Templates of forms for reports and financial data.

- Training and accounting manuals.

- Background on team leaders in the company presented in baseball card format and complete with photos.

- Address book of teams and leaders throughout the company.

- State of the company updates.

- Connection to outside databases.

If you are traveling from the home office to a commissary or from one commissary to another with the click of the mouse, a map and directions appear on your screen to help you in your journey (page 238).

If you are simply interested in knowing who the commissary leaders are, again, by clicking the mouse, you get the baseball card-version commissary leader complete with a picture (page 238).

Just like with your favorite baseball cards, you can find the team member's vital "stats" on the flip side, including when he or she was "acquired," the commissary's ranking, sales, and total operating expenses. It's both a fun and efficient way for us to keep score and to recognize the hitters in our company.

A WALK THROUGH THE SYSTEM

Pretend you are sitting at one of our Workbench stations, which is nothing more than your average PC. First thing you do is turn on your PC and get a screen that says "Selections," as on page 239.

Maps and Directions

The information in this section of the Workbench is current as of 9.7.90. Check the Change Revisions Library for any updates.

Legend

Burgerhoudt Region	◇
Macksood Region	■
Graf Region	◆
Lenzi Region	✪
MacPherson Region	✦
Range Region	◈
Whitacre Region	●

Click a Location

PRINT   ◄ ▲ ► MAP

Donald J. Vlcek, Jr.
Pres. Dominos Pizza Dist.
Acquired: 09/25/78

Past Positions:

Awards: 1982 Franchisees Person of the Year

Certification: JPR/IPO Cert, Dough Cert, Adizes (2day&Facilitator training), Crosby Quality College, Tom Peters Skunk Camp

Personal Stats: Married, 3 Children.

DET

STATS   PRINT   ◄ ▲ ► MAP

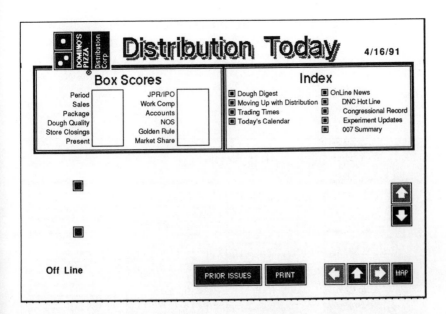

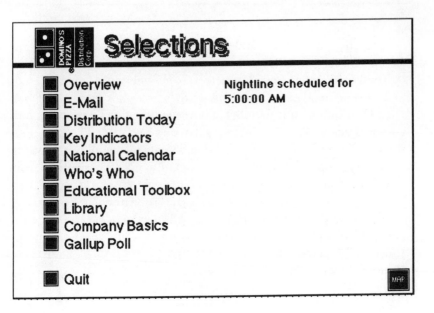

Touch the screen where it says map or click the mouse and you get the next template that says road map. From here, all you have to do is click and pick a subject and you are immediately at the next screen. Whenever you want to break out of where you are and get back, you are always just two clicks away.

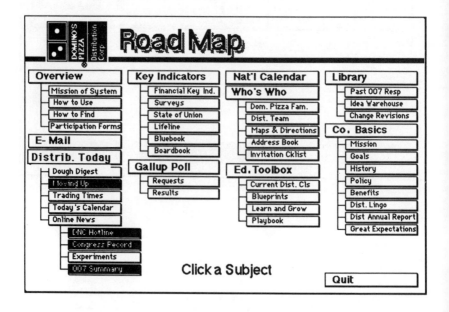

Let's click to overview and then to mission of system, where this screen appears (page 241).

You could decide to go one screen back, one screen forward, back to the overall road map, or to print what you see. It is as simple as that.

At Distribution, any member of our team gets much the same information I get, at the same time. Other files, available to all, include "Dough Digest," which offers information about one of our most important ingredients; "Moving Up," which includes information about promotions and changes within the company; "On Line News," "Trading Times," and "Today's Calendar," shown on page 241.

At any time you can go back to "road map" and make new selections. If you want to dip into "Key Indicators," you have your choice of "Surveys," "State of the Union," "Lifeline" (10-year financial history), "Bluebook" (current financial highlights), and "NPOs," shown on page 242.

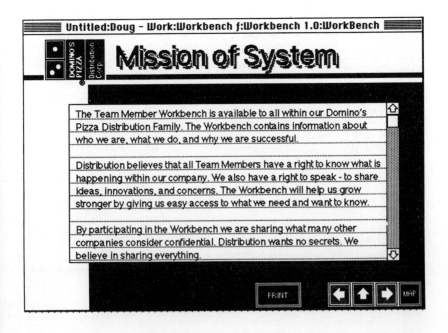

Mission of System

The Team Member Workbench is available to all within our Domino's Pizza Distribution Family. The Workbench contains information about who we are, what we do, and why we are successful.

Distribution believes that all Team Members have a right to know what is happening within our company. We also have a right to speak - to share ideas, innovations, and concerns. The Workbench will help us grow stronger by giving us easy access to what we need and want to know.

By participating in the Workbench we are sharing what many other companies consider confidential. Distribution wants no secrets. We believe in sharing everything.

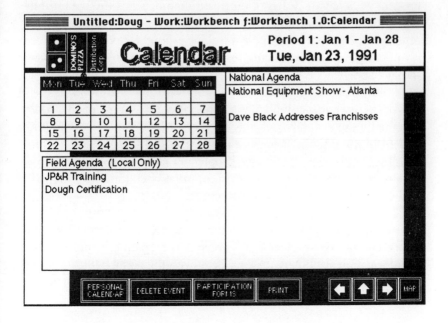

Calendar

Period 1: Jan 1 - Jan 28
Tue, Jan 23, 1991

Mon	Tue	Wed	Thu	Fri	Sat	Sun
1	2	3	4	5	6	7
8	9	10	11	12	13	14
15	16	17	18	19	20	21
22	23	24	25	26	27	28

National Agenda
National Equipment Show - Atlanta

Dave Black Addresses Franchisses

Field Agenda (Local Only)
JP&R Training
Dough Certification

Financial Key Indicators

Lenzi   Period: Week: Year:

	Sales	Actual Gross Profit	Pricing Gross Profit	Labor					
				Admin	Whse	Prod	D&S	Temp	Total
KS	$ 0	0%	0%	0%	0%	0%	0%	0%	0%
NM	$ 0	0%	0%	0%	0%	0%	0%	0%	0%
NTX	$ 0	0%	0%	0%	0%	0%	0%	0%	0%
TX	$ 0	0%	0%	0%	0%	0%	0%	0%	0%
VTX	$ 0	0%	0%	0%	0%	0%	0%	0%	0%
Totals	$ 0	0%	0%	0%	0%	0%	0%	0%	0%

	Projected TOE	NOS	Actual Inv	Past Dues	Lost Time Acc.	Veh. Acc.	Volume Disc.%	Pounds Per Hour
KS	0%	0%	0%	$ 0	0	0	0%	0
NM	0%	0%	0%	$ 0	0	0	0%	0
NTX	0%	0%	0%	$ 0	0	0	0%	0
TX	0%	0%	0%	$ 0	0	0	0%	0
VTX	0%	0%	0%	$ 0	0	0	0%	0
Totals	0%	0%	0%	$ 0	0	0	0%	0

PRINT   ◄ ▲ ►   MAP

AN OUTLET, A FORUM

Workbench provides team members with an outlet for their grievances and frustrations that might otherwise be bottled up and result in non-productive behavior. Each of our team members has the opportunity to register his or her input.

Could the system turn into a dumping ground for people who need to unload whatever is bugging them? I suppose it could. But so far it hasn't happened. We have received negative feedback from time to time, but, that's expected.

We knew when we implemented this system that some people could potentially use it to take potshots at others, but herein lies yet another benefit of the system. It forces each of us to be clear in explanation, direction, and focus. If you give people all the information you had as to why you made a particular decision, more often than not, they will end up agreeing with the road you chose.

An Educational Resource.   Another selection you can make on Workbench is the "Educational Toolbox." This path provides a wealth of information, whether you have been with the company for 15 years or you started yesterday. Numerous subtopics provide team members with instant access to company data.

Think of all the paper and money saved by not having to print 1,000 copies of all this material. Further, as updates are necessary, we change files in the computer rather than print new manuals, another savings. If someone needs to print a particular screen, or whole file, the option is always available. More often, they don't need to, all they need is to be able to refer to it at will.

Our category marked "Library" is where all the past 007 reports, responses, and resolutions are filed, along with "Idea Warehouse," which represents a potpourri of innovative ideas proven successful either at the home office or in the field.

NOT FOR EVERYONE

In addition to fostering a democratic workplace, Workbench also fosters a fish-bowl atmosphere. By that, I mean that everyone's performance is available for everyone else to see with a click of a button—mine, the regional managers, the commissary managers, and many of the team members.

The people who thrive in our system are the people who enjoy being part of this "big game" and regularly monitoring their performance in the context of everyone else's. This is not to say we pit individuals or divisions against each other, but rather we encourage

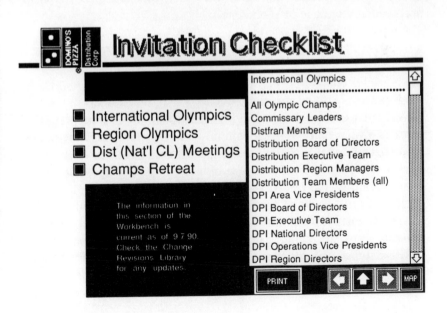

Invitation Checklist

- ◼ International Olympics
- ◼ Region Olympics
- ◼ Dist (Nat'l CL) Meetings
- ◼ Champs Retreat

The information in this section of the Workbench is current as of 9 7 90. Check the Change Revisions Library for any updates.

International Olympics

All Olympic Champs
Commissary Leaders
Distfran Members
Distribution Board of Directors
Distribution Executive Team
Distribution Region Managers
Distribution Team Members (all)
DPI Area Vice Presidents
DPI Board of Directors
DPI Executive Team
DPI National Directors
DPI Operations Vice Presidents
DPI Region Directors

PRINT   MAP

friendly competition that both challenges team members and yields greater corporate performance, much in the same way friendly competition is encouraged in the Distribution olympics.

Yes, we do lose people who like to play their cards close to their chest, but the democratization of corporate information in Workbench supports our mission and every one of our visions. The key is to continue to identify people who thrive under such conditions and to let them have as much freedom as possible.

Keeps All of Us on Our Toes. Workbench and other reinforcement tools force me as president to be open for all questions. But I get paid to face tough situations.

Yes, the up-front costs of designing and implementing Workbench were considerable. Today, we incur only on-line and long-distance charges and the cost of paying people to keep the data fresh. Our company's ability to transfer information rapidly and completely yields extraordinary operating efficiencies. Whatever bottlenecks, frustrations, breakdowns, and miscommunication occur within the company, in combination with the 007 reports, Workbench serves as an automatic, self-correcting mechanism.

We are only in our infancy in both understanding and using the system's capabilities to their fullest. As the microchip becomes more powerful, and information transmission less expensive, we are poised to broaden the scope of Workbench.

PUTTING THE SYSTEM TO WORK FOR YOU

In lieu of a chapter checklist, I'll close with low-cost suggestions for high-powered communications.

Whether you are a multinational corporation or an entrepreneurial firm of five people, you can employ Workbench-type principles in your operation. For example, using local-area networks or modems, divisions or departments, branch offices, or field representatives can easily report in and receive data.

If you are not wired for such transmittal, you can still put your corporate mission, goals, history, policies and benefits, and even your annual report and other intracompany communications on an inexpensive floppy disk and mail them to everyone on an interim basis.

Independent of the size of your budget, you can emulate many of our key selections on Workbench. A library of company problems and their resolutions is valuable to your staff. Similarly, a "who's who" directory, on-line or in hard copy, can help people get to know others in the company a little better.

Open to a New Way of Leading.   If you are concerned that movement toward a democratic workplace in your company will upset your power base, maybe it's time to look at your job and career relationship with your employees in another way.

The more they understand the tough challenges you face and why you are sometimes forced to make unpopular decisions, the greater their respect for you, and often, the less dissension within the ranks. As you become more and more at ease with relinquishing what has traditionally been closely held information, you begin to see there was little reason for it to be closely held in the first place.

As you share more information, you open up the possibility of having a more productive, loyal, and turned-on team than you thought possible. There certainly are risks: Some management people in your company will resist this openly; some employees won't be able to thrive under such a system. For a few, being exposed to such information will confirm their nagging suspicions.

Despite these developments, the benefits of a democratized workplace today are too compelling for you to ignore the issue. We have done it and it works. If we can expand our system, we will.

Chapter Sixteen

Communication
Unlimited

With all of the information available through Workbench, you might think it is enough to simply stop there. The communication aspect of Super Vision, however, is perpetual. We regard the monumental task of maintaining regular, clear, open, ongoing communications with team members as an every day activity.

We believe maintaining our vision for team members—"team members that can't think of a better company to work for"—requires going several additional steps to ensure they continually have the opportunity to have a wide and balanced view of company affairs.

In this chapter, we'll look at three vehicles we've used, the *Pepperoni Press*, WDPD, and the Satellite Network, in the attempt to fill in all the cracks when it comes to maintaining communications with team members.

THE PEPPERONI PRESS

On a weekly basis, we publish national, regional, and local sales figures by division in our company newspaper, *The Pepperoni Press*. The paper is published for all team members within the Dominos Pizza, Inc., family. The *Press* looks a lot like your morning newspaper. It is a

New managers taking over already-opened stores need to follow a checklist to ensure a smooth operational transition. See page 3.

HOTGRAM is here. See page 3 for details.

The Driving Force...............page 5

Sports & Fitness...............page 7

Vol. 653

The Domino's Pizza
Pepperoni PRESS.

A Weekly Look At The World's Largest Pizza Delivery Company

Average Sales
Week Ending 11-26
$9,500

$9,000

$8,000

We are No1

AWARD WINNERS—On the occasion of the recent visit to Japan by Gene Cabe, director of operations-Pacific Basin, and Sam Fine, vice president of Marketing, the Y. Higa Corporation hosted a gathering of its executives, store managers and MITs at the Tokyo American Club. The gathering publicly commemmorated the Higa Corporation receiving the Domino's Pizza Operations Super Eagle Award given by Dave Black for all-around outstanding performance.

Distribution price increases dramatically below consumer index increases

By Laura Johnstone
Distribution

Over the past 11 years, Distribution's prices to pizza stores have increased by only 1.9 percent, while other price and market indexes have all risen substantially higher, including:

* Consumer Price Index — up 89 percent since 1979
* Products Price Index — up 60 percent since 1979
* Pizza Price Index — up 33 percent since 1979 (a guideline set on pizza product raw materials)
* Distribution — up 1.9 percent since 1979

This information was calculated based on what a $10,000/week store paid for food in 1979 compared to what a $10,000/week store pays for food today.

In 1979 a $10,000/week store paid $2,065.46 per week for food, while at the end of 1988 the same store doing

two-color publication with the red and blue Domino's Pizza logo colors used throughout to highlight specific features.

Every issue contains a phone directory, which includes all of the major phone numbers throughout Domino's Pizza, Inc., Distribution, the International Division, and various regional offices. We want people to have this information. While we don't want to be inundated with calls, we want them to be able to reach us if they feel the need.

On the front page, we usually include late-breaking news. If our team members win an award, are cited within their community, or accomplish some unusual feat, it makes the front page. Similarly, if a division turns in a record performance, we will let everybody know.

If one of our commissaries or stores does something extraordinary for the community or suffers a setback due to some natural disaster or outage, that story will find its way into the *Press*.

Information from the summer survey, key indicators to our national performance objectives, and news of bonus payoffs are often presented.

The *Press* offers regular columns, one of which discusses the activities of competitors. Whether it is Pizza Hut, Little Caesar's, or other competitors, we name names, discuss their promotions and new products, and talk about their strategies in specific markets. In short, we inform our people as best we can so they can use that information to compete.

The *Press* also has features on various aspects of management, including break-even analyses, cost containment, security, recruitment, community relations, internal procedures, and other tips and techniques.

We encourage all team members throughout the corporation to contribute to the *Press*; we couldn't have a newspaper with such breadth and scope without wide participation.

Beyond Sunshine and Flowers

When you pick up the in-house organs of other companies, the few features included have obviously been assigned by the publication's editor under the direction of some higher-up. Such "news" isn't news at all. In the attempt to be informative, such publications can backfire and be viewed by employees as corporate propaganda.

As we see it, the only way to produce a weekly or monthly publication that is for, of, and by our team members is to include them every step of the way.

The *Pepperoni Press* is not all sunshine and flowers. We don't skirt controversial issues. Usually we put them on the front page for team members to read and consider. Yes, this is often in contrast to the type of information provided by top executives in other companies. Addressing the tough issues head on, however, and sharing as much information as you have with team members makes good business sense.

If your company is facing a tough challenge, negative press, or anything that will cause staff members to gossip, are you better off giving them your side of the story and including as complete information as you can, or would you rather have the rumor mill dictate impressions and understanding to your staff? For us, there is no question that it's better to level with our team members.

When Tom Monaghan has been confronted by various advocacy groups, we put it on the front page. Similarly, when reporters take potshots at any aspect of the company, parent or Distribution, we usually run a feature story out of the commotion.

You Can't Run and You Can't Hide. A Kentucky-based company's founder and CEO was undergoing treatment for cancer. This CEO and his executive staff decided to throw up a smoke screen for fear that employees as well as investors might panic. For months, all of the company's press releases, corporate memos, and in-house publications were used to mask the gravity of the leader's condition.

In truth, he was dying, and because the message the company disseminated lacked the ring of truth, the long-term damage was enormous. The quiet gossip in the corridors and washrooms speculated as to the state of the founder's health. The financial press picked up on the company vibes and diligently began probing for tidbits of information. Many investors, I'm told, felt extremely uneasy.

Granted, news of the impending death of the founder and CEO of a company is not easily disseminated. But consider the long-term detriment to the company. When employees, investors, and the financial press, added to creditors, suppliers, the entire community, and industry, engage in speculation as to the company's fate, you have to conclude that imparting the truth, as tactfully as possible in a timely manner, would yield a less challenging climate.

By presenting controversial or tough issues on the front page, we often are able to avoid losing considerable hours of team member productivity that would otherwise be devoted to their scrounging for answers. Often, the presence of such a feature on the front page is enough to quell any internal motion.

By leveling with team members on an organizational basis, more often than not, even decisions that were initially regarded as unpopular become widely embraced at all levels.

Suppose an article appears in the *Press* or is transmitted via Workbench explaining why we decided to make a certain decision regarding insurance benefits. By explaining the reasoning behind the decision, including the pros and cons of alternatives that were considered, we are often able to minimize a lot of the grumbling and anxiety that team members might experience were they not "in" on how the decision was reached.

The Innovator

Distribution publishes a special bimonthly magazine called *The Innovator*. Its editor, Laura Johnstone, remarked on its uniqueness: "Unlike many companies, we publish one single magazine that is distributed to our team members, suppliers, customers, community leaders, and parent company. This highlights the fact that we tell the same story to everyone we deal with. There are no mixed messages coming out of Distribution!"

Articles in *The Innovator* include Distribution operational and financial highlights, MVP profiles from around the country, discussions of company priorities, success stories from operations that are exceptional performers, forthcoming product rollouts, and product handling advice. Most articles not only describe successes or practices in place but also discuss their relationship to our company mission and priorities.

Your Employee Publications

The size of your company, how often you publish, or the size of your publication really don't matter. To achieve the same impact as *The Pepperoni Press* or *The Innovator*, the important principle is to have your publication really reflect what is going on in the company—have it be rooted in truth.

There are several ways to stimulate wider participation and coverage without increasing your budget. You could ask your editor to insert a small box on the first or second page that says, "Your contributions to this publication are welcome," with instructions on how to make submissions.

You also could instruct your editor to make wider rounds than usual. Have the editor interview the branch manager in the western part of the state or talk to the people in the loading dock, people who aren't usually heard.

As a rule of thumb, if you print someone's name in your publication, you can look forward to that person reading at least the next six months' issues, after which he or she will want to see his or her name in print again. And that's fine. Being heard or recognized, in any capacity, is an important tool for team member loyalty and long-term retention.

Photos Add Spice.   If you are not running photos in your publication, consider their inclusion. With the advent of optical scanners and desktop publishing, photos can become a regular, low-cost part of your publication.

Include a roster of important company phone numbers, including your own, in every issue. If you are concerned about a flood of calls, fear not. It may actually reduce the number of calls, or at least unnecessary calls.

The fact that you are willing to list your number and the important numbers throughout the company is a sign to your team members that you maintain an open posture and are ready to listen. If you don't want to include your private line, then list the number of your secretary.

Take Your Editor to Lunch

You may not have had regular sessions with your editor until now, but it might make sense to start. In a half-hour, you can direct him or her as to what kind of features you would like to see included in the publication. We are not talking the *New York Times* here—each feature doesn't have to be exciting or titillating.

A well-written column on how your insurance benefits work, an article on an upcoming companywide promotion, or a profile of a new manager will be widely read once your employees gain firm hold of the notion that this publication IS ABOUT THEM.

To balance any added expense for broadening your publication, consider the cost savings you will enjoy as a result of less employee downtime, potentially lower turnover, and the productivity-enhancing ideas that may find their way into print.

Last, consider the value of your time and how much can be saved when you deal squarely with the issues that your team members deserve to read about in your paper.

WELCOME TO STATION WDPD

Since many of our people in the field spend hours on the road, we decided to take advantage of this time to convey useful information in an enjoyable format. Over a two-year period, we produced a monthly cassette for wide distribution throughout Distribution that emulated a radio station format:

> *Welcome to the August edition of WDPD. The weather is starting to heat up and so is WDPD. So find a cool place, put your feet up, and take a listen. Keep those song requests coming in and we'll play them as soon as we can.*

Using our own production studio and imitating all the elements of a radio station, including a disc jockey, weather reporter, and special features, the monthly cassette ran between 35 and 45 minutes on each side.

A typical schedule included 4 to 5 minutes of company news, followed by 5 minutes of music, followed by 10 or 12 minutes where we might feature someone from dough, operations, the Equipment Resource Center, or myself. We would come back in with music for five minutes, followed by "Dr. Benefits" (see below), and close out the first side with an individual performance objectives success story.

Side two of the same cassette would continue with about three to five minutes of Distribution news, followed by music and perhaps a feature on our olympics. We'd then include a three-minute segment on JPR/IPOs, a couple of minutes on the Emporium, and maybe a feature on the Noid, followed by more music.

We kept all the "broadcasts" moving along in a manner that would both amuse and hold the interest of our team members.

Spelling It Out with "Dr. Benefits"

Most companies still employ a thick personnel, policies, and procedure manual that painstakingly describes how employees are to file claims, take vacation days, and receive various benefits. On WDPD, to convey the same type of information, we launched "Dr. Benefits." This was the brainstorm of Keith Deidrich from our company benefits team. Below is a typical script. Think about how this might sound on a "radio" broadcast acted out by a lively cast:

KYLE:

Hi, Nurse, is the Doctor around today? I need some help understanding sick/personal days.

NURSE INCENTIVES:

The Doctor's out today, but what kind of things do you need to know? Maybe I can help.

KYLE:

Well, how many days do I get every year?

NURSE INCENTIVES:

Let's see, you're an hourly team member and have been employed since last year, so you're entitled to five days of paid sick/personal time. If you were a salaried team member, you'd be entitled to seven days.

KYLE:

What if I hadn't started at the beginning of the year and instead started in, say, June?

NURSE INCENTIVES:

In that case, after you'd worked your 90 days, you'd be entitled to a portion of the five days. You'd get two and a half days for sick/personal time between June and the end of the year.

KYLE:

Hey, that's not bad! Does this mean that if I'm not sick this year, I'll be reimbursed for five days?

NURSE INCENTIVES:

No. Distribution's philosophy is that sick/personal days cannot be "cashed in" at the end of the year, and neither can they be carried over to the next year.

If you're sick, stay home, rather than risk coming in to work and infecting your teammates. Some team members might come to work ill if they thought they'd get money for sick days not used at the end of the year.

Other broadcasts of "Dr. Benefits" discussed maternity leave, health insurance, and other such matters.

A Forum for Introducing Innovations

If someone in one of the commissaries came up with an innovation that we thought everyone ought to know about, we would include it as a feature on WDPD. Here is a story that featured the Cross/Minnesota commissary:

> *Everyone here at Distribution understands the importance of customer service. But according to our mission, team members' satisfaction is just as important. Here is a story out of DNC Cross/Minnesota that shows how Distribution is the best place to work.*
>
> *As in all of our other commissaries, warehouse team members of DNC Minnesota are required to wear black steel-toed shoes. The commissary also wanted to have its delivery and service team members wear black steel-toed shoes.*
>
> *To make it more convenient, commissary leader Greg Cross referred to a distribution policy whereby the commissary will reimburse team members up to $50 annually for the steel-toed shoes they purchase for work. Region manager Jerry Graf tells us that the commissary took this one step further, so to speak. . . .*

The feature goes on to say the commissary was able to work out a volume purchase with a local shoe store, thereby keeping team members safe and comfortable at a discount price.

With some 35 to 45 minutes per side, WDPD gave us the opportunity to handle important issues as they arose on a timely basis. For example, to disseminate the word about our new accident reporting procedure, we featured the following:

> *Hey Distribution, listen up, cause I have some important information for you. There is a new procedure for reporting accidents in the field. It only requires one phone call to the Control Center and everything else is taken care of. . . ."*

At that point, Judy Cangealose, the distribution security coordinator, explained the new procedure. Then the announcer would come back on to say:

> *. . . this new and easy reporting procedure will take the burden off people in the field, because one call does it all. The Control Center is open 24 hours a day, seven days a week. They can be reached at the following number.*
>
> *We hope we can avoid unfortunate accidents, but it is nice to know if we do have one, Distribution has a reporting system that will simplify any problem.*

As a final example, the feature below conveyed "the 10 commandments for slip and fall prevention" in a manner that our team members enjoyed hearing. Sure, we could also give it to them in a memo, put it on Workbench, and highlight it in the *Pepperoni Press*, but how much more enjoyable it was to hear it over the "radio" like this:

> *Slip and fall accidents are dangerous and sometimes deadly. They make up 16 percent of all workmen's compensation claims and cost our company hundreds of thousands of dollars a year.*
>
> *We can't erase the costly accidents of last year, but we can prevent slip and fall accidents from happening now. Awareness and some commonsense tips can help keep your commissary safe.*
>
> *Here are the 10 commandments for slip and fall prevention:*
>
> (1) *Thou shall make sure your pathway is clear.*
>
> (2) *Thou shall close all cabinets and drawers after every use.*

(3) Thou shall secure electrical cords and wires away from walkways.

(4) Thou shall use a stepladder for overhead reaching.

(5) Thou shall clean up spills immediately.

(6) Thou shall repair or replace loose flooring.

(7) Thou shall make sure stairs and walkways are well lit.

(8) Thou shall mark wet areas clearly.

(9) Thou shall avoid bending, twisting, and leaning backwards when seated.

(10) Thou shall report damage areas immediately.

Following these commandments, we had several commissary leaders share some of their precautions for preventing slip and fall accidents. Mike Lemke of Lemke/Missouri reported his commissary added a grainy surface to the floor in the tray washing area, and it hasn't experienced any slip and fall accidents since. Randy Nielson of DMC Delaware and others briefly shared their tips.

It always adds so much more to the listening to break away from the disc jockey and have the guy or gal in the field give a first-person report. It feels like everyone in the company is willing to share their successes.

The people featured on the broadcast feel honored, and those listening get highly useful information. Everyone becomes more inclined to report whatever breakthroughs, large or small, they have enjoyed.

Your Own Broadcast

Are you thinking that this sounds good for Domino's Distribution, but you don't have the time, energy, or funds to produce your own version of WDPD? In any community you can hire a radio disc jockey for a couple of hundred dollars who will take you in the studio and in less than a few hours cut a professionally crafted 30- to 45-minute cassette.

Your employees are inundated with information from every direction. They have a lot to read and a lot to remember. Providing useful information to them in an alternative vehicle such as a cassette may be the vehicle for reaching a work force behind on their reading.

You don't need to prepare scripts in advance. Simply hand the announcer brief opening and closing statements and 10 questions that you would like to answer during the course of the "broadcast."

With the technology at radio stations, all of your "ers," "ums," and gaffs can be spliced from the recording for a final, near-perfect master that can be easily duplicated and disseminated.

Alternatively, you can produce your own cassette on desktop equipment. Your cassette need not be elaborate. It could start as simply as, "Hi, this is John Smith. Here are some issues I would like to address, on this eighth day of February, 1993."

You could then go on to discuss the key issues and simply sign off by saying, "That's all for this month's cassette. This is John Smith and thanks for listening."

Bulk tape copiers cost between $800 and $1,800. Blank cassettes of varying lengths can be purchased in bulk at $.45 to $.75 each. Cassette labels can be printed on any laser printer or duplicated on the office copier. If your company has anyone with broadcast capabilities or printing capabilities, you can make a flashier production, while still holding costs at a minimum.

All the Resources You Need.   Many of those among your junior staff have the capabilities to handle such a project. Such a coordinator could also interview others at your headquarters in person or field staff over the phone with a two-way recording answering machine. Production can run 30 to 40 minutes per side if it is broken up by interviews, music, and other niceties.

You could archive the various broadcasts, especially if they contain information that would benefit new hires. For example, if a broadcast highlights how a particular policy is administered, that broadcast would be valuable to anyone who joins the company for months or years thereafter, barring any dramatic changes.

If you have a large staff in the field who spend many hours on the road or if many of your employees commute long distances, single-issue cassettes can also be worthwhile.

Now, Our Own Show.   When you are interviewed on radio or TV, consider reproducing the interview on audio or videocassette so that all of your staff may benefit from the broadcast. Whenever one of your staff appears on radio or TV and the broadcast is appropriate for reproduction and distribution, go ahead—having better informed employees is always to your advantage.

THE SATELLITE NETWORK

The use of satellite transmission for training and information tools has caught on in many industries, including automotive dealerships, insurance, health, and retailing. Video conferencing—communicating from one location to another using one-way video and two-way audio—is nothing new in business, but we see it as a tool for far more than executive use. I believe we were one of the pioneers in this field by being of the first to place a satellite uplink on a truck and move it throughout the country covering various company functions and meetings. Team members like David Boyer, Gwen Hengehold, and Denise Gorsline would travel across country to cover our SWAT meetings, world record pizza sales attempts at Tom Nolan's Palm Springs pizza store, or national announcements at awards banquets or Distribution Olympic events.

Even if your employees catch only a glimpse of a broadcast, they will get to see you in living color making a presentation. That can be a much stronger connection to you than the few times they see you strolling around the corporate offices. You can't be everywhere, but your broadcasts and videos certainly can be.

We have the capability to offer our own live, nationally televised broadcasts to field operations, suppliers, and customers. To be frank, the cost of producing the satellite service is hundreds of times that of Workbench. In addition, many of our team members have an easier time turning on a computer than heading over to a video monitor and watching one hour or more of live broadcasts.

Nevertheless, the satellite network offers an enhanced capability to explore complex issues in depth. Suppose insurance is going up. We can write only so much about it in the *Pepperoni Press*. If the news comes via Workbench, it can look cold and uncaring. If I or one of the company's spokespeople deliver the same message via the satellite network, we are in a better position to rally the troops to realize there may be no other choice.

Sincerity shows off over the network in a way that is difficult to duplicate using other communication vehicles. Also, our team members tend to read hard copy or computer screens alone. Satellite broadcasts enable a whole crew to sit and receive information at the same time, thereby facilitating discussion.

With technology breakthroughs and innovation, the Satellite Network may one day become a visual Workbench where each team member can directly view current or previous broadcasts from a desk.

Your Own Videos

Producing your videocassettes need not be that expensive. If you lack the facilities, many of your corporate neighbors do not and may rent studio time for a reasonable fee. In addition, in almost every community today, local cable television stations are mandated to provide community access, although few citizens are aware of this.

For little or no fee, you may use the cable station facilities for several sessions, as long as the show you are producing is available for viewing by the local community, as well as your own company. This could be seen as a bit limiting. On further examination, however, many topics could serve a dual role, as do selected summer survey questions.

We've used the Satellite Network to transmit programs on the most recent developments in dough certification, our national performance objectives, and for special programs like our olympics. This is a smattering of what the Domino's Pizza Satellite Network can communicate.

What information can you convey that is useful for your employees and a good vehicle for community relations? You could explain the ground-breaking procedures for a new plant, highlight research breakthroughs, profile new members of your executive staff, or discuss some direct participation your company has in a community project.

As with audiocassettes, you don't want to inundate your staff with unnecessary or uninformative material, but when you do have a good topic, explore the possibilities.

COST-EFFECTIVE TOOLS

Our reinforcement tools only *seem* to be expensive.

One of the primary ways we have been able to keep operating costs down while increasing sales per employee is by holding the number of employees steady at 1,600. Kelley Hannan, who has been with our company for nearly two decades, was one of our top commissary managers and is now on our board of directors. He used to say the ideal number of people in a commissary matched the number of stores the commissary served.

For example, if there were 45 people in the commissary, that commissary served 45 stores. It was a good rule of thumb and it held up for many years.

Today, however, through better equipment, such as the reinforcement tools, more motivated employees, and greater operating efficiency, our 1,600 employees are able to serve 5,300 stores. As long as we are able to add new stores without significantly adding people, everyone, from myself to the lowest-paid person in the company, can look forward to steadily increasing wages and performance bonuses.

As a result of instituting the systems I've described, we achieved a 40 percent reduction in home office administration costs while maintaining effectiveness. Since these tools have been on-line, we have been able to reduce unnecessary requests, phone calls, and make-work; provide immediate corporatewide communication to all team members in the face of tough situations; and assemble a home office staff who are more responsive than ever to team members in the field.

As more "how-to" reports and company case histories are logged and stored on Workbench, as the Distribution olympics yields greater insights on efficiency, and as new applications of communication technologies are uncovered, we expect to become even more efficient and to reframe our mission and visions so as to embrace even greater challenges.

CHAPTER CHECKLIST

- Acknowledge that the monumental task of maintaining regular, open, ongoing communications with team members never ends.

- Actively seek additional measures to ensure that your employees continually have the opportunity to stay on top of company affairs.

- When one of your offices or branches does something extraordinary for the community, put that story on the front page of your in-house publication.

- Offer a regular column on the activities of your competitors.

- Encourage all employees throughout your company to contribute to the publication; you can't have a communication vehicle with much breadth and scope without wide participation.

- Ask your editor to invite contributions to the publication and to give people instructions on how to make submissions.

- Run employee photos in your publication.

- Instruct your editor to make wider rounds than he or she is normally accustomed to doing.

- Tackle controversial issues—put them on the front page for team members to read and consider.

- Explain your reasoning behind tough decisions, including the pros and cons of alternatives that were considered.

- Include a roster of important company phone numbers, including your own, or provide the number of your secretary.

- Hire a radio disc jockey for a couple of hundred dollars who will take you in the studio and in less than a few hours cut a professionally crafted 30- to 45-minute cassette, or . . .

- Produce your own cassette on desktop equipment.

- Identify those among your junior staff who have the capabilities to handle broadcast and cassette production.

- Archive your various broadcasts, especially if they contain information that would benefit new hires.

- When you are interviewed on radio or TV, reproduce the interview on audio or videocassette so your staff can benefit from the broadcast.

- Rent studio time from your corporate neighbors to produce a low-cost, high-quality video, or . . .

- Investigate access to local cable television stations in your community.

- Expect to become even more efficient, and look forward to embracing even greater challenges.

Epilogue

The future belongs to companies that effectively tap the ingenuity and drive of its work force and provide them with the leadership and tools to be successful. Super Vision works for us and for companies much smaller than we are.

As you work through the seven steps of Super Vision, you'll encounter some rough going—we did. We learned that looking back to previous steps provided the most keys to overcoming hurdles: Did you overlook a vital public? Is your mission off base or confusing? Are you using wrong key indicators or unrealistic performance levels? Do you have automatic rewards that include all team members? Super Visors need to ask these questions again and again—not only if something is wrong, but also to move forward.

Just to show what happens when you overlook a critical need, consider our experience with this book. This book would have been released earlier had I recognized the publisher's need that I comply to a schedule of deadlines with limited changes to the manuscript. Instead, I didn't consider the scheduling problems created by my drive to make this the best possible book by trying to improve every facet of it at every review. Had I anticipated this need and added a line to the mission statement or set a key indicator like "number of rewrites" or "deadlines missed," there would have been less frustration and an earlier publication. For this, I apologize to my co-writer Jeff David-son, to my editor Jeff Krames, to the project editor Jean Lou Hess, and to my staff for all their frustration. Thanks for your patience.

Please take a moment to complete the survey at the end of the book. I need your feedback to know if I otherwise fulfilled my mission as an author. Also, as you find success from these steps, I would appreciate it if you drop me a line at the address listed on the survey. I'd love to hear about it.

Bibliography

BOOKS

Blanchard, Kenneth, and Norman Vincent Peale. *The Power of Ethical Management.* New York: Morrow, 1988.

Davidson, Jeff. *Selling to the Giants.* New York: Tab/McGraw-Hill, 1991.

Hawkins, Paul. *Growing a Business.* New York: Simon & Schuster, 1988.

Monaghan, Tom, with Robert Anderson. *Pizza Tiger.* New York: Random House, 1986.

Peters, Tom. *Thriving on Chaos.* New York: Knopf, 1989.

Peters, Tom, and Nancy Austin. *A Passion for Excellence.* New York: Warner Books, 1987.

ARTICLES

Johnstone, Laura. "Distribution Price Increases Dramatically Below Consumer Price Index." *Pepperoni Press*, December 1, 1989.

Rutiglianio, Anthony. "Pizza Man Squashes the Wedding Cake." *Management Review*, September 1986.

"Towards an Electronically Democratic Workplace." *Modern Office Technology*, September 1989.

About the Authors

Don Vlcek, 41, transformed Domino's Pizza Distribution from a liability into Domino's Pizza, Inc.'s, most valuable asset. Appointed president on August 9, 1978, at the tender age of 28, Don quickly overcame $330,000 in losses in 1977.

Cited in Tom Peters' international best-sellers, *A Passion for Excellence* and *Managing Chaos*, Don's leadership and determination reversed the trend. Under his guidance, the company has become an internationally recognized model of an effective American organization.

Don has directed Distribution to be a lean company driven by the needs of its field operations. He installed a system that offers timely and continual personal recognition and helped create an atmosphere in which individual initiative may flourish. Instead of meeting additional growth with more regional offices and overhead, Don consolidated all support staff functions and dispersed a network of individual regional managers. He also began a unique communication system that ensures overnight response to any request from the field.

He is an outspoken critic of top-heavy administrative structure and is routinely asked to speak at high-level executive conferences, symposiums, and retreats, reflecting his views on achieving industry prominence, sales growth, market share, customer satisfaction, key supplier relationships, and higher levels of service. He is the recipient of numerous awards and citations including the Franchisee Person of the Year.

Jeff Davidson, 40, is the author of several books, among them: *Breathing Space: Living at a Comfortable Pace in a Sped-Up Society* (Mastermedia, Ltd., 1991); *Selling to the Giants* (Tab Books, 1991);

263

Power and Protocol for Getting to the Top (Shapolsky, 1990); *Blow Your Own Horn* (Berkley, 1991); *Marketing Your Consulting and Professional Services* (Wiley, revised 1990); and *Marketing on a Shoestring* (Wiley, 1988).

Jeff's works have been translated into Chinese, Japanese, Korean, Indonesian, Spanish, Portuguese, Dutch, and French. All told, his book have been selected by book clubs 17 times, four have been produced as cassettes, and two have gone on to mass-market editions.

Index

Reader Survey
Questionnaire

QUESTIONS

Circle yes or no in space provided

Was the book worth reading?	yes	no
Did you understand the seven-step process?	yes	no
Did the book increase your knowledge of effective business practices?	yes	no
Will you use some part of the methods presented in this book in your own business or on a personal project?	yes	no
Was the book enjoyable to read?	yes	no

LIST THE THREE MOST VALUABLE THINGS YOU GOT OUT OF THIS BOOK:

1. _____

2. _____

3. _____

LIST THREE THINGS THAT COULD HAVE BEEN IMPROVED ON OR ADDED TO THE BOOK:

1. _____

2. _____

3. _____

PLEASE INDICATE YOUR INTEREST IN
THE FOLLOWING:

Send me information on the Domino's Pizza Business
Consulting Innovation Network _____

Send me information about the Domino's Pizza
Chapter of Ducks Unlimited _____

I've enclosed my resume. Please direct it to:

___ store operations

___ commissary operations

___ office and field support operations

Geographic preference _____

*(Sorry, only qualified pizza store operations team members may
apply to franchise.)*

Please check:

___ Business person

___ Teacher or consultant

___ Domino's Pizza family

   ___ Corporate

   ___ Franchise

   ___ Supplier

Name _____

Address_____

_____

(Optional— but if you include, we'll send you a copy of this book's
survey results after 6/92.)

Please complete this survey and mail to:
Donald J. Vlcek, Jr., President
Domino's Pizza Distribution Corp.
30 Frank Lloyd Wright Drive
Ann Arbor, Michigan 48106

Also Available from Business One Irwin:

SECOND TO NONE
How Our Smartest Companies Put People First
Charles Garfield
A main selection of the executive program.
Discover how you can create a workplace where both people and profits flourish! Charles Garfield, the best-selling author of *Peak Performers*, gives you an inside look at today's leading businesses and how they became masters at expanding the teamwork and creativity of their workforce. Using his unique mix of practical strategies gleaned from our smartest companies, he shows how you can provide superior service to your customers, maintain a competitive edge during times of rapid transition, and inspire innovation, partnership, and total participation from your employees and managers.
ISBN: 1-55623-360-4 $22.95

BEING THE BOSS
The Importance of Leadership and Power
Abraham L. Gitlow
Discover the best ways to lead a corporate team so you can minimize internal conflict and improve morale. Gitlow shows how you can exercise power and authority to gain improved productivity, increased profits, and more satisfied employees and stockholders.
ISBN: 1-55623-635-2 $24.95

KIN CARE AND THE AMERICAN CORPORATION
Solving the Work/Family Dilemma
Dayle M. Smith
Smith shows how corporations can solve some of their staffing problems — including high turnover, absenteeism, recruiting failure, and declining productivity. Includes valuable checklists, forms, and guidelines you can use to determine the best programs.
ISBN: 1-55623-449-X $24.95

REBUILDING AMERICA'S WORKFORCE
Business Strategies to Close the Competitive Gap
William H. Kolberg and Foster C. Smith
Overcome today's reported shortage of skilled employees by implementing new management and training techniques designed to improve employee performance. Includes revealing interviews and case studies that show you how to make maximum employee performance a reality.
ISBN: 1-55623-622-0 $24.95

WORK IS NOT A FOUR-LETTER WORD
Improving the Quality of Your Work Life
Stephen Strasser and John Sena
If your job is adversely affecting your work life, let Strasser and Sena show you how to achieve success, fulfillment, and happiness! You'll find logical, action-based advice so you can resolve the situation by using alternative strategies to overcome career roadblocks.
ISBN: 1-55623-398-1 $19.95

All prices quoted are in U.S. currency and are subject to change without notice. Available at fine bookstores and libraries everywhere.